The Home Front and Beyond

American Women in the 1940s

American Women in the Twentieth Century

Series Editor: Barbara Haber, The Schlesinger Library on the History of Women in America, Radcliffe College

Pulling together a wealth of widely-scattered primary and secondary sources on women's history, *American Women in the Twentieth Century* is the first series to provide a chronological history of the changing status of women in America. Each volume presents the experiences and contributions of American women during one decade of this century. Written by leading scholars in American history and women's studies, *American Women in the Twentieth Century* meets the need for an encyclopedic overview of the roles women have played in shaping modern America.

Also Available:

Setting a Course: American Women in the 1920s
Dorothy M. Brown

Holding Their Own: American Women in the 1930s
Susan Ware

Mothers and More: American Women in the 1950s
Eugenia Kaledin

The Home Front and Beyond

American Women in the 1940s

Susan M. Hartmann

WITHDRAWN

Twayne Publishers · Boston

The Home Front and Beyond
American Women in the 1940s

Copyright © 1982
by G.K. Hall & Co.
All Rights Reserved
Twayne Publishers
A Division of G.K. Hall & Co.
70 Lincoln Street
Boston, Massachusetts 02111

Book design and production
by Barbara Anderson

This book was typeset in
10 point Janson with
Torino display type
supplied by
Composing Room of New England.

PRINTED ON PERMANENT/DURABLE
ACID-FREE PAPER AND BOUND IN
THE UNITED STATES OF AMERICA

Library of Congress Cataloging
in Publication Data

Hartmann, Susan M.
The home front and beyond.

Includes index.
1. Women—United States—History—20th century.
2. World War, 1939–1945—Women.   3. Women—Employment—
United States—History.   4. Women—United States—Social
conditions.   I. Title.
HQ1420.H34   305.4'0973   82-6209
ISBN 0-8057-9901-X   AACR2

10   9   8   7   6   5   4

softcover ISBN 0-8057-9903-6
10   9   8   7   6   5   4   3   2   1

Contents

About the Author

Susan Hartmann teaches history and women's studies at the University of Missouri—St. Louis. She has published *The Marshall Plan*, the award-winning *Truman and the 80th Congress*, and several articles on women's history.

Preface

Changes in a society's sex-gender system, the ways in which it distributes activities, roles, and power between women and men, take place very gradually. Only rarely do significant alterations in patterns of living and thought occur within the span of a few years. Consequently, to use a decade as the framework for investigating women's history is, in many respects, to establish an artificial structure. Yet, the field of American women's history, especially the study of their most recent past, is so new that a "decades-approach" serves as one means of gaining understanding that will eventually produce a more adequate scheme of periodization.

Moreover, the 1940s contained developments which sharply set off that decade from the preceding one and which established patterns that would shape women's lives for some years to come. Most obviously, the Second World War transformed the economy, made unprecedented claims on women and men, and disrupted social arrangements on a broad scale. In order to determine which of the changes endured and which were ephemeral, it is necessary to look beyond the war years. Developments in various aspects of women's status, of course, did not proceed along parallel lines or at a similar pace. Economic and reproductive patterns, for example, took their postwar shape before women's educational patterns became fixed. Yet, prevailing directions had crystallized by the end of the decade. From the vantage point of 1950 it is possible to discern how women's lives were permanently reshaped by war and economic regeneration and to understand women's own initiatives in the process of change.

The focus of this study is on women in the aggregate rather than on the unique activities or contributions of individual women. As much as is possible in a general study, I have tried to encompass the experiences of women across class and racial lines. In paying much greater attention to the public sphere than to the private domain, I do not deny the need for knowledge about women's interior lives, their intimate relationships, private activities, and self-perceptions. Instead, my emphasis reflects the limitations of time and space as well as my view that women's movement into the public realm represents the most substantial change of the 1940s.

Because women's experiences are linked with those of men and cannot be separated from the historical context in which they take place, I have begun this book with a survey of the major developments in American political, economic, and social life during the 1940s. (Those readers familiar with the period may wish to skip Chapter 1.) The second chapter summarizes women's status on the eve of the decade and provides an overview of women's history from 1940 to 1950. The most dramatic break with the past, women's service as full-fledged members of the military establishment, is examined in Chapter 3.

The next two chapters deal with women in the labor force. Chapter 4 explores the context of women's paid employment—the policies, practices, and motivations of the government, employers, and labor unions, and the environment they created for women workers. In Chapter 5, I focus on women themselves, with emphasis on the changing nature of their work and the changing nature of the female labor force. Women's education, primarily at the postsecondary level, is treated in Chapter 6.

In the seventh chapter, I discuss the legal system, its race-specific laws which constrained minority women, and its sex-specific statutes, most of which sanctioned inequality, but a few of which protected women and increased their public opportunities. Chapter 8 explores women's roles in the governing process, as members of pressure groups and political parties, and as officials, with particular emphasis on organizations and individuals who sought to advance women by changing public policy.

Women's roles as family members are discussed in Chapter 9, which analyzes changing marriage, divorce, childbearing, child-rearing, and housekeeping patterns. In Chapter 10, I survey the range of models available to women in popular culture. The concluding chapter assesses the relative importance of continuity and change in the various areas of women's lives.

I am profoundly indebted to those scholars who pioneered in establishing the field of women's history. My awakening interest in women's history could not have developed without the confirmation that what I considered important historical questions were not only legitimate, but were indeed essential to a more accurate rendering of the human past. As well as winning scholarly acceptance of the field, those historians of women have also been indispensable for their contributions to the developing methodology and conceptual tools of women's history. The encouragement I have received from women historians throughout the country has been matched by that from the Women's Studies faculty and students at the University of Missouri—St. Louis, who have never failed to inspire and sustain me.

Financial support from the Rockefeller Foundation, the University of Missouri—St. Louis, and the American Association of University Women enabled me to research and write the book. Equally crucial was the assistance I received from the staffs of the libraries and manuscript repositories mentioned in the Essay on Sources. I am also grateful to Karen Anderson, D'Ann Campbell, Madeline Davis, Carol Neuls-Bates, and Leila Rupp for permitting me to use their unpublished work.

I want to thank my editor, Barbara Haber, for her continued confidence in me and in this book. I have received enormous assistance from individuals who have read all or parts of earlier versions of the manuscript. For contributing insights and polish and for saving me from errors, I owe deep thanks to Karen Anderson, D'Ann Campbell, Katharine Corbett, M. C. Devilbiss, Linda Henry, Louise Knauer, Ann Lever, Leila Rupp, and Arlene Zarembka. I am also indebted to Richalyn Martin, June Hilliard, and Lanette Williams for their work on the preparation of the manuscript.

For less tangible support, I want to express special thanks to Richard Sheehan for his affection and encouragement; and to my parents, Marie and Herbert Meckfessel, whose love and nurture form my most vivid memory of the 1940s.

Susan M. Hartmann

University of Missouri—St. Louis

V-J Day on the White House lawn
Courtesy of Library of Congress

Chapter One

A Decade of War and Prosperity

As the 1940s began, American society confronted two critical questions. How could the economy be restructured to provide its people a decent livelihood and to insure future stability and growth? And, how could the United States best safeguard and promote its interests in an increasingly unstable and threatening world? Although the ensuing decade did not witness a complete resolution of these issues, by 1950 the nation had entered a period of economic expansion and prosperity and had devised a foreign policy based upon American predominance throughout much of the world. Attending these great changes were a number of developments which significantly altered the patterns of daily living for much of the population.[1]

The Great Depression cast a long shadow over the decade of the 1940s. When the economy hit its low point in 1933, the gross national product had plunged from $149.3 to $107.6 billion; national income stood at one-half its 1929 level; and more than 30 percent of the work force—12 million men and women—could not find jobs. In response to the economic crisis, the administration of Franklin D. Roosevelt had initiated federal programs of support to businesses and banks, farmers, workers, and the unemployed. Nonetheless, this unprecedented action, which increased the federal budget from $3 to $9 billion and which transformed the relationship between the government and the economy, failed to bring about recovery. Although the New Deal had stemmed the decline and had alleviated much suffering, by 1940 average real earnings remained below those of 1929, and more than 8 million Americans were still unemployed.

It was in resolving the second great issue, that of foreign policy, that Americans found a solution to the economic crisis. For, practically overnight, World War II turned the unemployment problem into one of a labor shortage and rocketed the economy into new heights of production and prosperity. Yet it was a war which most Americans had wanted to avoid. Still disillusioned at the results of World War I, they responded with alarm to the military aggression of Germany, Italy, and Japan, but hoped that that expansion could be checked without cost to the United States. While President Roosevelt pledged to keep the nation out of war, the United States reacted to Germany's conquest of France in June 1940 by strengthening its own defenses and increasing aid to sustain Britain in her solitary stand against Hitler. At the same time, the administration applied growing economic pressure in an effort to check Japanese aggression in the Far East. The Japanese attack on Pearl Harbor in December 1941 rested the question of the nation's appropriate role and plunged the United States into global war.

The demands of the military crisis launched the government into activities extraordinary even by New Deal standards. At home its major tasks were to maximize production in order to equip its fighting forces and those of its allies and to sustain its civilian population; and to find revenues to finance these enterprises. In meeting these needs the federal government extended its hand into the daily lives of individuals, limiting their choices in what they could buy, where they could live, how they could get to work, and even whether they could exchange one job for another. While individuals grumbled, these new restrictions were tolerated as temporary exigencies necessary to achieve the national goal of victory.

As the federal bureaucracy swelled from 1 million to 3.8 million, dozens of new government agencies were established. None was more powerful or more prominent than the War Production Board. Established to exercise general responsibility over the economy, that agency used carrots and sticks to get businessmen to convert factories to military production and to expand facilities, allocated scarce materials, coordinated production schedules, and decided what civilian goods could be produced. The War Manpower Commission allocated labor among the military, defense industry, agriculture, and essential civilian production. To avoid the loss of work hours through strikes, the War Labor Board was created to settle management-labor disputes in war industries. Other new agencies coordinated transportation, prepared propaganda, distributed research monies to industry and universities, censored outgoing and incoming foreign communications, and assisted war-impacted communities.

As the federal budget grew to $100 billion in 1945, new means were devised to procure revenue. Deficit financing provided about one-half the war costs as the national debt rose from $43 billion in 1941 to nearly $260 billion in 1945. While the government continued to borrow money by selling securities to Federal Reserve Banks, it also launched massive campaigns to sell war bonds in low denominations and got 25 million workers to purchase $25 bonds through payroll savings plans. Increased taxes provided the remaining half of the Treasury's needs. New legislation increased corporate taxes, raised the excess-profits tax to 90 percent, initiated the income-tax withholding system, and broadened the tax base. The number of Americans who paid federal income taxes rose from about 7 million in 1940 to more than 42 million in 1945.

Higher taxes and the encouragement of savings through war bonds were not sufficient to limit the inflation which resulted from increasing consumer purchasing power chasing a limited supply of goods. The government succeeded in curtailing the rise in prices to 29 percent between 1939 and 1945, and most of that increase came before the Office of Price Administration issued a general freeze in 1943. Along with its control over prices, the OPA also managed the distribution of goods by rationing scarce commodities as well as items where production depended on raw materials or services in short supply. Such commodities included gasoline, fuel oil, sugar, coffee, meat, canned goods, and shoes. While the OPA controlled prices, the War Labor Board kept wages in line.

The ultimate form of government control was, of course, its power to conscript men into the military forces. Of the more than 16 millions who served in the armed forces, 10 million men were drafted, including fathers after 1943. The fox-hole or the battle-ship was not the typical experience for most military personnel; more than one-fourth fulfilled their obligation stateside, and just one of eight actually saw combat. In comparison with America's allies, the human cost of war was relatively small—the United States suffered 1,016,245 casualties, including 405,399 deaths.

Although individuals, businessmen, farmers, and workers chafed under one or more of the restrictions imposed to further the war effort, the nation as a whole enjoyed unexampled material welfare. The labor force expanded from 56,180,000 in 1940 to 65,290,000 in 1945. Workers saw their average yearly real earnings rise from $754 in 1940 to $1,289 in 1944, the increase resulting not simply from increased rates of pay, but also from overtime work and expanded employment in already high-paying jobs. Union membership grew from under 9 million in 1940 to almost 15 million, or 35 percent of the nonfarm labor force, by 1945. Farm income more than doubled as production rose, even though the total farm population declined by 17 percent. During the Depression more than half of all Americans lived below the poverty line; by the end of the war just over one-third were poor. Another third earned incomes which placed them in the middle class.

These gains were based on the remarkable productive capacity of the economy. Manufacturing output and the GNP doubled during the war and Americans enjoyed more consumer goods than before the war, despite shortages and the diversion of manufacturing to war materials. The military crisis intensified the consolidation of business as antitrust prosecution halted and the government favored the largest firms with defense contracts.

Not all Americans benefited from the war-induced prosperity. Indeed, for those of Japanese ancestry the war destroyed not only their material well-being, but took away their very physical freedom. The War Department evacuated more than 110,000 Japanese-Americans, two-thirds of them United States citizens, from the West Coast and settled them in concentration camps under the control of the War Relocation Authority. In barren barracks surrounded by barbed-wire fences with armed guards, families lived in one room, sharing communal toilets and dining facilities, and had access to only meager education and recreation. Justifying the relocation on grounds of military security, the army found support from a public moved not only by panic after the Japanese attack on Pearl Harbor, but also by longstanding racial prejudice and economic envy. The Supreme Court condoned this gross violation of civil liberties, implicitly holding that the presumed military necessity overrode the Bill of Rights.

An older, much larger minority group, while continuing to endure intense discrimination and segregation, succeeded in turning the military crisis to its modest advantage. Hit the hardest by the Depression, black Americans had at the same time experienced a more sympathetic hearing in the White House, attention from the left wing of American politics, and the decline of racist assumptions among scholars and intellectuals. With greater confidence and heightened expectations, black leaders determined that victory abroad be accompanied by a war against racism at home. Threatening a massive demonstration in Washington, D.C., in 1941, they wrested from Roosevelt an executive order banning discrimination in defense production. Such a ban was easier to write than to enforce. Established to implement the executive order, the Fair Employment Practices Committee reached a satisfactory resolution of only one-third of the 8,000 complaints brought before it. Moreover, the armed forces continued to practice segregation and discrimination, while blacks in Detroit and Harlem were killed and injured in the two largest manifestations of racial violence during the war.

Nonetheless, the war did stimulate modest gains for black Americans. The number of black skilled workers more than doubled, and they increased their presence in semiskilled jobs by an even larger measure. While in 1939 the income of nonwhite male workers had stood at just 41 percent of that of their white counterparts, by 1950 the percentage had grown to 61. In 1944 the Supeme Court outlawed the white primary, one of the devices used to deny blacks the vote in the South. During the war the black press had grown more assertive, the National Association for the Advancement of Colored People had increased its membership from 50,000 to 450,000, and a new organization, the Congress of Racial Equality, had been founded to attack racism through direct action. Moreover, the war greatly accelerated black migration from the rural South to northern and western cities, a movement which continued unabated after the war. Those 1.5 million blacks who left the South during the 1940s not only improved their economic prospects but also acquired political power which they and white liberal supporters exerted on the Democratic party and the postwar administration of Harry S Truman. Such pressure led in 1948 to Truman's order to desegregate the military and to his proposal for a ten-point civil-rights program. Although the Fair Employment Practices Committee died with the end of the war and Congress refused to pass civil-rights legislation, developments in the 1940s improved the status of black Americans and provided the catalyst for the civil rights movement which would explode a decade later.

Blacks were not the only Americans on the move during the 1940s. In addition to those who left home for military service, the Census Bureau estimated that 15.3 million people moved during the war, half of those having crossed state lines. Some of the migration consisted of servicemen's families moving to military base areas, but most of it resulted from the lure of jobs in defense industries. With more than half of the shipbuilding and almost half of airplane production located on the Pacific Coast, California alone gained 2 million new inhabitants, as San Diego County grew by 43.7 percent and the Los Angeles area added 440,000 to its population. Southern seaport areas around Mobile, Alabama, Hampton Roads, Virginia, and Charleston, South Carolna, also mushroomed, as did midwestern industrial centers such as Detroit.

The population explosion in war industry and military base locations created both material and psychological strains. Scarce housing forced families to double up or to live in crowded trailers or makeshift dwellings, while it was not uncommon for war workers on different schedules to share a bed. Public transportation systems were jammed as gasoline rationing compelled workers to curtail use of their automobiles. Schools were sometimes congested to the point of requiring two shifts, and medical services were taxed to the limit. Tensions between old residents and newcomers were strained not only when the migrants were black: prejudice against "hillbillies" and others of different cultural backgrounds inhibited community cooperation to solve the problems of congestion and inadequate institutions and services.

The higher standard of living enjoyed by most Americans compensated for the inconveniences and deprivations experienced during the war. The big question was whether this standard could be sustained in peacetime. With still vivid memories of the Depression, Americans feared an economic crisis as millions of soldiers returned to an economy no longer stimulated by massive government orders. Such fears did not materialize. To be sure, there was considerable economic dislocation in the immediate postwar period. After the defeat of Germany in May 1945, but before the surrender of Japan in August, employment in shipyards and aircraft and arms plants was cut in half. The government cancelled $35 billion of war contracts within one month of V-J Day, and between June 1945 and June 1946 it discharged 9 million service men and women. Unemployment climbed from 1 million in 1945 to 2.3 million in 1946. After controls were lifted in mid-1946, the Consumer Price Index jumped 30 percent. Most unions had honored the no-strike pledge during the war, but in 1946, as overtime ended and weekly earnings dropped, unions struggled to maintain their members' income. Four and one-half million workers struck, halting production in the steel, automobile, electric, coal, maritime, and railroad industries.

Despite these blows, the American economy weathered the reconversion process and escaped the anticipated crisis. A number of factors cushioned the impact of sharply reduced government spending combined with the veterans' return. Consumers had saved billions of dollars which they were eager to spend on the houses, cars, and appliances denied them during the Depression and war. Wartime profits provided businesses with funds to convert to civilian production and invest in new plants and equipment. American grants and loans—$38 billion for the first four postwar years—enabled a war-devastated Europe to purchase American products. Defense spending dropped after the war but did not sink to prewar levels, while nondefense expenditures rose from $17 billion during the war to $25 billion in 1947. A rising birthrate, from 19.4 (births per 1,000 population) in 1940 to 24.5 in 1949, further sustained consumer demand.

The nation's gratitude to its returning warriors provided an additional cushion. Under the Servicemen's Readjustment Act of

1944, veterans were entitled to one year of unemployment compensation, low-interest loans to purchase homes, farms, and small businesses, and assistance for job-training and education at all levels. By October 1948 unemployment compensation to veterans amounted to $2.7 billion, and 1.3 million had received home loans. More than 7.6 million veterans had been approved for job-training and educational assistance which included tuition, books, and subsistence allowances. In the fall semester of 1948, more than 1 million veterans were attending colleges and universities, constituting close to half of total enrollments. This aid to veterans and their families directly benefited almost one-quarter of the population and by stimulating demand assisted the economic system in adjusting to peacetime conditions.

Their wartime savings enabled most Americans to participate in the postwar boom and to enjoy a vastly higher standard of living. Between 1946 and 1950 they purchased 21.4 million automobiles, more than 20 million refrigerators, 5.5 million electric stoves, and 11.6 million television sets. More than a million new housing units were constructed in each postwar year, and owner-occupied houses increased from 15.2 million in 1940 to 23.5 million in 1950, so that by the end of the decade a majority of families owned their own homes.

Yet economic stability proved elusive. By 1948 inflation had replaced recession as the primary economic concern. While wages and salaries increased by 23 percent between 1945 and 1950, the cost-of-living index went up 36.2 percent. Indeed, the average family's income had increased significantly during the war—from $3,664 in 1941 to $4,650 in 1944 (in 1950 dollars)—but during the postwar period its purchasing power declined slightly, to $4,461 in 1950. Prices continued to rise even during the first postwar recession which began in 1949. Unemployment climbed to 7 percent by early 1950, abating only when the Korean War provided a stimulus to economic recovery. Nor had the United States solved the problem of equitable income distribution; at the end of the decade about one-third of the population lived below the poverty line.

The Democratic administrations of the 1940s had sought economic stability in part through expanded federal protection of lower income groups. But Roosevelt's proposal for an "economic bill of rights" had faltered over his own military and foreign policy priorities and the growing conservative mood of Congress. His successor, Harry S Truman, sought to consolidate and expand New Deal reform, but he lacked FDR's charisma and political skills, faced a Republican-dominated Congress from 1946 to 1948, and, like Roosevelt, gave priority to matters of foreign policy. Over Truman's veto Congress passed the Taft-Hartley Act, which restricted labor-union activities, and it rebuffed his call for civil-rights legislation, a national health program, federal aid to education, and an agricultural plan that would benefit consumers as well as farmers. Congress did pass the Employment Act of 1946, which affirmed federal responsibility for a healthy economy but failed to provide the machinery for effective government action. Truman's other relatively modest achievements included a public housing program that was small compared to need, expansion of social security coverage and increased benefits, and a higher minimum wage. Such reforms helped to sustain the postwar economic boom and marked the permanence of the new era of government responsibility for economic well-being ushered in during the New Deal. While the Democrats were able to mobilize majorities in the elections of 1948 and 1950, they perceived no mandate for innovative social and economic policy. The behavior of elected officials reflected a certain complacency, one which accepted the social-welfare legislation of the 1930s and supported its cautious expansion, but which rejected more substantial domestic reform.

Such satisfaction, of course, belied the fact that the United States had not developed an economy capable of distributing an adequate livelihood to all its citizens. Yet the productive system had improved so much since 1940 that foreign dangers had replaced economic problems as the primary challenge to national well-being. By 1950 the question of the United States role in the global arena had been determined, but in ways which would have been unthinkable in 1940.

Far from eliminating the threat to American security, the nation's victory in World War II placed it in an international position that seemed to render it even more vulnerable than it had found itself in 1940. That vulnerability involved a paradox. On the one hand, the United States emerged from war as the most powerful nation in the world with an economy—unlike all others—even stronger than it had been before the war. But on the other hand,

Americans were constantly reminded that they faced a foreign threat greater than ever before, a threat requiring constant vigilance and preparedness. American leaders identified that menace as the Soviet Union bent on an expansionist course designed to impose communism throughout the world.

Soviet-American relations, strained during the war, reached the breaking point as the victorious Allies sought to order the postwar world. The critical question was the fate of Eastern Europe. Having made the largest contribution to the defeat of Hitler, and having suffered the heaviest losses (including the lives of 20 million citizens), the Soviet Union felt justified in claiming predominant influence in those Eastern European countries which it had defeated or liberated, just as the Western Allies directed the affairs of occupied Italy, Greece, and Japan. Most importantly, Soviet leaders determined that the nation's security demanded friendly governments in neighboring countries such as Poland through which Germany had invaded Russia. The United States was unwilling to employ force against the Soviets in Eastern Europe, but by 1947 it had committed the nation to a policy of containment.

The containment policy failed to distinguish between Soviet power and leftist movements. American policymakers assumed that any Communist success, or even non-Communist revolution, constituted the expansion of Soviet power and thus a direct threat to American security. They pursued containment by seeking to retain the United States monopoly over atomic weapons, by entering unprecedented peacetime alliances, and by providing economic and military aid to any nation which seemed vulnerable to Soviet pressure or Communist parties. By 1949, the United States had extended aid in Greece, Turkey, Western Europe, and China and was beginning a program of assistance to Third World countries.

While American aims advanced in Western Europe and the Middle East, containment was not a universal success. In 1949, the Chinese Communists defeated the United States–supported forces of Chiang Kai-Shek. And in that same year, the United States lost its nuclear ascendancy when the Soviet Union exploded its first atomic bomb. To a people unaccustomed to persistent intervention in global affairs and who had assumed that World War II would end the international crisis, the containment policy was difficult to live with. Even more frustrating were those situations where containment failed.

The contradiction between the assumed American omnipotence and the inability of the United States to work its will throughout the world contributed to an epidemic of domestic anticommunism by the late 1940s. In the preceding decade opponents of the New Deal had claimed that Communists in the government were subverting American institutions; such charges intensified with the deterioration of the international situation in the early postwar years. But Republicans were not alone in raising the specter of domestic communism. In defining foreign policy objectives to the public, officials in the Truman Administration inflamed fears by exaggerating the Soviet threat and by equating communism with Soviet influence. In 1947, Truman himself established a Federal Employee Loyalty Program to probe into the past and present associations of every government employee. Congressional committees investigated the political beliefs and associations of individuals within and without government. The Red Scare spread beyond Washington as state governments instituted loyalty oaths and conducted their own investigations, as labor unions and the movie industry purged Communists, as educational institutions cracked down on radicals, and as leaders of such organizations as the American Legion, the Catholic Church, and the United States Chamber of Commerce warned of the Communist threat within American society.

In personal terms the Red Scare meant the loss of job and reputation for thousands of Americans. Few distinctions were made among those who were currently members of the Communist party, those who had belonged in the past to the party or front organizations, those who had associated with Communists or fellow travelers, and those who merely criticized United States foreign or domestic policies. Nor was it conceded that one could adhere to communism and still be a loyal American. Instead, as individual rights were violated, a repressive atmosphere arose which stifled intellectual discourse and limited criticism of American institutions. By calling into question the loyalty of those who might advocate alternatives to current foreign or domestic policies, the postwar anti-Communist hysteria contributed to the entrenchment of the prevailing social order.

While the Second World War worked profound material changes in American society and thrust the nation to an unprecedented global presence, the forces of continuity remained strong. To be sure, the war increased the role of the federal government and the power of the Presidency; it contributed to the growth of organized labor and of big business; it stimulated large-scale migration; it promoted a new consciousness about racism; and, above all, it lifted the economy from depression to prosperity. But it was that very economic prosperity along with the renewed confidence in American institutions induced by victory which contributed to a mood of conservatism and complacency. Having weathered the strains and inconveniences of the military crisis, most Americans were more interested in holding on to their wartime gains, in maintaining things as they were than in social and economic experiments aimed to alleviate the inequities and injustices that remained in the social fabric. That continuing attachment to the prewar social order and values was nowhere more apparent than in the area of sex roles and women's status.

NOTES AND REFERENCES

1. This chapter relies on major secondary sources for its overview of Amerian history in the 1940s. The best studies of wartime America are John M. Blum, *V Was For Victory: Politics and American Culture During World War II* (New York: Harcourt Brace Jovanovich, 1976); Alan Clive, *State of War: Michigan in World War II* (Ann Arbor: University of Michigan Press, 1979); Richard R. Lingeman, *Don't You Know There's a War On? The American Home Front, 1941–1945* (New York: G. P. Putnam's Sons, 1970); Geoffrey Perrett, *Days of Sadness, Years of Triumph: The American People, 1939–1945* (New York: Coward, McCann & Geoghegan, Inc., 1973); Richard Polenberg, *War and Society: The United States, 1941–1945* (New York: J. B. Lippincott Co., 1972).

Postwar society and politics are treated in Joseph C. Goulden, *The Best Years, 1945–1950* (New York: Atheneum, 1976); Robert Griffith and Athan Theoharis, eds., *The Specter: Original Essays on the Cold War and the Origins of McCarthyism* (New York: New Viewpoints, 1974); Alonzo L. Hamby, *Beyond the New Deal: Harry S. Truman and American Liberalism* (New York: Columbia University Press, 1973); Godfrey Hodgson, *America in Our Time* (New York: Random House, 1976); Geoffrey Perrett, *A Dream of Greatness: The American People, 1945–1963* (New York: Coward, McCann & Geoghegan, 1979).

For foreign policy, see Stephen E. Ambrose, *Rise to Globalism: American Foreign Policy, 1938–1976* (New York: Penguin Books, rev. ed., 1976). Statistics in this chapter come from the annual volumes, United States Bureau of the Census, *Statistical Abstract of the United States* (Washington, D.C.: Government Printing Office); United States Bureau of the Census, *Historical Statistics of the United States, Colonial Times to 1970* (Washington, D.C.: Government Printing Office, 1975); and from Herman P. Miller, *Income of the American People* (New York: John Wiley and Sons, 1955).

GI's being welcomed on their return home at the end of WWII
Courtesy of Culver Pictures, New York

Chapter Two

Woman's Place in War and Reconversion

The critical events of the 1940s reshaped women's lives in many ways as they did those of men. As family members, women benefited from the war-induced economic boom and, as workers, they enjoyed unprecedented opportunities for employment. Government propaganda stressed women's critical importance in the war effort, and the new government controls imposed restraints on the economic choices of women and men alike. Although women were not subject to conscription, World War II afforded them their first opportunity to serve as regular members of the armed forces. The postwar period brought a sharp retraction of employment prospects for women workers, but as family members and consumers women did benefit from the relative economic prosperity which followed the war. As citizens, women engaged in the foreign policy debate attending the onset of the Cold War, and the political behavior and beliefs of women as well as of men in the public realm were subjected to the scrutiny of anti-Communist crusaders.

Although women and men shared similar experiences in the 1940s, the historical subordination of women and the division of labor according to sex meant that major political, economic, and social forces had a differential impact on women and that they responded to these developments in different ways. The sexual division of labor assigned women primary responsibility for the material and psychological maintenance of the family and men the primary responsibility for its economic support. Thus, women were viewed above all as wives and mothers, and their own concerns were more firmly rooted in the family. Economically dependent upon men in the family unit, women also had limited opportunities to influence policies and decisions in the public realm. Their domestic responsibilities along with systematic discrimination outside the home sharply limited women's participation in the public sphere—whether as blue-collar workers, professionals, culture-makers, or political activists. A dual labor system in the public sector paralleled the sexual division of labor within the home: the great majority of jobs were designated either as male or female, and only occasionally, such as in secondary school teaching, did men and women do the same work. Women's jobs were clustered in the areas of light manufacturing, service, and clerical work, where lower wages prevailed and opportunities for advancement were scarce. Although American society clung to these major tenets of the traditional sexual order, and although ideas about sex roles continued to be manifested in actual behavior, the Second World War modified women's position both in the home and in the world outside.

The extent to which World War II altered women's lives and social norms can be fully understood only with reference to the Depression decade. During that crisis, women as workers suffered unemployment and intensified discrimination, while most government relief and recovery programs were designed for men. The resurgence of labor activity in the 1930s increased the number of women union members, but left the vast majority of female workers unorganized. As family members, women found their domestic work expanded as they sought to compensate for reduced family income. The Depression forced postponement of marriage and contributed to a declining birth rate. Finally, women were put on the defensive as a general consensus hardened around the position that married women should not work outside the home.

The majority of adult women experienced the Depression as wives rather than as paid workers. More than 90 percent of all women married, but only 15 percent of all married women were in the labor force in 1940. As family income declined, wives had to substitute their own labor for goods and services which they had formerly purchased. Home canning, baking, and sewing for family consumption increased, and women also endeavored to supplement family income by taking in laundry or boarders or preparing food and clothing to sell. While their household production expanded, women's traditional function of providing emotional maintenance likewise increased as they coped with the psychological strains created when husbands no longer could live up to the traditional standard of masculinity—that of family provider. Crowded living conditions, resulting from a scarcity of affordable housing and the fact that family members spent more time at home, further taxed women's customary responsibility for maintaining smooth domestic relationships. Only in the area of child-rearing did women's domestic duties decrease in the 1930s. Hard-pressed families had fewer children, and the birth rate dropped from 25.1 in 1925 to 18.7 in 1935, rising only to 19.4 by 1940.[1]

Those women who sought to sustain themselves and their families through employment outside the home found themselves on the defensive. Ignoring the fact that low-income married women, particularly blacks and immigrants, worked outside the home with much greater frequency than their white middle-class counterparts, public discussion of the issue of working wives focused on the latter. In the 1920s writers had addressed the issue with some degree of openness and had exhibited relative tolerance for the working wife, *if* she could simultaneously fulfill her primary duties as wife and mother. But even this limited acceptance vanished when unemployment rates skyrocketed in the 1930s. In the Depression decade, those wives who worked outside the home were viewed as selfish, greedy women who took jobs away from male breadwinners. A Gallup poll in 1936 reported that 82 percent of the respondents believed that wives with employed husbands should not work outside the home, and that three-fourths of the women polled agreed.[2]

Such attitudes were manifest in the policies of public and private employers during the 1930s. Section 213 of the Economy Act of 1932 required that when federal agencies reduced personnel, those employees who were married to persons holding federal jobs should be the first to go. While the law was not sex-specific, 75 percent of those dismissed were women. Executive orders in several state and local governments replicated this policy, and state legislatures considered seriously bills of this nature as late as 1941. Specific discrimination against married women was practised by a majority of school districts as well as by private employers. It was particularly intense in white-collar jobs among utility companies, banks, and insurance firms. As Lois Scharf has pointed out, these white-collar jobs were in a most rapidly growing area of female employment, they were attractive positions for single women and some men, and they had considerable public visibility. Little objection was made to married women factory operatives and none at all to those in domestic service.[3]

Women's organizations focused considerable energies against employment discrimination, and won repeal of Section 213 in 1937 as well as a few favorable court decisions. But they were unable to protect the position of women in the more desirable employment areas. During the 1930s, women's advancement in professional and white-collar work was retarded. While the figure for men increased slightly, the percentage of women workers who were professionals declined from 13.6 in 1930 to 12.3 in 1940. Both in absolute numbers and as a percentage of all elementary and secondary school teachers, women lost ground in the 1930s. In teaching and administrative positions in higher education, women's percentage likewise fell.[4]

Nonetheless, the Great Depression failed to reverse general, long-term trends in women's employment. Indeed, by almost every measure, women's participation in work outside the home increased during the 1930s. Women's share of the labor force grew from 22 to 25 percent, while the percentage of all adult women who were in the work force rose from 24.3 to 25.4. The proportion of married women who were employed grew from 12 to 15 percent during the decade, while married women increased their share of the female labor force from 29 to 35.5 percent. Such changes were consistent in direction, if not in rate, with trends that had been evident since the turn of the century.[5]

That these trends were sustained during the Depression was due to the sexual stratification of the work force and to material exigencies felt by individual women in the economic crisis. Throughout the twentieth century, occupations had been sex-linked and men and women did not usually compete for the same jobs. The Depression dealt a sharper blow in areas of the economy with high concentrations of male workers, such as mining and heavy industry, while areas in which female workers predominated, such as service and clerical fields, suffered less contraction. In fact, women's unemployment rates were lower than men's, although the gap narrowed by the late 1930s. Where they were not in direct competition with men for jobs, women were able to maintain their relative position in the world of work. Moreover, women were pushed into the labor market as unemployment suffered by customary breadwinners reduced family income.[6]

The quantitative increase in women's participation in productive activity was not accompanied by qualitative gains. While close to one-third of all female workers were engaged in clerical occupations in 1940, one of every four was a domestic servant, and more than one-fourth were semiskilled workers. More than half of all black women workers were in domestic service. The median wage or salary income of men in 1939 was $962; for women it was $568, and for nonwhite women, $246. The resurgence of labor union activity in the late 1930s had a limited effect on women as workers because the great organizing drives led by the new Congress of Industrial Organizations (CIO) were in such industries as steel and automobile where most production workers were men. By 1940, women were just 9.4 percent of all union members, though they were 25 percent of all operatives.[7]

The ideological consensus that women belonged at home rather than in the marketplace contributed to the inferior status and pay of women when they did leave the home. The sex-segregated labor market resembled the division of labor in the family: women factory workers were concentrated in the production of clothing, food and other goods formerly made by women in the home; and women in fields like health care, education, and even clerical work were seen as performing wifely and motherly functions. The conventional norm that males were the providers justified low wages for women, rationalized discrimination in hiring against women, especially those who were married, and checked the aspirations of women themselves. Thus, although larger economic realities and the needs of women and their families contradicted in practice the theory of "woman's place," that ideology continued to have a powerful effect.

The heightened opposition to women workers in the 1930s forced those groups which spoke for women's interests on the defensive. The Women's Bureau of the Department of Labor, the National Women's Trade Union League, the American Association of University Women, the National Federation of Business and Professional Women's Clubs, and the National Woman's party found it necessary to concentrate their energies on defending the right of married women to work. Instead of moving forward with their agendas designed to enlarge the status and opportunities of women, they had to fight a rear-guard action. In attempting to counter the statements and practices of government officials, employers, and labor leaders that denied both women's right and their need to work outside the home, these organizations collected data and conducted investigations to show that women were not taking jobs away from unemployed men. In protesting economic discrimination, even those women's organizations with the most feminist orientation paid lip-service to the dominant norm by emphasizing a positive relationship between women's family responsibilities and their employment and by stressing their need to work over their right to employment.[8]

The material deprivation, the economic discrimination and the psychological discouragement experienced by women during the Depression made the Second World War all the more important in improving their lives and status. Because the nation mobilized for war required the active support of every member, the media continuously made women aware of their importance, not alone as mothers, wives and homemakers, but also as workers, citizens, and even as soldiers. As their value in extrafamilial roles increased in the public consciousness, women also benefited from real opportunities to earn income, to enter new employment fields, and to perform in a wide variety of areas that had hitherto been reserved for men.

Although the popular ideology that women's primary role was in the home survived the war both in public discourse and in the beliefs of most women, the military crisis did create an ideological climate supportive of women's movement into the public realm. In the first place, the public depiction of the war as a struggle for freedom and democracy provided symbols for women to enlist in their own cause. Moreover, where the Depression had encouraged public criticism of women workers, the labor shortage of the war years necessitated appeals by government and employers for women to take jobs. The need for female labor lent a new legitimacy to the women worker and made government, employers, and labor unions more willing to consider the needs of women. Finally, wartime propaganda enhanced the importance of women as citizens and assigned them significant public responsibilities.

Material gains were even more substantial than the liberalization in public portrayals of appropriate female activities. Between 1940 and 1945, the female labor force grew by more than 50 percent, as the number of women at work outside the home jumped from 11,970,000 (with an additional 2.19 million unemployed) in 1940 to 18,610,000 (420,000 unemployed) in 1945. The proportion of all women who were employed increased from 27.6 to 37 percent, and by 1945 they formed 36.1 percent of the civilian labor force. Three-fourths of the new female workers were married; by the end of the war one of every four wives was employed.[9]

Women's employment grew in every occupational field but that of domestic service. Their most spectacular gains, however, were in factory work, particularly in those industries producing defense materials where their numbers mushroomed by 460 percent. While the women who replaced men in aircraft factories, ordnance plants and shipyards were most numerous and visible, the labor shortage also opened doors for women musicians, airplane pilots, scientists, athletes, and college professors.[10]

Women enjoyed higher incomes in the war economy as their wages in industry increased both absolutely and in relation to men's. Female gains were highest in war manufacturing, where they worked in formerly male jobs, but their earnings also rose in industries where women were traditionally concentrated, as well as in office work and in service industries. The general labor shortage elevated women's earnings, but of greatest importance were the opportunities for women to work in jobs where rates were historically higher. In addition, women, though not to the same extent as men, worked longer hours during the war, and government and union equal pay policies, while never systematically applied, helped to raise women's income.[11]

While women's productive capacities contributed critically to the nation's wartime needs, war also expanded their role as citizens. The two-thirds of the adult female population not employed found ample opportunity to assist the war effort. Federal agencies with responsibilities for military personnel, civil defense, war bonds, and rationing established advisory panels of women to interpret government programs and to enlist female support. Millions of women volunteered their energies to the Red Cross and the Office of Civilian Defense; provided recreation for military personnel at USO canteens; gathered information for the Office of War Information; sold war bonds; and collected anti—black market pledges. Even when their "war work" involved canning, saving fats and making household goods last longer, such traditional domestic tasks were infused with a larger public purpose. While sometimes trivializing and patronizing, private advertising and government propaganda did enhance the importance of women beyond their customary familial roles.[12]

Public awareness of women's real and potential contributions to national goals was manifested in legislative action which chipped away at some of the legal and civil disabilities suffered by women. Four state legislatures enacted equal pay laws during the war, and several others removed their bans against women jurors. In direct contrast to attitudes and practices during the Depression, a number of states passed laws protecting married women from discrimination in employment. In addition, for the first time Congress seriously considered an equal pay bill and an equal rights amendment to the Constitution.[13]

Of course, the war also changed women's lives in adverse ways. Millions of women suffered the temporary or permanent loss of husbands, fathers, brothers, and sons. More than 400,000 men lost their lives and another 671,000 returned wounded from the war. To the loneliness and anxiety experienced by servicemen's wives was added material strain, for the government allotments to dependents of enlisted men were modest and did not always arrive with regularity. The more than 7 million women who changed residence during the war were cut off from familiar relationships and had to adjust to new, usually crowded communities. Because women spent more time at home and bore primary responsibility for their families' physical maintenance, they experienced more intensely the shortages of housing, food, and clothing.

Less apparent at the time were the limitations placed upon women's aspirations by the very agencies that were encouraging women to assume larger functions outside the home. The nation desperately needed the services of women during the war, but it was equally resolutely attached to the traditional sexual order. Indeed, as war brought social dislocation of an inordinate degree, the institution of the family with wife and mother at its core took on even more significance. Americans adjusted to women's new prominence in the public realm because that position was defined in terms which denied the erosion of cherished social norms.

The public discourse on women's new wartime roles established three conditions which set limits on social change. The first was that women were replacing men in the world outside the home only "for the duration." Particularly during the later stages of the war, employers and public officials asserted that women workers were proud of their contributions to the war effort, but were eager to return to the home and would gladly relinquish their jobs to returning soldiers. The second condition was that women would retain their "femininity" even as they performed masculine duties. Photographs of women war workers emphasized glamour, and advertising copy assured readers that beneath the overalls and grease stains there remained a true woman, feminine in appearance and behavior. Finally, the media emphasized the eternal feminine motivations behind women's willingness to step out of customary roles. Patriotic motives were not ignored; but also highlighted was women's determination to serve their families albeit in novel ways. In the public image, women took war jobs to bring their men home more quickly and to help make the world a more secure place for their children.[14]

Thus, as women moved into the public sphere, they were reminded that their new positions were temporary, that retaining the traditional feminine characteristics was essential, and that their familial roles continued to take precedence over all others. Margaret Hickey, who chaired the Women's Advisory Committee to the War Manpower Commission, rightly wondered if society's wartime courtship of women had been "honorable."[15] It was not surprising that American society "used" its women during World War II, for that has ever been the experience of all nations and all citizens during military crises. What is noteworthy is that American society managed a temporary disruption of traditional social norms within a larger context of continuity in the sexual order. The conditions implied in the invitation to women to take war jobs both facilitated public—and female—acceptance of altered behavior patterns and thwarted a significant restructuring of sex roles.

Whether by force or by choice, women did leave the labor force as the war ended. By 1946 the female labor force had declined from its wartime peak of 19,170,000 to 16,896,000. Women's share of the civilian labor force decreased from 35.4 percent in 1944 to 28.6 percent in 1947; and the proportion of all women in the job market fell from 36.5 percent to 30.8 percent. Even at their low point, however, these figures were higher than those for 1940, and by 1947 they had begun to climb again as the long-term trend in female employment reasserted itself. At the end of the decade the number, but not the proportion, of employed women was slightly higher than that of the wartime peak. Close to 29 percent of all women were in the labor force and they constituted 30 percent of all workers.[16]

What these overall figures do not reveal is the redistribution of women workers as the war ended. Women had made their major wartime gains in manufacturing, particularly in heavy industry, and it was here that they suffered the most extensive setbacks. Between June and September 1945, one of every four women had been dropped from factory jobs. In the automobile industry (which produced military goods during the war), where women had filled one-fourth of all wartime jobs, their proportion had been reduced to 7.5 percent by April 1946, a pattern which was repeated in ship-building, steel, and other durable-goods industries. Thus, the breakdown of the sex-segregated labor market necessitated by World War II did not survive. Women who remained in the labor force found their earnings reduced as they moved back into traditionally female jobs in light industry. As they shifted to clerical, service, and sales positions, they also lost the protection of labor unions.[17]

The ideological climate of the postwar era also circumscribed female activity. Public concern about family stability did not disappear during the war. Indeed, increased geographical mobili-

ty, growing rates of juvenile delinquency and child labor, a rising
divorce rate, the prolonged separation of between 3 and 4 million
families, and growing incidence of illegitimacy all produced considerable anxiety about the institution most people considered to
be the very foundation of social order. Largely representing the
acceleration of trends in existence before the war, these developments drew heightened attention in a nation undergoing intense
social dislocation. Not surprisingly, social scientists and social-
welfare experts routinely included working mothers among the
causes of family instability. After the war, women's services continued to be recognized as important to the nation as a whole. But
social stability had replaced military victory as the national goal;
and women were needed as wives and mothers rather than as
workers.[18]

Women whose behavior conformed to the intensified emphasis
on home and family were not simply manipulated by public appeals. Living conditions during the war enhanced the attractiveness of traditional family life and the customary division of labor
between wives and husbands. Shortages of food and clothing,
rationing, the unavailability of household appliances, and inadequate housing all had made housekeeping more arduous and time-
consuming. A steep surge in the birth rate during the war and
thereafter expanded women's childrearing responsibilities. Many
women who had taken on a job in addition to their domestic duties
were eager to extricate themselves from this double burden. Moreover, the emotional deprivations experienced by women separated
from husbands during the war made women willing to concentrate
their energies on rebuilding family relationships. An outpouring of
literature concerning the return of veterans to civilian life reinforced such personal needs by instructing women about their
crucial roles in the veterans' social readjustment. These books and
articles called upon women to strengthen the male ego, relinquish
some of their own independence, and, above all, to adapt their
needs and interests to those of their returning men.[19]

While women were assigned the primary role in veterans' readjustment to family life, the nation as a whole assumed responsibility for veterans' economic well-being, and this, too, contributed to
a disparity in status between men and women. The GI Bill of
Rights provided benefits for all veterans, but since the 350,000

women who volunteered represented just around 2 percent of all military personnel, its overwhelming impact was on men. Particularly in the areas of civil-service job preference, reemployment rights, and education, millions of men received advantages that were available to just a few women. Thus, while in absolute numbers women in the postwar period increased their representation in employment and in education, their overall proportion, relative to men, declined. A reasonable response to the sacrifices made by soldiers, the GI Bill, nonetheless, increased the gap between men and women in opportunities and status.

Those organizations which had historically represented women's interests were not oblivious to this relative decline in women's position. But while they defined and combated the limitations on women's aspirations, they were unable to generate a movement sufficiently powerful to sustain and further the wartime gains. While women's organizations had been able to unite around specific goals during the war, conflicting interests and priorities continued to impair their effectiveness. The major conflict was over the proposed Equal Rights Amendment, a controversy which in part reflected the barriers that class and race posed to a united womanhood. Large organizations like the American Association of University Women and the National Federation of Business and Professional Women's Clubs focused on goals attractive to their largely middle-class constituencies and failed to address the needs of lower-income women.[20] Even had they been able to bridge class and race lines, women's groups faced stubborn external obstacles. The retreat to the home of millions of women, based in part on personal decisions, was encouraged and reinforced by a powerful media appeal. Moreover, the onset of the Cold War drew both national attention and the consideration of women's organizations away from women's rights to the apparent international crisis, and the anti-Communist crusade discredited individual women leaders while it induced caution in the activities of women's organizations. Organized womanhood survived the 1940s, but with a voice both fragmented and stilled.

That many of the crisis-induced changes in women's lives were reversed by the end of the 1940s does not cancel out the importance of World War II in altering sex roles. The contradiction between women's behavior and deeply entrenched social beliefs had never been greater, and the resolution of that disharmony failed to return women to the status quo ante bellum. Although those conventional standards survived and reasserted themselves after the war, women's behavior in the public realm had undergone considerable change and would continue to develop in altered patterns. Moreover, a substantial number of women acted under the sheer imperative of economic necessity: whatever the popular consensus, they were compelled to order their lives in response to their own material needs and those of their families. The war and changes in the structure of the American economy afforded enlarged opportunities to meet these needs. Even the most dramatic assault on traditional sex roles, the incorporation of women into the armed forces, survived the return to normalcy.

NOTES AND REFERENCES

1. See Ruth Milkman, "Women's Work and the Economic Crisis: Some Lessons from the Great Depression," *Review of Radical Political Economics* 8 (Spring 1976):73–97; United States Bureau of the Census, *Historical Statistics of the United States, Colonial Times to 1970* (Washington, D.C.: Government Printing Office, 1975), p. 49.

2. For popular attitudes in the 1920s and 1930s see Leila Rupp, *Mobilizing Women for War: German and American Propaganda, 1939–1945* (Princeton, N.J.: Princeton University Press, 1978), pp. 51–73; and Lois Scharf, *To Work and To Wed: Female Employment, Feminism, and the Great Depression* (Westport, Conn.: Greenwood Press, 1980).

3. United States Department of Labor, Women's Bureau, "Official

Action as to Employment of Married Women," April 1940, Papers of the Consumers' League of Ohio, Box 40, Western Reserve Historical Society, Cleveland, Ohio; for a full discussion of married women workers, see Scharf, *To Work and To Wed.*

4. United States Bureau of the Census, *Statistical Abstracts of the United States: 1952* (Washington, D.C.: Government Printing Office, 1952), pp. 115, 188 (hereafter *SA*); Winifred D. Wandersee Bolin, "American Women and the Twentieth Century Work Force: The Depression Experience," in Mary Kelly, ed., *Woman's Being, Woman's Place: Female Identity and Vocation in American History* (Boston: G. K. Hall, 1979), pp. 296–312.

5. Peter Gabriel Filene, *Him/Her/Self: Sex Roles in Modern America* (New York: New American Library, 1976), p. 219.

6. Milkman, "Woman's Work and the Economic Crisis," pp. 78–81. She does point out that women's unemployment was probably undercounted.

7. *SA: 1952*, pp. 188, 270; *Changes in Women's Occupations, 1940–1950*, United States Department of Labor, Women's Bureau Bulletin 253 (Washington, D.C.: Government Printing Office, 1954), p. 11; Ruth Milkman, "Organizing the Sexual Division of Labor: Historical Perspectives on 'Women's Work' and the Labor Movement," *Socialist Review* 10 (January–February 1980):125–29.

8. See, for example, Ruth Shallcross, *Should Married Women Work?* (New York: Public Affairs Committee, 1940); Scharf, *To Work and To Wed*, pp. 60–65.

9. *SA: 1952*, p. 178; International Labour Office (hereafter ILO), *The War and Women's Employment: The Experience of the United Kingdom and the United States* (Montreal: ILO, 1946) pp. 175–76.

10. Ibid., pp. 171–74; United States Department of Labor, Women's Bureau, "Consultation on the Postwar Employment of Women," April 1946, Records of the Women's Bureau, 54-A-78, Box 11. (Citations for Women's Bureau records reflect their arrangement at the time of research. These records are now in the National Archives, arranged in the customary manner.)

11. ILO, *The War and Women's Employment*, pp. 206–18.

12. Eleanor F. Straub, "Government Policy toward Civilian Women during World War II," Ph.D. dissertation, Emory University, 1973, pp. 3–8; Office of War Information, "Women in the War," August 15, 1942, Records of the War Manpower Commission, Reports and Analysis Services, Historical Section, National Archives, RG 211. For examples of advertisements, see *Advertising's Part in Civilian Mobilization: Second Portfolio of Fifty Outstanding War Advertisements* (New York: Advertising and Selling, 1943).

13. United States Department of Labor, Women's Bureau, "The Legal Status of Women in the United States of America: Trends in Political and Civil Laws, 1938–1945," Papers of the American Federation of Labor, Series 8A, Box 22, State Historical Society, Madison, Wisconsin.

14. See Rupp, *Mobilizing Women for War*, pp. 137—66.

15. Margaret Hickey, "What's Ahead for the Woman Who Earns," March 14, 1946, Papers of Frieda Miller, Folder 199, Schlesinger Library, Radcliffe College.

16. *SA: 1952*, pp. 177—79; Rupp, *Mobilizing Women for War*, p. 186.

17. Women's Bureau, "Consultation on Postwar Employment of Women," p. 8; Frieda Miller, "The Womenfolk Take Stock," August 21, 1946, Records of the Women's Bureau, 58-A-850, Box 3; Frieda Miller, "Why Women Work," *American Federationist* 54 (February 1947):14—16.

18. Sidonie Matsner Gruenberg, ed., *The Family in a World at War* (New York: Harper and Bros., 1942), pp. 1—20; Francis Merrill, *Social Problems on the Home Front* (New York: Harper and Row, 1948), pp. 25—48; William H. Chafe, *The American Woman: Her Changing Social, Economic and Political Roles, 1920—1970* (New York: Oxford University Press, 1972), pp. 149—50, 176—78.

19. Susan M. Hartmann, "Prescriptions for Penelope: Literature on Women's Obligations to Returning World War II Veterans," *Women's Studies* 5 (1978):223—39.

20. Susan M. Hartmann, "Women's Organizations during World War II: The Interaction of Class, Race, and Feminism," in Kelley, ed., *Woman's Being, Woman's Place*, pp. 313—28.

Members of the Women's Army Corps disembark in North Africa, 1943
Courtesy of the National Archives

Chapter Three

Women in Uniform

The American women most sharply wrenched away from the customary patterns of female behavior during the 1940s were those who served with the armed forces. Their experience was not entirely novel. As nurses, cooks, seamstresses, laundresses, and later as clerical workers, women had worked directly for the military in every war since the Revolution. In those crises women had served as unpaid volunteers, as civilian employees of the services, or as volunteers in temporary or quasi-military bodies. Two elements were new to women's military service in the 1940s: they were utilized in nearly every activity short of combat, and they achieved permanent, regular status in the military establishment. The process by which women were integrated into the armed forces revealed the power of war to refashion sex roles, but also demonstrated the tenacity of conventional beliefs, as military leaders and public officials sought to meet exigencies with the least disruption of the prewar sexual order.

Women directly assisted the war effort in diverse capacities and in a variety of organizations. One thousand aviators served with the Women's Airforce Service Pilots (WASP); their status was civilian, but their service paralleled that of the women's military corps. The largest number of women joined the female corps of the military branches: 140,000 served with the Women's Army Corps

(WAC); 100,000 with the navy's WAVES; 23,000 with the Marine Corps Women's Reserve (MCWR); and 13,000 with the coast guard's SPARS. A small number of women physicians were commissioned directly with men into the medical corps of the army and navy. Finally, 60,000 women joined the Army Nurse Corps (ANC), and another 14,000 the Navy Nurse Corps (NNC). With the exception of these two units, women's opportunity to serve on an equitable basis was achieved only after considerable controversy.[1]

Because nursing had been a feminine profession from the beginning, little opposition arose to the use of women to tend the wounded even when such duties brought them under enemy fire. Their employment of civilians as nurses had led military officials to recognize the advantage of permanence and control when they created the Army Nurse Corps in 1901 and the Navy Nurse Corps in 1908. Although these were military organizations, members received neither full military rank nor pay and allowances equal to those of male military personnel. After World War I, their ranks had been reduced to fewer than 1,000, but women in the nursing corps were immediately drawn into war service with the first Japanese attacks on Pearl Harbor and the Philippines. Sixty-six army nurses spent the entire war at Bataan and Corregidor, serving most of that time under Japanese captivity.[2]

Once the nation was at war nurses volunteered for military service at a rate surpassing that of any other profession. More than 100,000 volunteered, and the 76,000 who served represented 31.3 percent of all active professional nurses. They saw duty in every theater, often right behind the front lines. Nurses accompanied the American invasions of North Africa and Italy, and were serving in France on D day plus four. They dug their own foxholes, lived under rugged field conditions, and cared for wounded men under enemy fire. In return, they finally won equal pay and allowances and full military rank.[3]

Male nurses discovered that not just women suffered from sex-role stereotyping. While women were commissioned as second lieutenants in the ANC and as ensigns in the NNC, men were denied comparable status. The military tended to assign men with professional nursing credentials to medical departments, but they generally served in the lower ranks. Men who had graduated from nursing schools and found themselves classified as corpsmen or medics protested at the waste of their skills when they were "taught" bandaging and litter-carrying along with military skills not related to nursing. Efforts of the American Nurses' Association to obtain legislation granting these men status in the military comparable to that of women nurses were unsuccessful.[4]

Black nurses also faced impediments to their full utilization in war service, even though the supply of nurses was scarce. The military treatment of black nurses paralleled its policy of segregation and discrimination against all blacks in the services, and it also mirrored their civilian status in the profession. The vast majority of nursing schools refused to admit blacks, and the American Nurses' Association tolerated white-only units in fifteen states. A few black women had been admitted to the Army Nurse Corps during the last months of World War I, but the small peacetime corps reverted to an all-white status. In 1941, the surgeon general announced that fifty-six black women would be admitted to serve only black patients. As casualties mounted and black organizations pressured military officials, their numbers in the ANC grew to 500 by 1945. When the war ended, just four were serving in the navy, which had admitted them only that year. A few black units were sent overseas, but for the most part black nurses made their contribution to victory by caring for black soldiers and prisoners of war.[5]

While nurses were actively sought for military duty, women physicians had to fight for the opportunity to serve in the military medical corps. Women who applied were told that the "qualified persons" authorized by law to receive temporary commissions referred to male doctors only. A few women, including Dr. Barbara Stimson, niece of the secretary of war, joined the British Medical Corps, while the American Medical Women's Association organized a campaign to reverse the War Department's stand. Assisted by the increasing need for military doctors and supported by numerous women's organizations and opinion leaders—but not by the American Medical Association—in April 1943, they won legislation enabling women physicians to join the army and navy medical corps. Although the number of women affected was small, the legislation was significant in expanding women's options as citizens and professionals. Moreover, because some medical schools had been rejecting women in order to save places for potential military doctors, the laws helped to bolster women's already precarious access to medical training.[6]

The combination of military needs and pressure from women themselves also worked to win women a place in the regular branches of the armed services, a step which represented the most startling departure from precedent. By World War II, the nature of war and of the military establishment had changed so as to foster the use of women's services. The global scope of American involvement, the increasing complexity of modern war, and the development of military technology had reduced the proportion of military personnel directly engaged in battle. During World War II 25 percent of military personnel never left the United States, and only about one in eight actually saw combat. In World War II only 34.1 percent of army personnel was engaged in purely military occupations. Thus, the increasingly "civilian" nature of many military duties, more than 10 percent of which were administrative and clerical, made possible the employment of women in the defense establishment.[7]

Most military leaders, however, were not quick to grasp this possibility, despite the precedent of World War I, when more than 10,000 women had served in the navy and marine corps and several thousand civilian women had performed clerical and communications duties for the army in France. As the situation in Europe deteriorated during 1939 and 1940, both army and navy staffs considered the utilization of women, but neither branch would make a commitment to the establishment of women's corps until prodded by women themselves. In the spring of 1941, Republican Congresswoman Edith Nourse Rogers of Massachusetts gave political voice and focus to the demands of women's organizations and individual citizens when she informed Chief of Staff General George C. Marshall that she planned to introduce legislation creating a women's corps. Fearing the establishment of a corps not to its liking, and specifically opposed to full military status for women, the War Department then began to prepare a bill that it could comfortably sponsor. Acceding to the army's insistence that the women's corps not be part of the army, Rogers introduced the War Department's bill to establish the Women's Army Auxiliary Corps (WAAC) in May 1941.[8]

Navy officials likewise responded to Rogers's initiative, despite the reluctance of most of its bureaus and offices. The only two to demonstrate enthusiasm were the head of the Bureau of Aeronautics, the newest and least tradition-bound branch of the navy, and the chief of naval operations, who perceived the potential of women in communications work. Nonetheless, the momentum generated by the army's legislation suggested that further hesitation might result in legislative imposition of a corps that the navy could not effectively administer. For reasons of discipline, security, and convenience, Secretary of the Navy Frank Knox wanted the women's units in the navy, and such a bill was introduced in March 1942.[9]

In justifying their requests for the establishment of women's corps, military officials stressed manpower considerations. Arguing that the employment of women could release men from non-combatant duties, they also insisted that women were better suited for certain jobs. By the summer of 1941, Marshall had recognized the inexpediency of using men in the many military positions that women were regularly performing in the civilian sector. Army Assistant Chief of Staff John H. Hildring testified that "we have found difficulty in getting enlisted men to perform tedious duties anywhere nearly as well as women will do it." Defense officials routinely mentioned switchboard operators, typists, clerks, dietitians, and laundry operators in providing examples of how women would be assigned. Finally, they argued that for reasons of security, permanence, and flexibility it was necessary to have support personnel under military control. Civil service employees, unlike military personnel, could resign at will, were not subject to transfer, and had limitations on their hours of work. In rationalizing its request for women's service, the military's emphasis on expediency and control was not unique, for such considerations also directed its approach toward male personnel. Where it did treat women differently was in its assumptions that all women were by nature better fitted for a specific and limited set of duties.[10]

The arguments of women themselves had a different focus. Individual women as well as organizations like the General Federation of Women's Clubs and the American Association of Univer-

sity Women, asserted above all women's right to full participation
in all the responsibilities of citizenship. In addition, women advocates were sensitive to the plight of those earlier women who had
served with the army during World War I and had been denied
hospitalization and other benefits after the war. The woman most
active in the establishment of the corps, Congresswoman Rogers,
combined appeals to expediency and justice. Along with military
leaders she promoted a women's corps as a solution to military
labor problems, and she too maintained that women were better
qualified for certain kinds of work. But she also suggested that
women might be used in technical and mechanical occupations.
Moreover, Rogers had observed the inadequate care provided for
women serving in France in the First World War and had cam-
paigned without success to obtain veterans' compensation for
them. "I was resolved," she said, "that our women would not again
serve with the Army without the protection that men got." Finally, Rogers urged passage of her bill on the grounds that women
both wanted and deserved equal opportunity to serve their
country.[11]

Overt opposition to the women's corps legislation was relatively
weak due largely to the reluctance of legislators to hinder the
military in a time of national crisis. Those who did speak and vote
against the bills expressed anxiety about disturbing the traditional
sexual order and the "sanctity of the home." These opponents did
not question women's capabilities with the exception of one con-
gressman who maintained that women were not trained to the
unquestioning obedience necessary for military order. But they
did argue that women should not be distracted from their domestic
duties: "Who will do the cooking, the washing, the mending, the
humble homey tasks to which every woman has devoted herself;
who will rear and nurture the children . . . ?" And, they suggested
that women in the military would reflect unfavorably on American
men: "What has become of the manhood of America, that we have
to call on our women to do what has ever been the duty of men?"[12]

In the face of a global war, such opposition scarcely prolonged
the debate. The House passed the WAAC bill, 249–86, in March
1942, and the Senate followed in May by a vote of thirty-eight to
twenty-seven. With the ground broken by the army legislation,
both houses approved the navy bill establishing the WAVES after

little debate and without roll-call votes. In November, the coast guard established the SPARS, and the marine corps its women's reserve in February 1943. After experiencing legal and practical difficulties in administering an auxiliary corps, the War Department moved to support full army status for women, and in June 1943 Congress converted the WAAC to the WAC.[13]

Given the rationale for incorporating women into the military it is not surprising that women's service reflected the gender-based division of labor in the civilian economy. Of the 55,000 Waves who took advanced training, one-third were in yeoman ratings, the clerical category; 30 percent were trained in hospital work; and another 14 percent as storekeepers. Their work in aviation attracted most publicity, and every navy pilot received some instruction from a woman once the WAVES got underway; yet only 13.7 percent of the Waves were trained in aviation. Like its naval counterpart, the United States Army Air Force was most innovative in utilizing women, but even in that branch about half of the Wacs did administrative and office work. Similarly, 62 percent of the Women Marines were in clerical and supply specialties. Because the primary military interest was in maximum procurement and utilization of personnel, women were most often assigned to work they normally did in civilian life, and relatively few were trained in masculine skills. As the war progressed military officials modified their assumptions about female capabilities, and the variety of duties performed by women expanded. By the end of the war, for example, Wave officers were being assigned to air crews on flights to Hawaii. Nonetheless the great majority of servicewomen were engaged in the traditional female areas of office work, communications, and health care.[14]

The military policies and procedures which treated women differently from men reflected both expediency and caution. While male officers focused primarily on the most efficient use of personnel, they occasionally sacrificed this consideration to Congressional and public opinion. Women leaders were more sensitive to the issue of equality and were reluctant to accept special privileges for women or to tolerate disadvantages. Wave Commander Mildred McAfee objected to the proscription against female supervision of male personnel, and such a ban created inefficiency in both the army and the navy, but male officers were unwilling to ruffle "too many feathers in Congress." In 1944, the marine corps got around the ticklish problem of female authority by ruling that it was proper for a woman officer to direct men when her orders were construed to be emanating from her male superior. To Mc-Afee the limitation of Waves to stateside service hindered recruitment, prevented women from feeling that they were full-fledged members of the navy, and insulted women with the implication that they could not be trusted abroad. Because of strong opposition in Congress, the navy refused to press for overseas duty until 1944, when Waves and Women Marines were permitted to serve in the American Theater. Waacs had been sent to North Africa early in 1943, and thereafter army women served in every major overseas theater, although the majority remained on the home front. The traditional military ban on social relations between officers and enlisted personnel applied to Wacs, and McAfee urged that women be granted no special consideration, yet the Navy Department relaxed the proscription for Waves on the grounds that the public expected a greater degree of social democracy for women.[15]

On other issues concerning the differential treatment of men and women, Captain McAfee and her counterpart in the WAC, Colonel Oveta Culp Hobby, saw eye to eye with their male superiors. They accepted the prevailing view that women's family roles were paramount. Married women could enlist, but mothers with children under fourteen were ineligible for the WAC, and the navy and marines excluded those with children under eighteen. While the enlisted man's wife and children were automatically eligible for a family allowance, dependency benefits were granted to a woman's relatives only upon proof that she in fact provided their main support. Waves were rarely allowed to resign to be with sick parents, but such permission was granted more often to women than to men, according to McAfee, "not as a favor to the women but in response to social pressures, which gave family obligations for a woman volunteer priority over military demands." The military establishment recognized the primacy of women's domestic relationships in demobilization regulations which allowed earliest discharges to women whose husbands had been mustered out.[16]

Military policies regarding servicewomen were designed with an eye to recruitment which posed a major problem through most of the war. At first women were turned away as the number of volunteers surpassed the WAAC quota of 12,000. But after the allotment was increased to 150,000 the army was unable to fill it. According to military studies, resistance sprang primarily from unsympathetic public opinion generated largely by male servicemen. Many soldiers' hostility faded quickly once they came into actual contact with Wacs, but only a minority ever observed military women firsthand. Some draftees did not want to be replaced by women so that they could be cannon fodder. Others resented publicity suggesting that women recruits were sometimes superior to men. Most simply could not shed their preconceptions about women's capabilities and their appropriate roles.[17]

The spread of vicious rumors about WAC immorality in 1943 dealt a severe blow to recruitment and demonstrated the extent to which women in uniform violated timeworn beliefs. These rumors circulated among civilians as well as among enlisted men and officers, and were based on the assumption that women's military contributions could only take the form of sexual favors. Reports that Wacs were frequently drunk, that they were sexually promiscuous, that the army provided them contraceptives, and—contradictorally—that hundreds of them were pregnant, circulated so widely that the president and secretary of war were compelled to make a public defense of enlisted women. At the same time military policies regarding conduct, discipline and sexual behavior were designed to protect the women's corps from such slander. Concurring with Director Hobby's belief that contraceptives should not be issued to women "for social as well as public relations reasons," Secretary of War Stimson made clear to army personnel that regulations concerning prophylaxis applied to men only. The Wac slanders caused navy officials to delay distribution of pamphlets and movies on sex hygiene for Waves and to drop completely a movie on contraception. Military discipline mirrored the double standard prevalent in civilian society: in the few cases where men and women marines were found jointly guilty of sexual misconduct women were punished more severely. Military regulations on the one hand held women to more stringent standards regarding their conduct, but at the same time recommended that women not normally serve time in the brig.[18]

Although charges of lesbianism were less frequent than rumors of heterosexual promiscuity, military officials were quick to act against any sign of what they and virtually all of society considered a perversion. As a result women were punished not only for actual behavior, as they were for heterosexual misconduct, but also for "homosexual tendencies." Marine corps officials used naval-intelligence agents to investigate cases of suspected lesbianism, and women marines could be discharged for homosexuality upon diagnosis of a psychiatrist. In all the women's units the numbers of women discharged for lesbianism were tiny. Nonetheless, in an environment conducive to the development of female comradeship, public suspicions and official policy encouraged women to set limits on their relationships with fellow volunteers.[19]

Military officials also bowed to racial attitudes and practices dominant in civilian society. Black women were admitted to the WAAC from the very beginning, and they represented almost 10 percent of the first group of women selected for officer training. Yet enlisted women were segregated in barracks, mess halls, and recreational facilities and were sent to the field in all-black units. Because blacks had been denied equal access to educational and economic opportunities in civilian society, black recruits were on the whole less skilled and consequently were assigned to less desirable classifications. While white women were also misassigned, black women with special skills were more often underutilized because the segregation policy did not allow them to be scattered among WAC detachments where their abilities could be employed. At Fort Devens, Massachusetts, four black women refused to report for duty when despite their training as medical technicians they were assigned menial hospital tasks. No Negro Wacs served overseas until 1945, when a postal batallion was sent to England, and later to France, to sort mail. As their male counterparts, black servicewomen also endured attacks and insults from civilians, especially in the South. When Negro Wacs attempted to sit in the white section of a Kentucky bus station, their uniforms did not protect them from being called "nigger wenches" and beaten by a local police officer. An army court martial thereupon tried one of these women for disorderly conduct, but found her not guilty.[20]

As civil rights groups and black women's organizations sought more equitable treatment for Negro Wacs, they also put intense pressure on the government to end the navy's policy of total exclusion. Taking literally the WAVES' purpose to release men for sea duty, the navy rejected black women's applications. Since virtually all black men were confined to messmen ratings, the navy reasoned that there were none that black women could replace. Not until October 1944 did President Roosevelt order the navy to begin a program for the incorporation of black Waves. With less than a year of fighting remaining, fewer than 100 served in World War II. The navy's belated admission of black women did give them one advantage over their sisters in the WAC: they were integrated into existing units from the beginning.[21]

That gender stereotypes were as firmly embedded in American society as racial prejudice was evident in the ongoing struggle of the women officers against the efforts of men both to trivialize and to glamorize women's military service. WAC leaders had to specify that Wacs be referred to as "women" or "soldiers," not as "girls," while women in all the branches tried to restrain the use of "cheese-cake" publicity with its emphasis on romantic appeal. At the same time they sought to limit material which emphasized excitement and adventure, believing that such publicity raised false expectations and belied the routine, often dull and drab reality of most women's military service. Where private enterprise dictated the images of servicewomen, these guidelines often did not prevail. Newsreels frequently referred to women as "girls" or "gals" and stressed the most dramatic as well as the more frivolous aspects of servicewomen's experience, such as their underwear and their patronage of beauty shops. The exasperation of Colonel Hobby with the press's flippant treatment of servicewomen was evident in her final news conference. Asked by a reporter if she had bought any new civilian hats, she responded, "Do you mind if I don't end this conference on a note of levity?"[22]

While they worked to dignify servicewomen and to highlight the seriousness of their contributions, women's corps leaders challenged little of the conventional wisdom about women's natural attributes and their appropriate roles. Acutely aware that military service represented a crucial test of women's capabilities, they sought a climate that would give women the best chance of meeting the challenge and were convinced that popular sentiment would not tolerate substantial deviations from traditional roles. Reflecting studies which suggested that a primary deterrent to recruitment was women's fear of losing their femininity or of being considered unfeminine, WAC publicity policy sought to impress the public that Wacs, were "just as feminine as before they enlisted," that, in fact, they developed "new poise and charm." Army policy prohibited pictures of women soldiers smoking or drinking and urged avoidance of reference to military activities requiring strenuous physical exertion. Colonal Hobby sought to portray women's service in terms of their traditional feminine relationships and responsibilities, and she recommended advertising copy which pointed out that servicewomen would be hastening the return of their sweethearts and husbands by "only performing the duties that women would ordinarily do in civilian life." Captain McAfee sought to reassure the public about Waves' postwar plans: they would be "as likely as other women to make marriage their profession."[23]

A product both of the need to appeal to prevailing public attitudes and of the views of the women officers, military propaganda encouraged a larger, yet still limited, vision of women's capabilities and responsibilities. Films, posters, and advertisements asserted the equivalency of women's duties and contributions—they were doing a "man-sized" job, marching "shoulder to shoulder with men," for it was "a woman's war, too," and they were getting equal pay. Moreover, women were pictured in nontraditional activities, training pilots and working on motor vehicles. But this media image also emphasized women as relatives of men, portraying the admiration of men for their wives, daughters, sweethearts and sisters who enlisted, encouraging women to sign up in order to bring their men safely home and to ensure a secure future for their children. Finally, the propaganda called attention to those skills traditionally associated with the female nature. The army needed women's "delicate hands" for "precision work at which women are so adept," and it required women in hospital work because "there is a need in a man for comfort and attention that only a woman can fill."[24]

Assumptions about innate feminine characteristics also played a significant role in postwar deliberations about the future of women in the armed services. Impressed with women's wartime contributions, military leaders believed that any future emergency would require the utilization of women and wanted to retain a nucleus of trained women to provide a base for swift expansion. Moreover, the rapid deterioration in Soviet-American relations suggested that a new crisis was close at hand. Facing a shortage of personnel in the immediate postwar period, officials told Congress that women's manual dexterity, patience, attention to detail, and enthusiasm for monotonous work made them superior to men in clerical work, communications, cryptography, and hospital work. At the same time they assured legislators that women's primary interests remained rooted in the home. One of the most enthusiastic WAC supporters, General Dwight D. Eisenhower, predicted that "after an enlistment or two enlistments women will ordinarily—and thank God—they will get married." In May 1948 Congress responded to the services' requirements by passing the Women's Armed Services Integration Act, which gave women permanent, regular status in the defense establishment. Full equality however, continued to elude women. They were limited to 2 percent of total strength, they could not advance higher than the rank of lieutenant colonel or commander, and married women could not enlist unless they were veterans. Moreover, the range of occupations available to women narrowed in the postwar military because officials believed that "unfeminine" work was unacceptable to public opinion in peacetime.[25]

Despite these limitations, a new option was available to women as a result of World War II. During the crisis women most frequently enlisted out of patriotism and a desire to promote victory. Of the later volunteers almost half joined for educational and vocational opportunities, 20 percent for adventure and travel, and only 9 percent for patriotic reasons. For these women military service became a means to individual development and self-fulfillment. Public opinion had also shifted to support women's presence in the armed services. Postwar polls showed that 53 percent of the public favored women in the peacetime military (35 percent were opposed, and the rest had no opinion). While women registered approval slightly more frequently than did men (54 to 52 percent), women under thirty expressed the most enthusiasm.[26]

Public acceptance of women's military role did not mean that servicewomen returning from World War II received a hero's welcome. In general, women were better prepared than men to return to civilian life. Few had been wounded or disabled; they were older and better educated than the average soldier, and many had held jobs before their tours of duty. Women veterans had fewer dependents, and they had freely chosen military service. Yet they did have readjustment problems which they met with little public sympathy or official support. In the mass of literature written to ease the veterans' return, women were scarcely mentioned. They had access to the hundreds of veterans' centers established throughout the country, but most of these services were geared to helping and advising men. Servicewomen could join the American Legion as full-fledged members, but the Veterans of Foreign Wars confined them to the ladies auxiliary established primarily for relatives of VFW members.[27]

Federal law guaranteed to women most of the benefits offered to male veterans. Women were entitled to reemployment in their former jobs; readjustment allowances while they sought work; veterans' preference in civil-service employment; federal grants to continue their education; and government loans to purchase homes or establish businesses. The discrimination experienced by ex-servicewomen derived from the assumption that women were economic dependents, not supporters. To receive assistance for dependents, women had to prove that they provided the major support, while such standards did not apply to men. The veterans' preference law gave widows and wives of disabled veterans their husbands' preference rights to federal jobs. But when veterans' organizations lobbied against a similar provision for husbands of female veterans, Congress acquiesced.[28]

Employment posed the biggest problem for women veterans. Hiring officials frequently did not recognize their reemployment rights. Even some government agencies were unaware of their prior claim to federal jobs, although by 1947, 41,000 had taken federal employment. While military experience gave male veterans an advantage in job-hunting, some employers actually counted women's service experience against them. Two-thirds of a group of 150 women veterans in New York reported discrimination in their efforts to find jobs. Women were particularly discouraged in their efforts to obtain employment commensurate with the skills and experience they had acquired during the war. In a 1946 survey of former Wacs, less than half of those employed were able to use the experience they had gained in the service on their new jobs.[29]

One group of women had to make the transition from war service to civilian life with no assistance whatsoever. These were the 1,074 Women's Airforce Service Pilots (WASP) who from 1942 to 1944 flew military planes throughout the United States and Canada for the Army Air Forces (AAF). The use of women in this unlikely capacity resulted from military needs and from the experience of women in aviation during the two prewar decades. Although women had been only a tiny minority of all pilots, they had been highly visible as the commercial aviation industry employed them to demonstrate and sell planes and sponsored them in races. These opportunities, too, had been based on expediency. The fledgling aviation industry's need to promote public acceptance of air travel led it to utilize women, because if a mere woman could pilot a plane, then flying must be safe.[30]

Jacqueline Cochran and Nancy Harkness Love were two of the women who had gained prominence in the era of industry's support for female pilots. As early as 1939 they began to suggest that women fliers be used for noncombat missions. Army Air Force officials resisted as long as the numbers of male pilots were sufficient for the airplanes available, and in early 1942 Cochran organized twenty-five American women to serve with the British Air Transport Authority in England. By the fall of that year, aircraft production had increased, more pilots were needed, and the AAF authorized Love to begin a small program which would use highly experienced women to ferry planes. Subsequently, the War Department called Cochran back from England to establish a training program to prepare larger numbers of women. In mid-1943 these two programs were reorganized into the WASP, a civilian organization, with Cochran as director. The WASP faced no recruiting problems as more than 25,000 women applied for fewer than 2,000 places in the program. In order to prevent "complications" for her new enterprise, Cochran persuaded an experienced black woman to withdraw quietly her application and to dissuade others of her race. The WASP remained all-white.[31]

Wasps piloted virtually every type of military aircraft, including transport planes, the mammoth B-29 bombers, and the newest and fastest fighter craft. In all, they logged over 60 million miles. Women eventually comprised half of all the Ferry Division's fighter plane pilots, and made 75 percent of all deliveries in the

United States. Wasps also flew at air bases, towing targets for air-to-air and ground-to-air gunner trainees who often fired live ammunition. They served as test pilots and flew simulated strafing, smoke laying, radar jamming, and searchlight tracking missions. Some Wasps were called upon to perform operations that male pilots found too tedious or too dangerous; and they flew the newest, riskiest aircraft to convince male pilots that these planes were easy to handle. Although the WASP accident rate was below that of male civilian pilots, thirty-eight women lost their lives.[32]

As was true for women in the military units, Wasps were subjected to policies and practices which treated them differently than their male counterparts. Women's monthly pay was $280 per month, while civilian men received $350. At first women were ordered grounded during their menstrual periods, but AAF officials dropped the regulation when they found it was not being enforced. While male pilots routinely hitched rides in military planes back to home bases, Wasps were denied this convenient, time-saving practice. They could not fly in the same cockpit with a man, and they could not carry male passengers. Ultimately most devastating to Wasps was their inability to achieve military status, and consequently, their ineligibility for military and veterans' benefits.[33]

The first opportunity for military status came in 1943 when the WAAC was converted into the WAC and made a full part of the army. At that time the Army Air Force favored the enrollment of women pilots in the WAC, but Cochran preferred a separate organization and won AAF officials to her side. An effort by the AAF to commission women directly as it had done with male civilian pilots under 1941 legislation met the same objection that had confronted women physicians: "qualified persons" referred to men exclusively. By 1944 when AAF officials finally went before Congress to request militarization of the WASP, the program itself was in jeopardy because men wanted the Wasps' jobs. Fourteen thousand flight instructors and trainees had recently been released as the government terminated its civilian training programs. Many of these men were now called for active duty and protested against being assigned to ground or flight crews instead of securing pilots' commissions. In addition, fliers were returning from combat who wanted to stay in the army as ferry pilots. AAF representatives argued to skeptical legislators that it was utilizing both men and women in the most efficient manner based on each individual's qualifications and that justice demanded military status for these women who met the AAF's highest standards. Legislators, however, paid heed instead to the cries of male pilots, the civilian aviation industry, and the American Legion. The House defeated the WASP militarization bill in June 1944, and by the end of the year, the last Wasp had been ejected from her cockpit. [34]

In the postwar years women pilots failed to regain even the place they had held in aviation before 1940. Despite their wartime experience, they stood little chance for pilot jobs in competition with more than 200,000 former military pilots. Women did find work in the airlines industry, but in offices or behind ticket counters; their place in the skies was limited to serving as stewardesses. Not until the 1970s would small numbers of women begin to pilot planes for commercial airlines and the air force. As women began to break again the sexual division of labor in aviation, Congress belatedly responded to a full-scale campaign of former Wasps and granted them veteran status in 1977. [35]

Despite their unequal treatment, military service was a positive experience for most of the 350,000 women who volunteered. Sixty-five thousand of them took advantage of veterans' benefits for college or graduate study. A few reenlisted and pursued life-long careers in the military. War service itself expanded the horizons of these women as it took them far from home and placed them in novel situations. Pride in newly discovered capabilities was nearly universal. Whether it was the ability to persevere in arduous, routine duties, to perform work that only men were considered capable of before, or to carry out responsibilities under near-combat conditions, servicewomen experienced profound satisfaction in rising to the diverse challenges of military service. Above all, they enjoyed the opportunity to fulfill the most demanding role of citizenship.

It was military expediency that afforded women this opportunity. In the twentieth century, transformations in warfare had produced a military establishment capable of utilizing women, and the feminization of areas in the civilian economy had created an occupational structure which provided women with skills required by the military. Global war, with its heavy demands on manpower, forced military and civilian leaders to recognize the implications of these developments. Their satisfaction with women's war service led them to accept women's military contributions on a permanent basis when a new crisis, that of the Cold War, sprang up in the ruins of World War II. At the same time, expediency operated to sustain gender distinctions. Reflecting the importance of placating public and legislative opinion, military policies and propaganda supported the conventional wisdom that women needed special protection, that they possessed innate feminine characteristics, and that their familial and domestic roles were paramount. Governed by its need for the maximum use of personnel, the military employed women for the most part in traditionally female jobs and did little to effect any permanent alterations in the sex-based division of labor. Thus, military women experienced the expansion of woman's sphere, but within parameters that assaulted as little as possible prewar realities or attitudes. In important respects, their more numerous civilian sisters experienced a similar balance of change and continuity.

NOTES AND REFERENCES

1. National Manpower Council, *Womanpower* (New York: Columbia University Press, 1957), pp. 285—98.

2. Mary M. Roberts, *American Nursing: History and Interpretation* (New York: Macmillan, 1954), pp. 28—30, 171, 342—45; Phillip A. Kalisch and Beatrice J. Kalisch, "Nurses under Fire: The World War Experience of Nurses on Bataan and Corregidor," *Nursing Research* 25 (November—December 1976):409—29.

3. Roberts, *American Nursing*, pp. 342—52; "The Nurses' Contribution to American Victory: Facts and Figures from Pearl Harbor to V-J Day," *American Journal of Nursing* 45 (September 1945):683.

4. Roberts, *American Nursing*, pp. 319—22; Jacob Ross, "Men Nurses in the Military Service," *American Journal of Nursing* 47 (March 1947):146.

5. Mabel K. Staupers, "Present Status of the Negro Nurse in the Army Nursing Corps," *Aframerican Woman's Journal* 1 (Conference Issue, 1941):34; Jesse J. Johnson, ed., *Black Women in the Armed Forces, 1942—1974* (Hampton, Va., 1974), pp. 47—48.

6. Mary Roth Walsh, *"Doctors Wanted: No Women Need Apply:" Sexual Barriers in the Medical Profession* (New Haven: Yale University Press, 1977), pp. 226—30.

7. Morris Janowitz and Roger W. Little, *Sociology and the Military Establishment* (Beverly Hills, Calif.: Sage Publications, 3rd ed., 1974), p. 47.

8. Mattie E. Treadwell, *The United States Army in World War II, Vol. VIII, The Women's Army Corps* (Washington, D.C.: Department of the Army, 1954), pp. 6—10, 15—18.

9. Susan M. Hartmann, "Women in the Military Service," in Mabel E. Deutrich and Virginia C. Purdy, eds., *Clio Was a Woman: Studies in the History of American Women* (Washington, D.C.: Howard University Press, 1980), p. 196.

10. Ibid.

11. Ibid., p. 197.

12. Ibid.

13. Ibid., pp. 197—98.

14. Ibid., p. 198; Joy Bright Hancock, *Lady in the Navy: A Personal Reminiscence* (Annapolis, Md.: The Naval Institute Press, 1972), p. 138; Lt. Col. Pat Meid, "Marine Corps Women's Reserve in World War II," Historical Branch, G-3 Division Headquarters, United States Marine Corps, 1964, p. 29.

15. Ibid., p. 40; Hartmann, "Women in the Military Service," p. 199.

16. Ibid.

17. Treadwell, *The Women's Army Corps*, pp. 98, 688—91; Kate A. Arbogast, "Women in the Armed Forces: A Rediscovered Resource," *Military Review* 53 (November 1973):15.

18. Hartmann, "Women in the Military Service," p. 199; Ruth Cheney Streeter, "History of the Marine Corps Women's Reserve: A Critical Analysis of Its Development and Operation, 1943–1945," December 5, 1945, p. 229, Schlesinger Library, Radcliffe College.

19. Ibid., pp. 230–37; Treadwell, *The Women's Army Corps*, p. 625.

20. Johnson, *Black Women in the Armed Forces*, pp. 6, 15; Treadwell, *The Women's Army Corps*, pp. 589–601; Charles Houston to Mary McLeod Bethune, April 26, 1945, Papers of the National Council of Negro Women, Series 5, WAC, National Archives for Black Women's History, Washington, D.C.; Truman K. Gibson to Bethune, August 18, 1945, ibid.

21. "U.S. Naval Administration World War II, Bureau of Naval Personnel, The Negro in the Navy," pp. 15–17, 98–99, Unpublished manuscript in Naval History Library, Washington, D.C.; Jacqueline Van Voris, "Quiet Victory: The Waves in World War II," pp. 133–38, unpublished manuscript in Operational Archives, Naval History Division, Washington, D.C.; Correspondence and memoranda in the Records of the Bureau of Naval Personnel, Boxes 2329–31, National Archives, Record Group 24.

22. Hartmann, "Women in the Military Service," p. 200; Treadwell, *The Women's Army Corps*, p. 723.

23. Hartmann, "Women in the Military Service," pp. 200–201.

24. Ibid.

25. Ibid.; Mary Lou Calene, "Changing Acceptable Occupations for Military and Civilian Women: The Effects of Two World Wars," M.S. thesis, Naval Postgraduate School, Monterey, Calif., 1975, pp. 44–45.

26. Hartmann, "Women in the Military Service," p. 201.

27. Nancy McInerny, "The Woman Vet Has Her Headaches, Too," *New York Times Magazine*, June 30, 1946, p. 18; Susan Perry, "Female Veterans: Their Fight Is Not Over," *Graduate Woman* 74 (May/June 1980):18–23; Treadwell, *The Women's Army Corps*, pp. 737–39.

28. Ibid., p. 738; Davis R. B. Ross, *Preparing for Ulysses: Politics and Veterans during World War II* (New York: Columbia University Press, 1969), pp. 193–95.

29. McInerny, "The Woman Vet Has Her Headaches, Too," pp. 38–39; Perry, "Female Veterans," p. 23; Treadwell, *The Women's Army Corps*, pp. 737–39; United States Department of Labor, Women's Bureau, *Facts on Women Workers*, September 30, 1947, p. 2.

30. Joseph J. Corn, "Making Flying 'Thinkable': Women Pilots and the Selling of Aviation, 1927–1940," *American Quarterly* 31 (Fall 1979): 556–71.

31. Victor K. Chun, "The Origin of the WASPs," *American Aviation Historical Society Journal* 14 (Winter 1969):259–62; Sally Van Wegenen Keil, *Those Wonderful Women in Their Flying Machines: The Unknown Heroines of World War II* (New York: Rawson, Wade Publishers, Inc., 1979), pp. 47–51, 97–111, 164; Jacqueline Cochran, *The Stars at Noon* (Boston: Little, Brown and Co., 1954), pp. 127–28.

32. Keil, *Those Wonderful Women in Their Flying Machines*, pp. 3–4, 248–49, 256; Chun, "The Origin of the WASPs," p. 262; Len Famiglietti, "How Women Flew in Wartime," *Air Force Times*, April 26, 1976, p. 34.

33. Keil, *Those Wonderful Women in Their Flying Machines*, pp. 105, 118–19.

34. Treadwell, *The Women's Army Corps*, pp. 784–85; Cochran, *The Stars at Noon*, pp. 119–20; Chun, "The Origin of the WASPs." p. 261; Keil, *Those Wonderful Women in Their Flying Machines*, pp. 265–306.

35. Corn, "Making Flying 'Thinkable,'" pp. 70–71; Keil, *Those Wonderful Women in Their Flying Machines*, pp. 307–16; Frances W. Kerr, "Women in Aviation," Release of the Women's Bureau, Department of Labor, August 4, 1946, p. 2.

Workers building the SS George Washington Carver, 1943
Courtesy of the National Archives

Chapter Four

The Environment of Women's Employment: Government, Employers, and Labor Unions

The sheer number of women involved made shifts in female employment patterns the most dramatic wartime change in women's status. As the Women's Bureau and other supporters of women's right to work constantly pointed out, women, like men, worked primarily because they needed the income. While World War II added some new motivations to women's economic behavior, material considerations remained dominant. What fluctuated during the decade of the 1940s was the context in which women made economic decisions. Whether a woman worked or not, the nature and conditions of her employment, the kinds of training she afforded herself—all were greatly influenced by general economic forces as well as by the specific policies and practices of the government, employers, and labor unions. Women did not just simply respond to these external forces, but their own initiatives cannot be understood without reference to the larger environment in which they acted. The critical factor in that environment was the degree to which the nation required female labor.

As the European war intensified in the summer of 1940, the government took measures to strengthen national defense capabilities, and employers began to respond to the increasing demand for war materials. Both employers and government officials, however, were slow to grasp the need for or potential of women's labor in defense industries. Even after the Japanese attack on Pearl Harbor brought the United States into global conflict, employers reported few plans to hire women. A survey of 12,512 defense plants in January 1942 disclosed that employers would hire women in less than one-third of the job openings anticipated in the next six months, and that fewer than 20 percent of the skilled, managerial and professional positions would be open to women. The War Department itself took the position that defense producers "should not be encouraged to utilize women on a large scale until all available male labor in the area has first been employed."[1]

The surge of defense production sparked economic recovery, but at least initially it affected men and women in disparate ways. Women were laid off by the thousands as plants producing civilian goods converted to war production and employers hired men in the new defense jobs. Fully ninety percent of the jobs listed with the Seattle Employment Service in 1941 were for men only. Between 1940 and 1942, male job-seekers registered with government employment services declined by 29 percent, while female applicants decreased by just 12 percent, and women's share of job placements declined from 46.8 to 37.1 percent. In 1940 and 1941 women throughout the country wrote to the Women's Bureau that they were unable to secure jobs and were barred from training programs.[2]

Because defense employers were reluctant to hire women—even those with previous industrial experience—women had meager opportunities in the newly established government training programs. Federal and local administrators of the largest program, Vocational Training for War Production Workers (VTWPW), would not establish courses for women because the law required that programs be directed to the needs of defense producers. A government report on training programs for blacks in Memphis matter-of-factly reported that none of the courses was designed for women because "there was practically no local call for Negro women in the industries for which special training was a requisite." As late as February 1942, the director of the program for the Detroit area, a prime defense production center, declined to provide training for women unless a specific job awaited them. At the time of Pearl Harbor, women were less than five percent of trainees under VTWPW, and almost one-third of these were in sewing and stenographic courses. Their proportion of the college-level trainees in the Engineering, Science and Management War Training program (ESMWT) was even smaller.[3]

In the meantime, the Women's Bureau along with several national women's organizations sought to alert the nation to the contributions women could make to war production. The Women's Bureau consulted with trade unions and employers and began to issue bulletins describing the kind of jobs women could do and recommending specific measures for the efficient employment of female workers. While government officials acknowledged the utility of research on women workers done by the Women's Bureau, they refused to concede women a role in developing policy for defense production. Even when the War Manpower Commission (WMC) established a Women's Advisory Committee in September 1942, its role was limited to that of making recommendations. Indeed, at the first several meetings of the WMC's Management-Labor Policy Committee, Margaret Hickey, who chaired and represented the Women's Advisory Committee, was not even provided a seat at the table where the men deliberated. Throughout the life of her committee, its members voiced frustration at their ineffectual status, but efforts to increase their authority and effect were consistently rebuffed.[4]

The expansion of women's opportunities for jobs and training depended upon the intensification of production imperatives and the withdrawal of millions of men into military service. By mid-1942 employers were willing to hire women in 70 percent of the anticipated semiskilled positions and 63 percent of the professional and managerial openings. Possibilities for women to obtain training increased at a similar pace. Between March 1942 and March 1943 their share of the enrollments in preemployment vocational training increased from 8.7 to 32.4 percent. In the ESMWT program, women's enrollments went up from 9.4 to 22 percent.[5]

In close harmony with shifting labor needs and supply, the intense courtship of women by employers and government lasted from late 1942 to 1944. The War Manpower Commission sponsored local recruitment campaigns in areas of critical labor shortages, and with the Office of War Information launched national media appeals to draw women into the labor force. While the initial spotlight was on work in war materials production, by 1943 the emphasis had shifted to jobs in civilian goods production and service industries. Propaganda appealed to women on a variety of levels. War work was often presented as glamorous and exciting as well as an opportunity to earn good wages. But the dominant appeal was that of patriotism. Women were urged to fulfill their duty as citizens and thereby hasten victory, and they were warned of the dire consequences to individual soldiers and to the nation posed by idle women. As Leila Rupp has pointed out, this appeal to patriotism was less threatening to traditional social norms because it carried the implication of impermanence.[6]

Throughout the war, government officials bemoaned what they considered the inadequate response of women to recruitment campaigns, and articles in the popular press criticized women for being "slackers." Yet, although labor shortages plagued particular locations and temporarily slowed production, the nation succeeded in mobilizing a labor force sufficient to produce the materials for victory. Without resorting to a draft of civilian labor, it was able to expand the civilian work force by 13 million, of which women contributed half the number.[7]

Nearly a million of these women were hired by the federal government itself. The wartime proliferation of federal activities required the addition of more than 2 million civilians to the 920,310 already employed in 1939. As they had in the private sector, men benefited from the initial expansion and in fact slightly increased their proportion of federal jobs between 1939 and 1940, but between 1941 and 1944, women constituted one-half of the new employees. The number of women in civil-service jobs jumped from fewer than 200,000 in 1939 to more than 1 million in 1944, a 540 percent increase. Their share of federal positions increased from 18.8 to 37.6 percent. Although clerical work continued to be the typical female job, by 1943 women were being hired as mechanics and press, crane, and tractor operators as well as in professional classifications usually filled by men. During the war, all new civil service appointments were limited to the duration plus six months. Thus, the postwar prospects for these new employees depended upon the degree of contraction of the federal bureaucracy and the extent to which veterans would want civil service jobs.[8]

While the government itself hired women in large numbers and promoted their training and recruitment, it also moved to improve the conditions of women's employment. Since the early 1900s, state legislatures had passed a body of laws designed to protect women workers, and the Women's Bureau had as a top priority the expansion of legislation regulating the hours and conditions of women's work. As production demands mounted, however, employers sought release from restrictions on night work and women's hours in order to utilize fully a tightening labor supply. In response to pressures from employers and such government agencies as the War Production Board, most states relaxed their standards to permit nighttime work and longer hours. Nonetheless, while the Women's Bureau lamented the breakdown in labor standards, it noted that most changes were only for the duration. Women did work longer hours: in twenty-five manufacturing industries their average weekly hours increased from 38.1 to 41.2. But the hours for male workers increased even more. Moreover, while many women with family responsibilities found longer hours burdensome, others welcomed the opportunity to increase their earnings.[9]

Of more uniform benefit to women workers was the government's promotion of equal pay. Both the War Production Board and the War Manpower Commission established the principle, but it was the National War Labor Board (NWLB) which had the power to effect that goal in its resolution of labor disputes. In the fall of 1942, the board ordered equal pay for women who did "work of the same quality and quantity" as that of men, and enforced that ruling in a series of subsequent decisions. Between November 1942 and January 1944 it received reports from more than 2,200 companies which had voluntarily eliminated wage differentials. Government policies both generated significant publicity for the right of women to equal compensation and eliminated actual discrimination. The overall results, however, were modest. In the first place, the NWLB could act only if unions initiated the issue in contract negotiations. Moreover, the board let stand inequalities among departments within a single plant and among different plants owned by a single company. It also refused to overturn historical differentials in rates for "men's" and "women's" jobs.

The government's equal pay policy benefited women when they directly replaced men, but failed to challenge the traditional practice of paying lower rates in jobs done by women regardless of the skill and energy required.[10]

The need to increase the labor supply and to reduce absenteeism also prompted the government to address the dual responsibilities of female workers. It recognized that shortages of food, consumer goods, medical care, and transportation made even more difficult the burden of combining paid employment with domestic duties. The government publicized the problem and encouraged businesses and community institutions to develop such programs as expanded shopping hours and prepared food services to ease women's load. Its suggestions did not, however, include a redistribution of labor between men and women in the home. Nor did it follow the British model of providing direct services for working women or requiring that employers do so.[11]

The government's approach to women with the most critical problem—those with children—was characterized by ambivalence. Official policy discouraged mothers with small children from working outside the home: "Now, as in peacetime, a mother's primary duty is to her home and children." At the same time, officials recognized that financial need compelled some mothers to work and that in localities with severe labor shortages production goals would require the employment of mothers. In addition, War Manpower Commission policy urged employers not to discriminate against women with children and upheld the right of each mother to make her own decision regarding employment. Bowing to these realities, the Children's Bureau nonetheless warned mothers that their personal care was critical to the normal development of infants. Group care for children under two years would result in "slower mental development, social ineptness, weakened initiative, and damage to the child's capacity . . . to form satisfactory relationships." Thus, when mothers could not nurture their children on a full-time basis, the Children's Bureau recommended foster-family day care as the next best alternative. Moreover, a Woman's Bureau publication addressed to employers of women pointed out official opposition to the employment of mothers of children under fourteen, and urged that such applicants be questioned closely about provisions for their children's care.[12]

Despite such ambivalence, the war did prompt the federal government to respond for the first time to the needs of working mothers. During the Depression it had supported nurseries through the Work Progress Administration (WPA), but this program had been a welfare measure, aimed at providing jobs for unemployed teachers, aides, custodians and the like, and at assisting low-income families whose children attended the centers at no charge. In 1942, these nurseries began to enroll children of defense workers and to charge fees. Upon the abolition of the WPA in 1943, the Federal Works Agency administered an expanded program of child care, expending nearly $50 million by the end of the war. At its peak, the program enrolled 130,000 children in more than 3,000 centers. The day-care program depended upon local initiative to design a program and to demonstrate that defense production depended upon child care services. It was clearly perceived by its sponsors as a war emergency program, and it served a tiny proportion of all working mothers.[13]

Employers in the private sector made dramatic changes to facilitate the absorption of 6.5 million additional women into the work force. Companies abandoned the sexual segregation of the labor force as they hired women by the thousands to perform jobs which had always been reserved for men. One of the sturdiest bastions of male exclusivity, shipyard production work, opened its doors to women in 1942, and by 1943 women accounted for 10 percent of total employment. In the intensifying labor shortage, employers were willing to try women at most jobs, and by 1943 women appeared as steel workers, lumberjacks, train conductors, and surface miners.

As employers now welcomed women, they also relaxed their opposition to particular groups of women. In reversing its ninety-year-old ban against married women in August 1942, Swift and Company joined thousands of firms in abandoning a company policy as well as a cherished social norm. A critical teacher shortage moved school boards throughout the country to end their discrimination against married women, and some even appealed specifically to wives to return to teaching. The old notion that married women were depriving male breadwinners of jobs was made even less valid by wartime conditions. The concern about women's primary responsibilities to their families continued, but could not withstand employers' need for workers or the nation's need for production. Some managers even professed preference for married women as more stable and conscientious than their single sisters.[14]

Prejudice against black women and older women diminished less readily. Ten months after Pearl Harbor, black women numbered fewer than 100 among the more than 30,000 women in Detroit war industries. The war did enable black women to move out of farm and domestic labor into better jobs in service and manufacturing industries, but as a rule employers turned to them only as a last resort. The number of black women in manufacturing increased four-fold, but their wartime gains lagged behind those of white women and black men. Older women also faced discrimination. Industry-produced guides for employing women routinely suggested that those in the twenty to forty to forty-five age category made the best workers, and some companies set thirty as the maximum. The worsening labor supply situation in 1943 did expand opportunities for older women, but the war did not erode employers' preference for youth.[15]

Employers who hired women to fill men's jobs remained conscious that their new workers were female and took special measures to accommodate them. Defense manufacturers with contracts which assured them their production costs plus an agreeable profit were most willing to make changes because the government absorbed the extra expense. They also undertook adjustments in working conditions, wage scales, benefits and in the productive process itself because they viewed them as essential to maintaining a work force capable of achieving production goals.[16]

A most typical practice was the use of counselors. Some companies had employed them before the war, but the practice became widespread when firms found themselves with thousands of new workers strange to the ways of factory life. Employers hired men to counsel male employees, but they considered the woman counselor to be even more necessary, especially when large numbers of women were hired for the first time and there were no female production supervisors. Their functions were three-fold. Women counselors interpreted company policies and rules to women and oversaw their enforcement. In addition, they sought to make male workers and foremen more receptive to women and understanding of both their special problems and their capabilities. Finally, women counselors discussed both job and personal problems with female workers and assisted them in obtaining services like child care, transportation, and housing. Although organized labor did not like this paternalism on the part of employers, the Women's Bureau found that by 1943 women's counselors had been established in almost all the factories it surveyed.[17]

Even more important was the restructuring of the manufacturing process to accommodate women. A 1943 National Industrial Conference Board study of 155 plants with more than 600,000 workers found that the great majority had made changes in formerly male jobs. To compensate for the inexperience and lesser physical strength of most of their female workers, management reengineered the production process, breaking down jobs into simpler operations and applying technology to decrease the amount of strength required. When Brown and Sharpe, for example, diluted the toolmakers' job into lathe operating, milling, and drawing, it could utilize women in these separate operations with considerable less training than that required for toolmakers. Other companies found that women could perform male jobs when conveyor belts, automatic elevators, mobile cranes, and electric push buttons replaced human energy. The dilution of old crafts and the application of technology represented historical trends in American industry which the war only accelerated. While they allowed for the rapid integration of new workers and made some labor less physically taxing, they also diminished the variety in work, the control over the work process and the pride and satisfaction that had once attended highly skilled labor.[18]

The war also induced many companies to endorse equal pay for women both in principle and in practice. The National Association of Manufacturers advocated the principle, and most munitions plants, aircraft factories, and shipyards started women in men's jobs at equal rates. Cost-plus contracts enabled employers to compensate women equitably at no cost to profits, and pressure from unions and the NWLB moved more recalcitrant companies. These factors, however, did not prevent employers from assigning women different job classifications and paying them less, even for work comparable to men's. Moreover, although the war compelled some breakdown in the dual labor system, the majority of female workers continued to be employed in women's jobs, and employers maintained the historic gap between wages in men's jobs and women's jobs.[19]

A few companies approached the problem of recruiting and retaining labor on a broader scale. Recognizing the double burden of women with families, they sought to alleviate women's domestic duties by providing specific services in the plant. The Kaiser Corporation attracted most attention for the child care centers established in its Oregon shipyards, but numerous other firms, including Grumman Aircraft, Curtiss-Wright, Hudson, and Douglas Aircraft, operated or subsidized day care for their employees' children. Other plants installed shopping, laundry and repair services and provided meals which workers could purchase to take home to their families. Lucrative war contracts along with fairly nominal fees paid by workers enabled companies to provide these services without jeopardizing high profits. Unique in recognizing the connection between household work and production, these innovations helped relatively few women, and then, only for the duration.[20]

Employers' attitudes about their new workers varied as much as the measures they undertook to accommodate women workers. While few employers echoed so bluntly a statement by the National Foremen's Institute that women were "a distinct type of human being socially, sexually, psychologically and physically," their public comments routinely pointed out sex differences. A most frequent assumption was that women relished the kind of monotonous, repetitive work that would drive men crazy. Women were also thought to be more emotional and more concerned about their appearance even eschewing jobs that would overdevelop muscles. The widespread belief that women did not like female supervisors along with the assumption that women were temporary workers justified employers' resistance to promoting women. A National Industrial Conference Board survey of 131 plants in 1943 disclosed that more than half had no plans to advance their female employees. Firms like N. A. Woodworth and Scoville Manufacturing Company, which conducted supervisory training programs for women, were in the minority.[21]

Employers who had previously shunned women now compared them favorably with men. General Motors President Charles E.

Wilson found women "more enthusiastic and showing much better spirit. . . ." Other executives praised women for their greater conscientiousness, loyalty, and tractability and pointed to their better safety records and more painstaking care of machines and tools. These employers were obviously celebrating what they considered a more docile and easily controlled labor force. In addition, whether intentionally or unwittingly, the male-female comparisons served to divide workers. One shipyard production expert bluntly stated his interest in keeping a few female workers on after the war, "mainly as an incentive for greater efficiency and accomplishment from males. A limited number of women, properly employed, could possibly serve to good advantage in establishing the required tempo of production."[22]

Such intentions and public statements did not help to ease the resentment expressed by male workers when women invaded their domain. Some of the opposition derived from socially conditioned stereotypes which engendered a distrust of women as workers, suspicion of their motives, and the feeling that they could only be a disturbance or distraction on the job. More realistically, after a decade of high unemployment, men regarded any new workers as potential threats to their own livelihoods. The entrance of women into skilled crafts was especially alarming. Men who had prepared for jobs with years of apprenticeship resented women benefiting from the high wages and good working conditions for which men had so long struggled. Nor were they pleased when women received such special benefits required by protective labor laws as longer rest periods, more desirable shifts and newer restroom facilities. As jobs were diluted and broken down to accommodate less-skilled workers, men saw their special craft status decline. Moreover, older men whose seniority had moved them into easier jobs objected to returning to heavier work so that women could be used in the less strenuous positions. Finally, in wartime the epitome of masculinity was the soldier defending his country. Male workers not only fell short of this standard, but suffered the additional ignominy of doing work that even women could do.[23]

Much of their initial opposition to working alongside women evaporated as men recognized the manpower crisis and women proved themselves serious and competent workers. Not all men were as grudging as the longtime shipbuilder who insisted that women belonged in the home, but "as long as we have a war on our hands and as long as a manpower shortage exists, the average man worker has to steel himself to get along with them on the job." The acceptance of women in such traditional male bastions as ship-building, transportation, and foundries was usually a bow to ne-cessity only for the duration. But even in newer industries where women were accepted more readily, that toleration was condi-tional upon a sufficiency of jobs for male workers. One labor editor reported that workingmen were "scared stiff at the danger of widespread unemployment after the war," and another that male workers saw their future job security jeopardized by the wide-spread employment of women.[24]

Just as male workers differed considerably in their attitudes and behavior towards women workers so did the labor unions which represented them. Since its inception in 1937, the Congress of Industrial Organizations (CIO) had admitted all workers, and the ranks of its affiliates swelled with women as they took jobs in the auto, metals, and rubber industries. The American Federation of Labor (AFL) included among its affiliates the International Ladies Garment Workers Union (ILGWU) which was predominantly female, but many of its craft-oriented affiliates excluded women. Pressed by the manpower shortage, they reluctantly revised ad-mission policies. Even then, some welcomed women only for the duration. The International Brotherhood of Teamsters excluded women from union benefits and required them to sign a statement "agreeing to the fact that the local can withdraw their membership whenever in their judgment the emergency ceases." The majority of AFL and CIO affiliates accepted women without condition, and as total union membership soared to 15 million, women contrib-uted 3 to 3.5 million members, while their proportion climbed from 9.4 percent in 1940 to 21.8 percent in 1944.[25]

Especially among CIO unions, the war brought increasing con-sideration of the special needs and problems of their new members. Prior to the war the CIO's attention to women had been channeled into organizing the wives of members into auxiliaries; even when its focus shifted to women workers it frequently relegated these issues to the auxiliaries. In June 1941, the United Electrical, Radio and Machine Workers of America (UEW) held the first conference to address issues concerning female workers. The largest union in the country, the United Automobile Workers (UAW), sponsored similar meetings, established a Women's Bureau to recommend policies and programs affecting women, and urged its locals to set up women's committees. National UAW and UEW policies urged the protection of women workers through contract provisions securing equal pay and seniority, work standards, and maternity leaves. Nor were out-of-plant problems neglected. The CIO publicized the need for day care, lobbied in Congress for adequate funding, and worked with community groups to establish local centers.[26]

Female union members were dependent upon men to safeguard their interests, for women's representation in positions of power fell far below their share of union membership. The ILGWU had a lone woman on its executive board to represent the 225,000 women constituting 75 percent of its membership. No woman served on the executive boards of the AFL and CIO, and only the relatively small United Federal Workers had a female president. In 1944, when women were 30 percent of total membership, the UAW listed fewer than fifty women out of more than 2,000 convention delegates. The UEW, with female membership of 40 percent, set the most impressive example in its organizing staff, which was one-third female, but did not replicate this pattern in its national leadership. In all unions, women fared better at the local level, but even here did not hold power proportionate to their numbers. Of those UAW locals having women members, 60 percent had at least one woman on their executive boards, but women did less well on the important bargaining and grievance committees. Only on 37 percent of the former and 24 percent of the latter were women represented at all.[27]

Both the gains made by women through labor unions and the failure of unions to protect all of their members were apparent in the history of equal pay during the war. All unions endorsed the principle when women assumed men's jobs, and the UEW and UAW were especially vigorous in bringing equal pay disputes to the NWLB. In major contracts with Westinghouse and General Electric, the UEW reduced or eliminated pay differentials, and the UAW negotiated similar contracts with General Motors. Yet, even the most progressive unions could not enforce national policy on all of their locals. One-half of the midwestern locals investigated by the Women's Bureau in 1943 had equal pay clauses in their contracts, and 68 percent of UEW members were protected by such provisions. The most progress was made where women took over male jobs. Here the interests of male and female unionists coincided, for equal pay prevented employers from undercutting wage standards by hiring women at cheaper rates.[28]

What unions failed, in general, to challenge was wage discrimination where men and women were employed in different jobs, even when the skills and labor required were comparable. The UAW, for example, approved contracts which classified jobs as female and male, light and heavy, and allowed rate differentials. George Meany, writing in the *American Federationist*, proudly referred to a chart showing wage increases since the AFL had organized northern California cannery workers, seemingly unconcerned that the chart specified rates by sex and showed discrepancies of 15 cents and more per hour. Wage surveys during the war years demonstrated that women production workers gained absolutely and relative to men. But a 1944 study of twenty-five industries revealed the enormity of the existing gap: average hourly rates for all men exceeded those of women by 50 percent, and those of unskilled men were 20 percent higher than those for all women. Unions alone, of course, were not responsible for this discrepancy, but it did indicate how far organized labor had yet to go in achieving equal protection for all its members. As the war moved to a close, the protection women could count upon from unions became even more precarious.[29]

In 1944, those groups which had welcomed, even urged, women to take jobs began to roll up the welcome mat. No American was immune from the concern that the end of defense production and the release of millions of soldiers, would return the nation to the hard times of the 1930s. While public spokesmen of all sorts proposed a variety of means to ensure full employment, they all assumed that a partial solution was the retirement of millions of women to domesticity. Both in their public statements which sought to influence public opinion, and in their policies and practices, the government, employers, and labor unions transformed the environment of women's employment and narrowed the ground on which women could make economic decisions.

Most business leaders recognized women's important contribution to the war effort, the skills they had developed, their proven competence, and the need and desire of many to remain in the labor force. They noted that women's labor force participation was not something that had just arrived on the scene, and they recognized the injustice of treating women as a resource to be used and discarded. While they rejected extensive governmental intervention to secure full employment, they did urge cooperation among management, workers, and government officials to promote an expanding economy which could employ all who sought jobs. At the same time industrialists either assumed married women would withdraw from the labor market or they urged them to do so. Radio executive Mark Woods predicted in 1944 that "for nearly every man returning to his former job, there will be a woman returning to her former occupation—caring for the home." Frederick Crawford, chairman of the board of the National Association of Manufacturers, asserted that many women should drop out "for the sake of their homes as well as the labor situation." And TWA President Jack Frye insisted that most women in business were there on a temporary basis: "They intend—and rightfully—to return home after the war, or marry and make new homes." Thus, business spokesmen reiterated the prewar norm that married women owed their fulltime attention to the home and family. Acknowledging that the loss or disability of a husband would require employment for some married women, they failed to concede women's right to work. Indeed, the Chamber of Commerce objected that guaranteeing a job for everyone who wanted one would require a "rigid, regimented or planned society."[30]

In contrast, labor leaders believed that governmental measures could promote an expanding economy capable of providing sufficient jobs for all, and they consistently linked women's job prospects to the maintenance of a full-employment economy. While this was a realistic appraisal, it also implied a condition on women's right to work that was not present for men. Moreover, most labor leaders assumed considerable voluntary withdrawal on the part of women. Emil Rieve, president of the Textile Workers Union and CIO executive board member, asserted that full employment did not mean the wartime "supersaturated" employment situation: "If he can bring home enough money himself, the American worker does not want to see his wife, his 16-year-old daughter, and his

70-year-old father trudging off to the mill. . . . He wants to see . . . his wife making a home for the family." CIO spokesmen were especially supportive of women's right to work and recognized that not only need but also the desire for financial independence, status, and satisfaction motivated women to seek jobs. But their postwar program emphasized the need to safeguard the family through sufficient jobs at adequate wages for men combined with an expanded social security system for families without breadwinners. While such a program offered potential benefit to women forced into the labor market by material exigency, it also demonstrated the tenacity of the prewar social norm which assigned priority to women's domestic roles.[31]

Along with this climate of public opinion no longer supportive of women's economic aspirations came even more powerful economic and political realities. With the curtailment of government contracts, employers had no choice but to reduce employment. Moreover, they were bound by federal law to rehire veterans to their former or similar positions even when this meant discharging nonveterans with greater seniority. In addition, those companies with union contracts had to comply with seniority provisions as they reconverted to peacetime production. Within these limitations employers enjoyed considerable flexibility in determining the composition of their postwar labor forces. Those industries which had traditionally employed women would continue to do so in equal or higher numbers. But the prospects for women were bleak in areas where the war had initiated or greatly expanded their employment. Their low seniority combined with employers' preferences resulted in women's wholesale replacement by men.

Brewster Aeronautical Corporation, Bell Aircraft, United States Rubber, and Aetna Life Insurance were among major firms predicting in 1944 that female employment would fall to near prewar levels. A survey of postwar plans in 304 New York state war plants disclosed reconversion policies decidedly unfavorable to women. Most employers listed seniority as the major determining principle, but women tended to have the least seniority and the larger firms awarded seniority on a departmental rather than plant-wide basis. Moreover, companies employing one-fifth of the women included in the survey based their lay-off policies on need and assumed that men were the providers. By the early postwar period the effects of such policies showed in job listings. A United States Employment Service survey of three cities found that 60 to 80 percent of the job openings were for men only. And, as Detroit automakers expanded production in the spring of 1946, they sought men for 80 to 90 percent of the jobs.[32]

While union leaders firmly reiterated the seniority principle, urged locals to monitor lay-off and reemployment practices, and even opposed "superseniority" for veterans, they frequently failed to protect the seniority that women had accrued. Some contracts limited all women's seniority privileges to the duration, while others reserved this distinction for married women. In 1948, for example, six UAW locals in Racine, Wisconsin, had contract provisions which withdrew seniority from any woman who married. Local unions often violated the antidiscrimination policies adopted at UAW international conventions, and the executive board failed to use its full authority to defend its female members. Moreover, according to the Women's Bureau, most unions failed to assist women who were laid off in receiving fair treatment from state unemployment programs. The UAW's successful struggle with the Michigan Unemployment Compensation Commission to allow benefits to women unavailable to work all three shifts was exceptional. The wartime support of unions for their female members diminished as postwar strikes, inflation, opposition to antilabor legislation, and internal struggles with radicals claimed the lion's share of their attention.[33]

Neither could women count on federal efforts to maintain a favorable environment for their employment. Victory brought the demise of the War Manpower Commission and its Women's Advisory Committee as well as special offices in other agencies which had concentrated on women. Eliminated too were those programs which sought to facilitate women's employment by easing their domestic responsibilities. When federal funds for child care were discontinued in 1946, few cities had the will or the resources to assume full support. The federal government itself had 400,000 fewer female employees by 1947, and their proportion of civil service workers had dropped from 38 to 24 percent. The GI Bill gave veterans preference in government employment, and civil-service postwar policy was to receive applications only from veterans or persons dropped from federal agencies. Moreover, since unemployment benefits were under state control, the federal government could not even ensure that female applicants were treated fairly. The Women's Bureau alone remained to safeguard women's economic status, and its funding suffered from postwar budget cuts. [34]

Wartime necessity produced striking changes in the policies and practices of government, employers, and labor unions toward women workers. Access to traditionally male jobs, higher pay and more equitable wage scales, union representation, and occasional assistance with their domestic responsibilities created the most favorable environment that women workers had ever experienced. But that hospitable climate had an extremely brief life-span, shorter than the war itself. When the labor scarcity dissipated and threatened to become a surplus, employers resumed their preference for male workers, bolstered by the continuing assumption that men were the breadwinners and by veterans' legal and moral claims to employment. Organized labor's attention to its female members waned as it gave precedence to defending its wartime gains, fighting antilabor legislation and resolving internal conflicts. With victory, the federal government withdrew from its unprecedented economic intervention, and the postwar political climate contained a powerful current of opposition to programs involving government interference in or competition with private industry. Postwar economic growth enabled most women who needed or wanted work to find it, but under conditions which represented a considerable deterioration of their wartime economic status.

NOTES AND REFERENCES

1. "Survey of Employment Prospects for Women in War Industries, January to June, 1942," pp. 1–2, War Manpower Commission (hereafter WMC), Office of the Assistant Executive Director for Field Services, Records of the WMC, National Archives (hereafter NA), Record Group 211; Leonard J. Maloney to Liaison Officers, August 26, 1942, Records of Headquarters, Army Services Forces, Box 605, NA, Record Group 160.

2. Letters from Caroline Manning to Women's Bureau, October 1941, Records of the Consumers League of Ohio, Western Reserve Historical Society, Box 35; Bertha M. Nienburg, "War History Statement," n.d., p. 2, Records of the Women's Bureau, 55-A-485, Box 2, NA, Record Group 86; Karen Tucker Anderson, "The Impact of World War II in the Puget Sound Area on the Status of Women and the Family," Ph.D. dissertation, University of Washington, 1975, p. 25; Bureau of Employment Security, "The Employment of Women in War Production," May 1942, pp. 19–22, WMC, Reports and Analysis Service, Historical Section; Mary Anderson, *Woman at Work* (Minneapolis: University of Minnesota Press, 1951), pp. 246–50.

3. Bureau of Employment Security, "The Employment of Women in War Production," pp. 30–32; "Training Negroes for War Work," *Monthly Labor Review* 57 (November 1943):952–53; Elizabeth S. Magee to E. L. Oliver, January 31, 1942, Records of the Consumers League of Ohio, Box 35; W. E. Stirton to Victor G. Reuther, February 3, 1942, Papers of the United Auto Workers, War Policy Collection, Box 12, Wayne State Labor History Archives, Detroit, Michigan; for an overview of government

training programs, see Eleanor F. Straub, "Government Policy toward
Civilian Women in World War II," Ph.D. dissertation, Emory University, 1973, pp. 212–30.

4. Press release, "The Woman Worker Looks Ahead," January 25,
1942, WMC, Reports and Analysis Service, Historical Division, Records
of the WMC; Mary Anderson, "Women on the Labor Fronts," May 19,
1942, ibid.; "The Women's Advisory Committee to the War Manpower
Commission, 1942–1945," pp. 1–4, 37–47, Records of the Women's
Bureau, 56-A-284, Box 2.

5. Bureau of Program Requirements, "Developments in the Employment of Women," May 31, 1943, pp. 1–4, Records of the WMC, Office of
the Assistant Executive Director for Field Services.

6. Straub, "Government Policy toward Civilian Women," pp. 103–
25; V. C. Jones, "Unsung Heroines," Wall Street Journal, July 2, 1942;
Office of War Information, "Basic Program Plan for Womanpower,"
August 1943, p. 2, Records of the Office of War Information (hereafter
OWI), E41, Box 148, NA, Record Group 208; Leila J. Rupp, Mobilizing
Women for War: German and American Propaganda, 1939–1945 (Princeton:
Princeton University Press, 1978), pp. 139–57; Straub, "Government
Policy toward Civilian Women," 125–38.

7. Ibid., p. 144; Rupp, Mobilizing Women for War, pp. 112–13,
160–61.

8. Women in the Federal Service, 1923–1947, Women's Bureau Bulletin
No. 230, Parts I and II (Washington, D.C.: Government Printing Office,
1949 and 1950), pp. 5, 18, 31–33.

9. Straub, "Government Policy toward Civilian Women," pp. 230–
38; International Labour Office, The War and Women's Employment: The
Experience of the United Kingdom and The United States (Montreal: ILO,
1946), p. 202.

10. Straub, "Government Policy toward Civilian Women," pp. 239–
58; National War Labor Board Policy on Equal Pay for Equal Work for
Women," September 1945, Records of the Women's Bureau, 56-A-284,
Box 1.

11. "Need for Community Facilities to Aid Married Women Employed in War Industry and to Meet Their Household Responsibilities,"
October 24, 1942, Reports and Analysis Service, Historical Section,
Workers' Safeguard, Records of the WMC; Community Services for Women
War Workers, Women's Bureau Special Bulletin No. 15 (Washington,
D.C.: Government Printing Office, 1944).

12. Katherine F. Lenroot, "The Children's Bureau Program for the
Day Care of Children of Working Mothers," Records of the OWI, E82,
Box 244; Children's Bureau, "Policy of the Children's Bureau on the Care
of Infants Whose Mothers are Employed," December 1, 1944, WMC,
Field Service Reports, Office of the Assistant Executive Director for Field
Services; When You Hire Women, Women's Bureau, Special Bulletin No. 14
(Washington, D.C.: Government Printing Office, 1944).

13. Straub, "Government Policy toward Civilian Women," pp. 263–97; Howard Dratch, "The Politics of Child Care in the 1940's," *Science and Society* 38 (Summer 1974):175–77; Margaret O'Brien Stienfels, *Who's Minding the Children? The History and Politics of Day Care in America* (New York: Simon and Schuster, 1973), pp. 66–68.

14. "Specific Instances as to Increased Employment of Married Women," October 1942, Records of the Women's Bureau, 58-A-850, Box 2.

15. Research Department, UAW, "Employment of Negro Women in Detroit," October 9, 1942, Papers of the UAW, War Policy Collection, Box 6; International Labour Office, *The War and Women's Employment*, pp. 177–78, 183–85; *Supervising the Woman War Worker* (Deep River, Conn.: National Foreman's Institute, 1943), p. 23; *Recruiting, Selecting, Training Women for Automotive Service* (South Bend, Ind.: The Studebaker Corporation, 1943), p. 20; *Manpower Utilization: Case Materials from 329 Plants* (New York: McGraw-Hill, 1943), p. 22. An excellent account of employers' policies regarding black women is Karen Tucker Anderson, "Last Hired, First Fired: The Black Woman Worker during World War II," paper presented at the National Women's Studies Association meeting, May 1980.

16. D'Ann Campbell, "Wives, Workers and Womanhood: America During World War II," Ph.D. dissertation, University of North Carolina, 1979, Chapter 3 provides an overview of attitudes and practices of employers and male workers.

17. *The Employer Counsellor* (New York: Metropolitan Life Insurance Company, 1943); Mildred Davis to Emma Ward, February 21, 1943, Papers of Emma F. Ward, Sophia Smith Collection, Smith College, Northampton, Mass., Box 1; Mary Anderson to Louise C. Odencrantz, March 20, 1943, Records of the Women's Bureau, 55-A-556, Box 12; Women's Bureau, "Women in Personnel and Industrial Relations Work in War Industries," March 1943, ibid., 58-A-281, Box 32.

18. Geneva Seybold, "Wartime Pay of Women in Industry," National Industrial Conference Board, Studies in Personnel Policy No. 58 (New York, 1943), pp. 8–10; *Women in the Factory: A Panel Discussion* (New York: American Management Association, 1943), p. 8; Women's Bureau, *When You Hire Women*, Special Bulletin No. 14 (Washington, D.C.: Government Printing Office, 1944); International Labour Office, *The War and Women's Employment*, pp. 191–92.

19. Ibid., pp. 206–23; Women's Bureau, "Differentials in Pay for Women," November 1945, Papers of the American Federation of Labor, State Historical Society of Wisconsin, Madison, 8A, Box 22; William H. Chafe, *The American Woman: Her Changing Social, Economic, and Political Roles, 1920–1970* (New York: Oxford University Press, 1972), pp. 154–58.

20. Katherine Glover, *Women at Work in Wartime* (New York: Public Affairs Pamphlet 77, 1943), p. 18; *Reducing Absenteeism through Employer Education* (New York: Metropolitan Life Insurance Company, n.d.), p. 22;

Dratch, "The Politics of Child Care," p. 195–201.

21. *Supervising the Woman War Worker*, pp. 5–6, 25, 28–29; *Manpower Utilization*, pp. 22, 32, 122–25; Dale Cox, International Harvester Corporation, to Merle Thorpe, November 1, 1942, Records of the Women's Bureau, 54-A-78, Box 8; Seybold, "Wartime Pay of Women," p. 25; *Solving the Manpower Problem* (New York: American Management Association, 1942), p. 16.

22. *American Women at War* (New York: National Association of Manufacturers, 1942), pp. 6, 11, 25–28; *Women in the Factory*, p. 5; *Supervising the Woman War Worker*, p. 29; *Manpower Utilization*, pp. 32, 34, 41; J. D. Sharkey to Emma Ward, April 11, 1945, Ward Papers.

23. Katherine Archibald, *Wartime Shipyard: A Study in Social Disunity* (Berkeley: University of California Press, 1947), pp. 17–19, 27; Elinore M. Herrick, "Report on Women's Employment Program, Todd Shipyards Corporation," 1944, pp. 10–11, Elinore Herrick Papers, Folder 72, Schlesinger Library; *Personnel Management in War Industries, Vol. II* (Ann Arbor: University of Michigan, 1943), p. 134.

24. "What Men Workers Think of Women Workers," *Mariner*, December 11, 1943; Bureau of Special Services, Division of Research, "Opinion About the Wartime Employment of Women," May 29, 1944, pp. i–iii, 5–7, 9–11, 17–19, Records of the OWI, F82, Box 559.

25. Straub, "Government Policy toward Civilian Women," pp. 193–97; Ruth Milkman, "Organizing the Sexual Division of Labor: Historical Perspectives on 'Women's Work' and the American Labor Movement," *Socialist Review* 49 (January–February 1980):128–33.

26. Policies and activities of these unions regarding women are reported in *CIO News; The United Automobile Worker*; and *Ammunition*. See also "Women in Unions in a Mid-West War Industry," 1944, Records of the Women's Bureau 56-2-50, Box 1; and "Women in Trade Unions during the War Period," ibid., 55-A-485, Box 4.

27. Milkman, "Organizing the Sexual Division of Labor," p. 130; Rose Pesotta, *Bread Upon the Waters* (New York: Dodd, Mead and Co., 1944), p. 395; *United Automobile Worker* October 1, 1944, pp. 3, 5; *Ammunition*, December 1944, p. 21.

28. Straub, "Government Policy toward Civilian Women," pp. 200, 205; "Women in Unions in a Mid-West War Industry Area," pp. 13–14.

29. "Women in Trade Unions during the War Period"; George Meany, "Progress in the Cannery Industry," *American Federationist* 53 (August 1946):3–7; Milkman, "Organizing the Sexual Division of Labor," p. 132.

30. *American Women in the Postwar World: A Symposium of the Role Women Will Play in Business and Industry* (New York: Newsweek Club Bureau, 1944), pp. 14–16, 21–22, 26–30, 34–35; Charles A. Myers, *Personnel Problems of the Postwar Transition Period* (New York: Committee for Economic Development, 1944); Emerson P. Schmidt, *Full Employment: Its Policies and Economics* (Washington, D.C.: Chamber of Commerce of the United States, 1944).

31. Emil Rieve, "Assuring Full Employment—As Labor Sees It," January 11, 1945, pp. 3–4, Textile Workers Union of America Papers, 11A, Box 1, State Historical Society, Madison, Wisconsin; *American Women in the Postwar World*, pp. 11–13.

32. Pauline Arnold, "Where Will the Postwar Jobs Lie?" *Independent Woman* 23 (October 1944):318–20; New York Department of Labor, "Employers' Post-War Plans for Women Workers," January 1945, Records of the Women's Bureau 54-A-78, Box 9; Mary Elizabeth Pidgeon, "Reconversion and the Employment of Women," ibid., 58-A-580, Box 2; "Recent Trends Affecting the Employment of Women in Automobile Manufacturing in Detroit," July 26, 1946, ibid.

33. William H. Oliver to Emil Mazey, May 2, 1949, Papers of the United Automobile Workers, Reuther File, Box 20; "Women in Unions in a Mid-West War Industry Area," pp. 20–21; "Women in Trade Unions during the War Period," pp. 9–11; *United Automobile Worker*, May 1, 1945. For a good analysis of UAW policies and practices, see Nancy Gabin, "Women Workers and the UAW in the Post–World War II Period: 1945–1954," *Labor History* 21 (Winter 1979–80):5–30.

34. *Women in the Federal Service*, pp. 18, 31.

Welders arriving at Todd Erie Basin drydock, 1942
Courtesy of the National Archives

Chapter Five

Women's Work and the Female Labor Force

Within the context of a war economy and postwar reconversion women made occupational choices that altered significantly the shape of the female labor force and the nature of women's work. The leap in numbers of employed women was the most obvious. A second change was in the composition of the female labor force as increasing numbers of married women and older women took jobs. Third, the war redistributed women workers among job categories. Spurred by the military crisis, these developments represented the intensification of long-range trends related to the changing structure of the American economy and to the changing demographic characteristics of the female population. Although some of these transformations were halted and even reversed in the reconversion period, patterns of women's employment underwent considerable change in the decade of the 1940s.

D'Ann Campbell has pointed out that average yearly statistics understate the extent of women's labor force participation during the war years. In contrast to men, women were much more likely to move in and out of paid employment. While the female labor force grew by 6.5 million during the war, 2.3 million women left their jobs. In 1944, 37 percent of all adult women were reported in the labor force, but nearly 50 percent of all women were actually employed at some time during that year. Paid employment, then, constituted a part of the wartime experience of half or more of adult women.[1]

The greatest changes in wartime economic behavior took place among married women. One in every ten married women entered the work force during the war, and they represented more than 3 million of the new female workers, while 2,890,000 were single and the rest widowed or divorced. For the first time in the nation's history there were more married women than single in the female labor force. While housework and voluntary activities continued to occupy the majority of married women, the percentage of all wives who worked outside the home grew from 13.9 in 1940 to 22.5 in 1944. Women whose husbands were absent were more than twice as likely to seek jobs; half of all servicemen's wives were in the labor force. Women with children represented a significant portion of the wartime increase in female employment. More than half a million women with children under ten took jobs as their proportion of all women in this category increased from 7.8 percent in 1940 to 12.1 percent in 1944.[2]

Older women, too, made a major contribution to the war economy as more than 2 million women aged thirty-five years and older entered the labor force. Those in the thirty-five to forty-four age group increased their labor force participation from 27.3 to 37.2 percent, while the proportion of women aged forty-five and over at work grew from 16.4 to 21 percent. By 1945, half of all women workers were over thirty-five; slightly more than one in four was forty-five or older. The typical female worker had changed, from one who was younger and single to one who was older and married. This new pattern maintained itself through the postwar period.[3]

The war had less effect on the racial composition of the female labor force. The employment of black women increased from 1.5 to 2.1 million between 1940 and 1944, while the proportion of adult black women who were wage earners increased from one-third to 40 percent. Their share of the female labor force, however, declined from 13.8 to 12.5. The labor force participation rate of black women was so high before the war—more than one-fourth of married women with husbands present worked—that their wartime employment did not increase as much as that of white women. Moreover, the war economy improved employment prospects for black men and thus reduced somewhat the necessity which had driven black women into the labor market. By 1950, the participation rate for black women was just about where it had been in 1940, signaling a slow convergence of the economic behavior of white and black women.[4]

Although there were no systematic analyses of women workers' motivations, scattered surveys and public opinion reports indicate that financial considerations were paramount. Patriotic motives were certainly present, and these were frequently combined with the belief that war work would bring a loved one home sooner. As a woman in a rubber plant remarked, "Every time I test a batch of rubber, I know it's going to help bring my three sons home quicker." Nonetheless, most women worked because they needed the money. Besides those women who were the sole support of themselves and dependents, there were millions more whose wages meant the difference between sheer survival and modest comfort. The accumulated deprivations and debts from ten years of depression combined with unprecedented employment opportunities and a favorable climate of opinion provided powerful incentives.[5]

Servicemen's wives had particularly compelling reasons to seek work. War wives received a minimum of $50 per month, of which the government provided $28 and $22 was deducted from husbands' pay. Soldiers in the lowest seven ranks received monthly pay ranging from $50 to $138. Consequently, their wives worked to make up the income loss suffered as their husbands went to war. Moreover, employment allowed them to make their own contribution to the war effort and to their husbands' return, and work helped to ease the loneliness and make the time of separation pass more quickly.

The desire for self-expression, personal satisfaction, or escape from domestic monotony counted little in women's decisions to take jobs. In reality, most of the jobs available to them were arduous and routine and offered few attractions in terms of personal development or expression. Yet, once at work women discovered the nonmaterial satisfactions of employment. They enjoyed the companionship of fellow workers, the pleasure of mastering a new skill, the opportunity to contribute to a public good, and the gratification of proving their mettle in jobs once thought beyond the powers of women. One housewife reported to the Office of War Information, "Some just love their jobs. I think they for the first time in their life feel important." A working mother found that the "companionship of working with others is vastly more stimulating and rewarding than housework," and welcomed escape from the "narrowing effect that staying at home full time exerts upon my outlook in life."[6]

The wartime labor shortage did not erode all of the difficulties experienced by female workers. These obstacles deterred women from entering the labor force and posed problems for those who did seek jobs. In the first place, available jobs were concentrated in areas not accessible to all women. Geographical variations in the demand for labor were accompanied by temporal variations. Lay-offs due to production cut-backs began as early as 1943 and accelerated in 1944. Moreover, by 1943 employment opportunities for women lay more in nondurable-goods production and in service industries than in the higher-paying defense sector. While propagandists sought to present these jobs as essential war work, their relatively low wages and their distant relationship to military needs offered little inducement.

Black women confronted particularly stiff obstacles. All women had to await the scarcity of male workers for new job opportunities, but black women faced the additional barrier of racial discrimination. Although the federal government promoted equal opportunity and established the Fair Employment Practices Commission (FEPC) to protect the employment of minorities, the government itself contributed to the persistence of injustice. Even when black women proved discrimination, the FEPC could only recommend withdrawal of war contracts from the offending employer, an unlikely measure when maximum, uninterrupted production was the top priority. The War Department itself allowed managers of arsenals, plants, and depots under its supervision to refuse jobs to black women; in 1943 it posted an advertisement for "competent, white female help in the Pentagon Cafeterias and Dining Rooms." Black women in Cincinnati reported that when they applied to the United States Employment Service office they were ignored or referred to domestic or maintenance jobs.[7]

The experience of ten women in Cape Girardeau, Missouri, illustrates the multitude of barriers black women faced. These women, aged thirty to fifty-five, applied for and were refused jobs at a clothing plant which made WAC uniforms. Because their previous experience had been in domestic service, home sewing, and WPA sewing projects, plant officials insisted that the refusal was based on their lack of power machine experience. But, while the company had trained inexperienced white women, it did not train black women and promised to do so only if enough applied to warrant the establishment of a separate training unit. The chairwoman of the local ILGWU union gave some support to employers' claims that white employees would not work with blacks when she stated that white women would probably resent working alongside black women, but would not object to a separate unit with segregated facilities. Nor did black women receive help from USES personnel, who said they had never referred blacks to the factory because management had not specified that it wanted "colored" help. Five of the ten women had registered with the employment office and were classified only for housework. Finally, four of the women who filed the complaint had another handicap: they were over thirty-five, the age limit for trainees.[8]

Completion of training did not guarantee job opportunities even for young, single black women in areas where labor was scarce. Several of these had completed 200 to 600 hours of training on power sewing machines, but were refused jobs by St. Louis firms producing military uniforms. Three of them were able to find work in a cartridge plant, but none was able to utilize her training. Again, management insisted that white workers would not tolerate racial mixing, an assertion given some credence by the work stoppages which occurred when black women were employed in other Midwestern plants. Yet, as Karen Anderson has suggested, union-management educational efforts among whites and a firm commitment by employers could result in the smooth integration of black workers. Even in the North, the entrance of black women into new kinds of work was difficult and slow. It was not until late in 1944, for example, that black women in New York gained access to jobs as telephone operators. They needed extraordinary perseverance when told at employment offices, "We have not yet installed separate toilet facilities"; "A sufficient number of colored women have not been trained to start a separate shift"; "We cannot put a Negro in the front office"; "We do not employ colored." Black women filed more than one of every four discrimination complaints heard by the FEPC between July 1943 and December 1944. But even when these efforts and other pressures enabled black women to make inroads into new fields, they came so late that their relatively low seniority would subject them to the earliest lay-offs.[9]

Married women, black and white, encountered most obstacles to their economic aspirations. The manpower crisis softened but did not eliminate objections to married women who worked outside the home. To a 1943 Gallup poll question, "Would you be willing for your wife to take a full time job running a machine in a war plant?" only 30 percent of married men replied yes, and an additional 11 percent gave a qualified response. (Forty percent of the women polled indicated a willingness to take such a job, and another 17 percent said yes, with qualifications.) A *Ladies Home Journal* poll of wives at work indicated that 20 percent did not have their husbands' approval. These women also believed that husbands were more approving of their own wives working than of married women in general.[10]

It was married women with children who faced the most social disapprobation. Public opinion coincided with government policy to discourage mothers of young children from taking jobs. Working mothers were easy scapegoats as juvenile delinquency increased. No women could avoid hearing the charge that "mothers, proudly winning the war on the production line, are losing it on the home front." Women who sought jobs often faced scrutiny about their provisions for the children's care, a practice recommended by government officials. Nor were mothers immune to pressures from their own children, who felt both a decrease in personal attention and a loss of social status as their mothers took jobs.[11]

Married women who could ignore adverse public and family opinion still had to deal with practical difficulties attending their dual roles. For war made housekeeping more difficult and increased the strain of combining paid employment with customary domestic duties. The typical work week for women consisted of 48 hours, with one day off. Gasoline rationing and crowded public transportation meant that more time was consumed in getting to and from work. Scarcities of food and civilian commodities made shopping a major problem. Stores often sold out by early afternoon, and even when goods were on hand few retail establishments kept evening hours. Meal preparation was complicated by rationing and the difficulty of obtaining such customary foods as sugar, meat, and butter. Shortages of medical-care professionals made it difficult for working women to obtain health care for themselves and their children. The movement of service workers to higher paid factory jobs created shortages in services that provided alternatives to women's domestic labor. In Detroit, for example, laundries experienced a 40 percent drop in employment and would not even take new customers. As priority was assigned to military production, women could not obtain a variety of household goods that might lighten their domestic load: toasters, vacuum cleaners, percolators, irons, and electric refrigerators. The percentage of families owning washing machines, refrigerators, and vacuum cleaners actually decreased during the war. The availability of household help declined as former domestic workers moved into better jobs.[12]

Most women did not benefit from the modest efforts by employers, governmental and community institutions to ease women's domestic burdens. Moreover, the war scarcely disturbed the sexual division of labor within the family, except when the movement of men into the military or to defense production areas left women with total responsibility for the maintenance of the home. Suggestions in the media that men assume some of the household duties were rare. An article to that effect in the *United Automobile Worker* was placed on the women's page and it was addressed to women, not to men. Fifty-nine percent of the women surveyed by the *Ladies Home Journal* said that their husbands "helped" with the housework, but did not indicate how much of the responsibilities they shared.[13]

When the Women's Bureau surveyed more than 3,000 women in thirteen factories, it found that half of the married, widowed, or divorced women had the overall responsibility for the home and did the major part of the work. When interviewees described the help they received from household members, they mentioned other women much more frequently than husbands or sons. Family members as well as women themselves seemed to maintain prewar expectations regarding women's domestic roles. A forty-year-old woman described her day, which began at 5:45 A.M. when she rose to prepare her husband's breakfast and lunch before punching in herself at 7:00. She tried to shop during her lunch hour. "My husband got home at 4:15 and would have to wait until I got home at 5:45 and got his supper. Some nights he was mad." Another woman explained why she left her job, "My husband likes his meals on time, so he persuaded me to quit work."[14]

In the absence of either a significant redistribution of household labor or its removal into the public sector, women performed their dual roles in part by sacrificing sleep and recreation. When pressures were particularly intense, many unilaterally readjusted their work schedules. A mill worker with a husband and two daughters told how she coped with a full-time job and all the household work: "I was late sometimes because I didn't feel like getting up, and I just slept. I made up my time when I got to the mill." Surveys of absenteeism reported highest rates among women in the twenty-five to thirty-nine age group, confirming the extent to which their domestic burdens impelled women on occasion to disregard their employers' work schedules. While the press extensively aired the problem of absenteeism, there was a general awareness that it was women's age-old responsibilities rather than indifference to duty that caused them to miss work.[15]

Of all the traditional female duties, that of child care was most difficult to reconcile with work in the public sphere. The Census Bureau estimated in 1944 that 2.75 million employed women had 4.5 million children under the age of fourteen. The federal government's child-care program provided both nursery schools and centers for afterschool care, but at its peak in July 1944 it enrolled only 130,000 children in 3,100 units. Privately run centers accommodated relatively few more. Yet, child care centers reported throughout the war that they were not filled to capacity. Although day-care centers proved to be lifesavers to thousands of women, shortcomings in the facilities themselves combined with women's own preferences meant that the majority of working mothers used alternatives to group care in fulfilling their maternal responsibilities.[16]

Many women did not have access to child-care centers because of their location. Only defense-impacted communities could receive federal funds. The location of facilities at a distance from home or work combined with scarce transportation made it inconvenient if not impossible for all women to use them. Transportation was especially difficult for mothers with more than one child when units accommodating preschool and school-age children were in different locations. Nor did hours of operation suit the work schedules of all women. In Detroit, for example, where many factories began the shift at 6:30 A.M., nurseries did not open until 7:00. Because they closed at 6:00 P.M., they were unavailable to women on later shifts. The tendency of plants to rotate working hours among employees created further complications. The cost to parents was also a deterrent, especially before October 1943, when the Federal Works Agency mandated a ceiling of 50 cents per child per day. Even that was high to many potential users: 60 percent of the Minneapolis mothers who used child-care centers earned less than $24 per week and had to pay fees for two children. Moreover, in some areas, inadequate publicity meant that some mothers were not informed about existing facilities. While Hartford, Connecticut, had eighteen child-care centers, personnel directors in thirty-two local plants did not even know they existed.[17]

Even when conditions attending child-care facilities were optimal, women frequently chose alternatives. Before the war most day nurseries had catered to poor children, and women continued to associate child care with charity. They were hesitant about placing their children in a strange environment and worried about the qualifications of the centers' personnel. These women preferred to leave their children with a family member or with someone else whom they knew and trusted. Given a public consensus that working mothers were at best a necessary evil and that children were better off under individual nurturance, women's resistance to group care is not surprising. But they suffered financially, because public funds were not available for the individual care that the majority of mothers used.[18]

In addition to dealing with out-of-plant responsibilities, more than half of the female labor force had to make the adjustment to new jobs. Of the 19 million women at work in 1944, 6.5 million were new workers; 230,000 had been unemployed in 1941; and 1.5 million had shifted occupations. Even among the 85 percent of those women employed at the time of Pearl Harbor who remained in the same occupational category, a considerable proportion had changed jobs. Thus, women in consumer goods production moved into defense industries, while others shifted from stores and com-

mercial offices to clerical jobs in government and war plants. As
millions of women made these economic decisions, they produced
a major redistribution of the female labor force and changed the
nature of women's paid employment.[19]

The restructuring of the female labor force increased the proportions of women workers engaged in factory and clerical jobs.
Where factory jobs had employed one in five women workers in
1940, 1944 found 30 percent in such positions. Similarly, in 1940,
one in five had been in clerical work, but by 1944, more than
one-fourth of all women workers were so employed. The percent-
ages of employed women who were in sales and commercial service
occupations remained fairly stable at around 7 and 10, respectively. But there were relatively fewer women engaged in the
professions—a decline from 13.2 to 9 percent—and in domestic
service, which had occupied 17.7 percent of all working women in
1940 but only 9.5 in 1944. While the female labor force redistributed itself during the war, the actual numbers of women and
their proportion of all workers increased in every field but domestic service.[20]

The recomposition of the black female labor force was also
striking. Before the war, 70 percent were in the service occupations
and 16 percent in farm labor. Between 1940 and 1944, the proportion of black women in agriculture was cut in half. Where three in
five black women workers had been in private household service in
1940, fewer than one in two were so employed in 1944. The
percentage of black women workers in commercial service and in
factory occupations grew to nearly 20 percent each. Slight gains
were also registered in clerical, sales, and professional categories,
but fewer than 10 percent of the black female labor force were
engaged in each of these fields.[21]

The largest wartime gain in female employment was in manufacturing, where more than 2.5 million additional women represented an increase of 140 percent by 1944. Where one in five
women workers had been employed in manufacturing in 1940, one
in three were so occupied in 1944, and they constituted more than
one-third of all factory operatives. The greatest number of these
women, 3,270,000, were in defense industries, where female employment grew by 462 percent. Despite the relatively long hours
and the hard, monotonous work, factory jobs were attractive to

women workers. They were heavily publicized, and women in war and essential civilian goods industries enjoyed the wages which surpassed those in service jobs, in most office and sales work, and even in many teaching positions.[22]

Especially in the factories where they were newcomers, women experienced little upward mobility but tended to remain in the less skilled, more routine work. The assumption that women were around for the duration only made employers more likely to train them for just a single operation and made some women reluctant to learn new skills. At the wartime peak, women represented just four percent of skilled industrial workers. Their average weekly wages in 1944—$31.21, compared with $54.65 for men—reflected their lower places in the factory hierarchy as well as outright discrimination, their concentration in lower-paying industries and the fact that they worked less overtime. Black industrial women were usually in the lowest-level jobs. Although their participation in factory work quadrupled, black women were heavily concentrated in positions of janitors, sweepers, and material handlers. Especially in southern industries, even in War Department plants, these jobs were their only opportunities because managers would not integrate production lines.[23]

Factory work also brought millions of women under the protection of labor unions. That did not mean, however, that they participated in union affairs equally with men. The expectation that their work was temporary and that their household duties would leave little free time deterred women from active participation. In addition, many women were discouraged by union policies and the attitudes and behavior of male members. Steel-worker Elsa Graves spoke approvingly of union leaders' efforts on behalf of women, but criticized the rank-and-file men who believed that women worked only for "pin money" and expected their postwar withdrawal. Other women reported hostility from male unionists, a reluctance to entrust women with bargaining and grievance responsibilities, and unions' failure to strive vigorously for equal pay and seniority. Women members resented being treated as women rather than workers: UAW women urged that the women's page in the union's newspaper concentrate on employment problems rather than on attire and recipes. Even women who had devoted considerable energies to union activities and who had risen to leadership positions experienced sexism. When ILGWU President David Dubinsky instructed Vice-President Rose Pesotta to stop "playing the prima donna even though you are the only woman member of the Board," Pesotta likened her position to that of Dubinsky when he was on the AFL Executive Council: "There you were considered the *Jew* and her *[sic]* I am considered the *Woman* and at times I feel just as comfortable as you did."[24]

Although almost as great as in manufacturing, the movement of women into clerical work was largely unheralded. The more than two million women who took office jobs during the war constituted an 85 percent increase. Representing one-half of all clerical workers in 1940, women increased their proportion to 70 percent in 1945. While clerical wages increased from 15 to 30 percent during the war, hourly earnings of factory workers grew by 47 percent and weekly paychecks by close to 70 percent. Lacking the monetary appeal of factory jobs, office work did offer greater job security since it was a field that had become increasingly feminized in the preceding decades. The work was also less dirty and arduous and to many women carried more prestige. The war provided new, though limited, opportunities for black women: their employment in clerical work increased fivefold, but left them as less than 2 percent of all women in the field.[25]

Wartime gains for women in professional and semiprofessional work were so small that that category declined in proportion to other areas of female employment, and women failed to improve their position relative to men. This was due in part to the small increase of women teachers, a category that had occupied half of all women professionals before the war. A critical teacher shortage and relaxation of the ban against married women could not attract enough women to a field in which many positions paid less than defense industry work. A similar shortage occurred in nursing which had accounted for another 20 percent of women professionals in 1940. That field, too, was characterized by relatively low wages in addition to inconvenient schedules and sturdier barriers to the employment of married women. The absence of men did provide new opportunities for women lawyers, doctors, musicians, journalists, and scientists, but the numbers of women entering these jobs were not sufficient to alter overall trends. Moreover, most professional fields required considerable education: war work lured many women away from training in the sciences, for example, before they completed a full course of study. Even those who continued would not finish their professional training until the war was over and the male competition had returned.[26]

The wartime experience of musicians exemplified both the new professional opportunities for women and the limited amount of change that occurred. Before 1940, a handful of women found employment in major symphony orchestras, primarily as harpists or violinists, but most female musicians performed in all-woman orchestras or in amateur and community organizations. The wartime shortage of male instrumentalists not only opened the doors of leading orchestras to women, but also found them playing instruments traditionally associated with masculine skills. By 1945, for example, former members of the Women's Symphony Orchestra of Chicago occupied the chairs of principal French horn in the Chicago Symphony, trumpet in the National Symphony, and principal cello in the New Orleans Symphony. The Boston Symphony hired its first woman, a bassoonist, in 1945, and in St. Louis women won English horn, trombone, and percussion chairs. The New York all-woman orchestra, Orchestrette Classique, disbanded as its first desk musicians found positions in major institutions. During the war women trainees in the National Orchestral Association increased from 15 to 50 percent of the total. As was the case in other fields, the return of men forced women to relinquish some of these gains. The proportion of women apprentices in the National Orchestral Association, for example, dropped to 25 percent. But as the all-woman symphony movement faded, women retained a small foothold in major orchestras, where by 1953 they held between one and thirteen chairs in the eighteen leading institutions and claimed more than token places in the organizations of secondary rank.[27]

The redistribution of the female labor force that was more numerically significant, more beneficial to women workers, and more permanent, was their movement out of domestic service. The shift resulted in a net decline of 400,000 in that field. The wartime scarcity of domestic help drove up wages, from a weekly average of $9 before the war to $12 during the war, and offered opportunities for some women to earn as much as $20 or $25. But neither higher earnings nor somewhat improved conditions could keep women from choosing better-paying jobs in factories, offices, and service industries. Only two states set maximum hours and minimum wages for domestic servants. They were excluded from social security coverage, and the scattered efforts of the CIO to organize this fragmented, isolated, low-paid group of workers were unsuccessful. Domestic servants who had shifted jobs enjoyed the higher wages and better conditions as well as the independence, social contacts and "self-respect" that attended their new occupations.[28]

In contrast to white women, the number of black female household employees increased by around 50,000 during the war; domestic service became more racially polarized as the black share of all female household employees increased from 46.6 to 60.9 percent. But as a proportion of total black female employment, domestic service decreased from 60 to 45 percent as black women moved into factory and commercial service work. While the vast majority hoped to hang on to their new jobs, they realized that their position was precarious. A black woman who preferred her job as machine operator in a can company was "beginning to accept the fact that Negro women will be forced to return to domestic work."[29]

Black women were not alone in expecting and experiencing the postwar constriction of economic opportunity. Between 1943 and 1945 a number of agencies queried thousands of women about their postwar plans. Pollsters found that from 61 to 85 percent of women workers wanted to keep their jobs; among married women the positive responses ranged from 47 to 68 percent. Typically these women cited need as their primary motivation, but, sensitive to the climate of opinion, they expressed unwillingness to take work from returning veterans: "I'd stay if they want me without taking a man's place away from him." The vast majority were able to realize their plans, but not without experiencing a period of unemployment and the necessity of accepting lower-paying jobs. By early 1947, when postwar employment of women was at its depth, women had lost 1 million factory jobs, half a million clerical positions, 300,000 jobs in commercial service, and another 100,000 in sales. The professional and semiprofessional category alone increased, as it added 300,000 women. Women's share of all jobs had dropped from 36 to 28 percent. Nonetheless, nearly 17 million women remained in the labor force. This was 14 percent below the wartime peak, but represented a 17 percent increase since 1940.[30]

The shift of the American economy into peacetime production stimulated by the demand for civilian goods which had been blocked during the war enabled women to remain in the paid labor force. In addition, the withdrawal of more than 2 million women created opportunities for those who wanted to remain or to enter the labor market. Most of those who left their jobs went back to unpaid work as housewives and mothers. Rising marriage and birth rates contributed to this withdrawal: one year after V-J Day, the labor force participation of women in the twenty to thirty-four age group was 1 million below predictions based on prewar trends. The accumulation of wartime savings, the return of soldier-husbands, and favorable opportunities for men in the postwar economy diminished the financial motivations of some wives. Moreover, although the production of goods to lighten women's household work resumed, child care was a more difficult problem as publicly supported centers were disbanded. Government surveys of women who had been laid off, but who failed to return when work was available, confirmed the strains of combining housekeeping with paid employment.[31]

Although economists classified those women who left the labor force as "voluntary withdrawals," it is probable that many married women did not so much reject paid employment itself as they calculated that the kinds of jobs available in the postwar economy would not compensate for the strains involved in handling double roles. Women were let go from factory jobs at nearly double the rates of men, and female lay-offs were greatest in the higher-paying industries which had traditionally employed men. The jobs that were available to women carried less attractive wages and working conditions. In the first quarter of 1946, government employment agencies placed 40 percent of female applicants in household and other service jobs, 13 to 15 percent in semiskilled positions, and less than 5 percent in professional managerial or skilled work. In June of that year, 70 percent of jobs open to women paid less than 65 cents per hour, while only one-fourth of those for men paid that little. The 3.6 percent unemployment rate for women in 1948, only slightly higher than that for men, in all likelihood concealed the existence of additional women who had dropped out of the labor market discouraged by the conditions and wages of work available.[32]

Women who remained in the labor force were reshuffled from defense work into industries which had customarily welcomed them. As shipbuilding shrank dramatically, it became once again an exclusively male field. Women's share of the Detroit automobile industry jobs fell from 25 to 7.5 percent. In heavy industries such as electrical and other machinery, iron, and steel, women hung on to some wartime gains, but their share of jobs in durable goods manufacture was cut in half, and black women virtually disappeared. Women's proportion of jobs in the nondurable-goods industries declined much less as textile, apparel, and food industries absorbed former war workers.[33]

A Women's Bureau survey of women who had been aircraft, shipbuilding, and electrical equipment workers provided details of the postwar experiences of women workers. Three-fourths of these women were still in the labor force in the fall of 1946, and 45 percent of these had been able to keep their wartime jobs. Almost nine in ten had suffered a decrease in earnings as average weekly paychecks fell from $50 to $37. Even those women who kept their jobs earned less due to shorter hours. Harder hit were those who had to take work in other industries. A married woman who had earned $40 per week in an aircraft plant found employment in a hat factory at $29; a former electrician's helper at $48 per week received $28 as a saleswoman; and a wartime painter in an aircraft factory saw her weekly paycheck reduced from $51 to $34 as she moved to leather-goods production. Other war workers found employment in restaurants, laundries, telephone exchanges, and domestic service. Eighty percent of the women able to work in factory or clerical jobs were relatively satisfied with their work, but two-thirds of those in retail trade and service preferred other jobs.[34]

The loss of attractive opportunities created by the war economy did not hold back the increase in women's employment after 1947. By 1950, 28.6 percent of all adult women, 18.5 million, were in the labor force, where they constituted nearly 30 percent of all workers. More striking was the continuing propensity of wives to work outside the home. The percentage of working married couples rose from 11 to 22 percent during the 1940s. At the end of the decade, one in every four married women with husbands present was in the labor force, where they were 52 percent of all women workers. Two million of these had children under six. As Valerie Oppenheimer has shown, these women, in part, were responding to demand. The most rapidly expanding industries were those which had relied on female labor before 1940. But the pool from which they had drawn—young single women—could no longer provide a sufficient supply of workers. The war had broken down some of the resistance of employers to married women, and their postwar need for labor led them to accept, even seek, women whom they would not previously employ.[35]

Pushing married women into the labor force were the material needs of their families. Unemployment remained relatively low throughout the postwar period, but rising prices threatened economic security. Indeed, the average family experienced a slight decrease in purchasing power between 1944 and 1950. Moreover, the definition of need had been undergoing a gradual change since the 1930s. A survey of 9,000 women union members in 1952 found the need to help support their families the chief motivation for 60 to 80 percent of the married women. But significant numbers were at work for objectives beyond simple economic survival. The percentage of married women working to purchase a home ranged from 26 to 66 percent; between 14 and 26 percent worked to educate their children; and between 13 and 32 percent cited such specific goals as payment of medical bills, purchase of home furnishings, or the upkeep of automobiles. Although the proportion of working wives declined as husbands' incomes rose, at all income levels more wives worked outside the home at the end of the 1940s. Even when husbands earned between $5,000 and $6,000, an income higher than the $4,500 average for all families, one in five of their wives was in the labor market. The postwar expansion in production of household appliances and processed foods made work outside the home less stressful for married women, and it also provided a motivation for working.[36]

As women's labor-force participation grew, so did the gap between their earnings and those of men. Excluding the lowliest paid in domestic service, women's pay was 62 percent that of men in 1939, but only 53 percent in 1950. Part of the differential was due to women's greater tendency to take part-time work, which 20

percent of the female labor force did in 1950. Women's employment was also more intermittent so that they failed to accrue
comparable seniority. Discrimination against women, both in hiring for better-paying jobs and in promotion policies, contributed
further to the disparity. Moreover, the dual labor market which
had characterized the prewar period reasserted itself so that most
women worked in predominantly female occupations where labor
unions had made little headway and whose wages reflected the
assumption that women's labor was worth less than that of men.
Black women continued to be the lowest paid. Their male counterparts benefited more from the racial progress of the decade, and
the differential in median income between black men and women
increased during the 1940s. Relative to all women, black women
experienced a slight gain—but their median income was still less
than half that of white women by the end of the decade.[37]

While women continued to be segregated in female jobs, the
nature of their work did change during the 1940s. Clerical work
expanded to occupy the largest number of women workers, more
than one in four in 1950. Another one in five were factory operatives, about the same proportion as in 1940. A net decline of more
than 0.5 million reduced the proportion of employed women in
domestic service from nearly 20 to less than 10 percent. White
women gained more from this shift than black women, who in
1950 constituted a higher percentage of all household workers than
they had in 1940. Nonetheless, black women too left domestic
work: while that had claimed three of five employed black women
in 1940, it occupied two of five in 1950. As they participated in the
great migration from farm to city and from South to North and
West, black women also left agricultural work. Their labor became
more diversified as they moved increasingly into commercial service and factory work, improved slightly their presence in the
professions, and made some inroads into clerical and sales work.[38]

Although World War II did little to ameliorate permanently the
secondary position of women in the economy, it did contribute to
changes in women's economic behavior. By ending the Depression
and laying a foundation for postwar economic growth, the war
expanded job opportunities for women and added a greater ele-
ment of choice to their lives. It accelerated the movement of
women from farm and household labor into more attractive occu-

pations. The wartime labor shortage softened employers' resistance to married women and older women, and allowed them to prove their capabilities. In affording a taste of paid employment to women who would not otherwise have left their homes, it increased the propensity of married women to take jobs. While they continued to subordinate their paid employment to family needs and viewed work as a job rather than a career, women increasingly obliterated the lines which had defined a distinct and separate sphere.

NOTES AND REFERENCES

1. D'Ann Campbell, "Wives, Workers, and Womanhood: America during World War II," Ph.D. dissertation, University of North Carolina, 1979, pp. 31–32.

2. Ibid., pp. 13–30; Mary Elizabeth Pidgeon, *Changes in Women's Employment during the War*, Women's Bureau Special Bulletin No. 20 (Washington, D.C.: Government Printing Office, 1944), pp. 17–22; Leonard Eskin, "Sources of Wartime Labor Supply in the United States," *Monthly Labor Review* (hereafter *MLR*) 59 (August 1944):275.

3. Ibid., pp. 273–76; "The Special Problems of Older Women Workers," *MLR* 62 (March 1946):393–94.

4. *Negro Women War Workers*, Women's Bureau Bulletin No. 202 (Washington, D.C.: Government Printing Office, 1945), pp. iii, 16–18; Nora R. Tucker and Thomasina W. Norford, "Ten Years of Progress: The Negro Woman in the Labor Force," National Council of Negro Women, *Women United*, Souvenir Year Book, October 1951, pp. 39–40.

5. Bureau of Special Services, Office of War Information, Division of

Research, "Opinion About the Wartime Employment of Women," May 29, 1944, pp. 15–17, Records of the Office of War Information, Series E 82, Box 559; Emma Ward to Maude E. Withers, March 7, 1945, Ward Papers, Box 1, Sophia Smith Collection; Marie Green, "Family Agency Services to Working Mothers," M.S. thesis, Smith College, 1943, p. 21; Barbara Gray, "The Child-Care Problems of Forty-Six Working Mothers," M.S. thesis, Smith College, 1943, pp. 20–23.

6. "Opinion About the Wartime Employment of Women," pp. 16– 19; Nell Giles, "What About the Women?" *Ladies Home Journal* 61 (June 1944):23, 157–58; Rhoda Pratt Hanson, "I'm Leaving Home Part Time," *Independent Woman* 25 (December 1946):364.

7. Karen Tucker Anderson, "Last Hired, First Fired: The Black Woman Worker during World War II," paper presented at the National Women's Studies Association meeting, May 1980, pp. 3–5; Warwick B. Hobart, "Training and Utilization of Women in Selected War Establishments, December 1, 1942–April 1, 1943," Records of the Army Service Forces, Box 604, National Archives, Record Group 160; Truman K. Gibson, Jr., to Lt. Col. James T. O'Connell, March 2, 1943, ibid., Box 603; Anne Mason to Jeanetta Welsh, n.d., Nina Craig to John M. Baker, November 29, 1943, Mary McLeod Bethune to Paul V. McNutt, December 10, 1943, Papers of the National Council of Negro Women, Series 5, Folder 319, National Archives for Black Women's History, Washington, D.C.

8. Capt. John J. Blewitt to Administrative Assistant, Office of the Secretary of War, August 13, 1943, Records of the Army Service Forces, Box 602.

9. Capt. John J. Blewitt to Commanding Officer, June 8, 1943, ibid., Box 603; Anderson, "Last Hired, First Fired," p. 7; Eleanor F. Straub, "Government Policy toward Civilian Women during World War II," Ph.D. dissertation, Emory University, 1973, pp. 186–93; George E. DeMar, "Negro Women Are American Workers, Too," *Opportunity: Journal of Negro Life* 21 (April 1943):41–42.

10. George H. Gallup, *The Gallup Poll: Public Opinion, 1935–1971* (New York: Random House, 1972), p. 367; Giles, "What About the Women?" p. 157.

11. Straub, "Government Policy toward Civilian Women," pp. 297– 300; "Opinion About the Wartime Employment of Women," pp. 1–3, 5–6, 10–12; Eleanor Lake, "Trouble on the Street Corner," *Common Sense* 12 (May 1943):148; "The Intelligent Use of Women in Industry," Women's Personnel Conference, October 31–November 3, 1944, Seattle, Washington, pp. 20–21, Elinore M. Herrick Papers, folder 175, SL.

12. Campbell, "Wives, Workers and Womanhood," pp. 74–82, 84– 87; War Production Board, Office of Labor Production, "Problems of Women War Workers in Detroit," August 20, 1943, Records of the War Production Board, File 025.606, NA, Record Group 179.

13. "Pampered Husbands Should Be Educated," *United Automobile Worker*, August 15, 1943, p. 6; Giles, "What About the Women?" p. 157.

14. *Women's Wartime Hours of Work: The Effect on Their Factory Performance and Home Life*, Women's Bureau Bulletin No. 208 (Washington, D.C.: Government Printing Office, 1947), pp. 3–5, 49, 86–87, 159–60.

15. Ibid.; *MLR* 58 (January 1943):1–9; "Opinion About the Wartime Employment of Women," pp. 20–22.

16. "Building the Future for Children and Youth," April 1943, Office of Community War Services Policy Memoranda III, p. 19, Records of the Office of Community War Services, Record Group 215, NA; Federal Works Agency, Bureau of Community Facilities, "Summary of Information on the Child Care Program Receiving Assistance under the Lanham Act," Papers of the Child Care Centers Parents Association, folder 6, SL; Straub, "Government Policy toward Civilian Women," pp. 285–89.

17. Federal Security Agency, Office of Community War Services memorandum, untitled, December 9, 1943, Records of the Office of Community War Services, Policy Memoranda File; Anne L. Gould, "The Child Care Program and Its Relation to War Production," October 30, 1943, Papers of the United Automobile Workers, Women's Bureau, Jeffrey File, Labor History Archives, Wayne State University, Detroit, Michigan; Phyllis Fraser, "New England Shipbuilding Corporation: Report on Women," n.d., pp. 5–6, Herrick Papers File A-156, folder 77; John O. Louis, "Child Care Centers," *Public Welfare* 1 (May 1943):141–47; Constance McLaughlin Green, *The Role of Women as Production Workers in War Plants in the Connecticut Valley* (Northampton, Mass.: Smith College Studies in History, 1946), pp. 53–57.

18. Ibid.; Gould, "The Child Care Program and Its Relation to War Production," p. 5; Augusta H. Clawson, *Shipyard Diary of a Woman Welder* (New York: Penguin Books, 1944), p. 165; Straub, "Government Policy toward Civilian Women," pp. 292–94; "Opinion About the Wartime Employment of Women," pp. 24–29; Eleanor M. Hosley, "Is Day Care the Answer?" *Bulletin of the Child Welfare League of America* 22 (March 1943):1–3, 11.

19. Pidgeon, "Changes in Women's Employment," pp. 5–10.

20. Ibid., p. 9.

21. *Negro Women War Workers*, p. 21.

22. Pidgeon, "Changes in Women's Employment," p. 15; Campbell, "Wives, Workers, and Womanhood," p. 20.

23. Karen Beck Skold, "The Job He Left Behind: American Women in the Shipyards during World War II," in Carol R. Berkin and Clara M. Lovett, *Women, War and Revolution* (New York: Holmes and Meier, 1980), pp. 55–72; Green, *The Role of Women as Production Workers*, pp. 31–32; Campbell, "Wives, Workers, and Womanhood," pp. 136, 158; Alan Clive, "Women Workers in World War II: Michigan as a Test Case," *Labor History* 20 (Winter 1979):52–53; Hobart, "Training and Utilization of Women," pp. 22, 53, 57, 77.

24. "Women in Trade Unions during the War Period," November 1944, pp. 6–7, Records of the Women's Bureau, Box 5, NA, Record Group 86; "Women and the Unions," *Life and Labor Bulletin* 49 (February

1944):1−2; Green, *The Role of Women as Production Workers*, pp. 60−63; Office Staff of the Women's Bureau to Regional Representative, March 6, 1943, Papers of the Consumers League of Ohio, Box 41; David Dubinsky to Rose Pesotta, January 8, 1941, Pesotta to Dubinsky, February 20, 1941, Pesotta papers, New York Public Library.

25. Pidgeon, "Changes in Women's Employment," p. 9; Campbell, "Wives, Workers and Womanhood," p. 22; "Trends of Earnings among White-Collar Workers during the War," *MRL* 58 (May 1944):1033−48; "War and Post-War Trends in Employment of Negroes," ibid. 60 (January 1945):3.

26. Campbell, "Wives, Workers and Womanhood," pp. 112−18; "Effect of War on Employment of Woman Lawyers," *MLR* 57 (September 1943), pp. 502−503; *The Outlook for Women in Science*, Women's Bureau Bulletin No. 223, Part I (Washington, D.C.: Government Printing Office, 1949), p. 27; Marion Marzolf, *Up from the Footnote: A History of Women Journalists* (New York: Hastings House, 1977), pp. 52, 69−72, 140−41.

27. Christine Ammer, *Unsung: A History of Women in American Music* (Westport, Conn.: Greenwood Press, 1980), pp. 99−115, 200−203; Jerzy Bojanowsky, "Championing the Woman Orchestra Player," *Musical Courier* 131 (January 15, 1945):42; Mary L. Stoltzfus, "Eve in the Ensemble," ibid. 136 (December 1, 1947):9, 17; Hope Stoddard, "Ladies of the Symphony," *International Musician* 51 (May 1953):24−25; Carol Neuls-Bates, "Women as Orchestral Musicians in the United States, Circa 1925−45," in Jane Bowers and Judith Tick, eds., *Women Making Music* (Berkeley: University of California Press, forthcoming).

28. "Wartime Shifts of Household Employees into Other Industries," March 1946, Records of the Women's Bureau, 56-A-260; "Wartime Job Opportunities for Women Household Workers in Washington, D.C.," *MLR* 60 (March 1945):575, 583−84; Jo Ann Robinson, script for slide show on household workers, Papers of the National Council of Negro Women; Kathryn Blood, "Domestic Workers," January 1944, pp. 2−3, ibid., Series 5, folder 504; "New Defense Jobs," *Newsreel*, January 1943, pp. 2−3, Employment, Industrial Relations File, Sophia Smith Collection.

29. "War and Post-War Trends in Employment of Negroes," pp. 2−3; "Wartime Shifts of Household Employees," p. 3.

30. Lillian Sharpley, "Married Women at Work," M.A. thesis, Columbia University, 1945, pp. 41−59; "Women's Bureau Study of Women War Workers and Their Postwar Plans," February 1946, Records of the Women's Bureau, 54-A-78, Box 9; "Women War Workers' Post-War Job Plans," *MLR* 59 (September 1944):589; "Do You Want to Keep Your War Job in Peacetime?" *PM*, April 11, 1943; Mary Elizabeth Pidgeon, "Women Workers and Recent Economic Change," *MLR* 65 (December 1947):668; "Facts on Women Workers," May 31, 1947, p. 2 (mimeographed publication of the Women's Bureau).

31. "Postwar Labor Turnover among Women Factory Workers," *MLR* 64 (March 1947):419; "The Labor Force in the First Year of Peace," ibid.

63 (November 1946):676; Office of War Information, News Release, August 23, 1944, pp. 1–2, Records of the Office of War Information, E84, Box 568.

32. Ibid.; "Postwar Labor Turnover among Women Factory Workers," p. 411; "Jobs for Women Since the War," n.d. (c. September 1946), Records of the Women's Bureau 58-A-850, Box 2; *New York Times*, June 26, 1946; "Labor Force, Employment, and Unemployment," *MLR* 68 (February 1949):173.

33. Skold, "The Job He Left Behind," p. 68; "Recent Trends Affecting the Employment of Women in Automobile Manufacturing in Detroit," July 26, 1946, Records of the Women's Bureau 58-A-850, Box 2; Pidgeon, "Women Workers and Recent Economic Change," *MLR* 65 (December 1947):666, 668–69; Anderson, "Last Hired, First Fired," p. 17.

34. "Women's Bureau Survey of Ex–War Workers in Baltimore," pp. 7, 16, 37–40, 53–55, Records of the Women's Bureau, 55-A-556, Box 19.

35. "Expanding Occupational Opportunities for Women," *MLR* 71 (April 1953); *Handbook of Facts on Women Workers*, Women's Bureau Bulletin No. 242 (Washington, D.C.: Government Printing Office, 1952), pp. 20–21; United States Bureau of the Census, *Statistical Abstracts of the United States: 1952* (Washington, D.C.: Government Printing Office, 1952), pp. 177–78; Valerie Oppenheimer, *The Female Labor Force in the United States: Demographic and Economic Factors Governing Its Growth and Changing Composition* (Westport, Conn.: Greenwood Press, 1976).

36. Herman P. Miller, *Income of the American People* (New York: John Wiley and Sons, 1955), pp. 86–88, 109; *Women Workers and Their Dependents*, Women's Bureau Bulletin No. 239 (Washington, D.C.: Government Printing Office, 1952), pp. 45–47; Janet E. Heiniger provides an analysis of women's economic motivations based on data for the 1950s in an unpublished paper, "Working towards the Suburban Dream: Why Women Entered the Labor Force, 1945–1965."

37. Dorothy S. Brady, "Equal Pay—What Are the Facts?" *Reports of the National Conference on Equal Pay, 1952*, Women's Bureau Bulletin No. 243 (Washington, D.C.: Government Printing Office, 1953), pp. 14–17; "Expanding Occupational Opportunities for Women," p. 1; Miller, *Income of the American People*, p. 99.

38. *Changes in Women's Occupations, 1940–1950*, Women's Bureau Bulletin, No. 153 (Washington, D.C.: Government Printing Office, 1954), pp. 9–11, 82; C. Arnold Anderson and Mary Jean Bowman, "The Vanishing Servant and the Contemporary Status System of the American South," *American Journal of Sociology* 59 (November 1953):220, 227.

Wife and child of veteran in married students' village at the
University of Minnesota, 1949
Courtesy of Library of Congress

Chapter Six

Women's Education

Women's educational patterns in the 1940s reinforced their inferior position in the economy. Although the exigencies of war temporarily promoted somewhat greater opportunity for women to study in traditionally male fields, the war also contributed to the withdrawal of women from high school and college. As enrollments climbed in the postwar period, women graduated from college in ever-increasing numbers, but relative to men their educational attainments declined. Moreover, the content of their education prepared women for social and economic roles that sustained the polarization of the sexes. By 1950, the gap between women and men in higher education had lengthened, and women had also fallen further behind men in higher-level teaching and in administration positions.

The war reduced high-school enrollments as both boys and girls responded to new opportunities to earn money. But over the decade the prewar tendency for greater proportions of teenagers to complete high school persisted, and female graduates continued to outnumber males. The percentage of seventeen-year-old boys who completed high school increased from 48 to 54 during the 1940s, while that for girls rose from 54 to 61. Beyond high school, however, the educational aspirations and achievements of young women dropped below those of their male counterparts.[1]

Anticipation of marriage directed both the curricular choices and the future plans of high school girls. Surveys made by educational agencies in the early 1950s reported that only 62 percent of fully qualified high-school girls, but 78 percent of boys, planned to go on to college. High-school girls were less likely to take academic and general education courses, more inclined to pursue a commercial curriculum. The largest number of high-school girls, 35 percent in a 1955 national survey, were enrolled in typing, shorthand, and general business courses in preparation for jobs immediately after graduation. Such choices were consistent with the gender-differentiated advice of school counselors and compatible with the economy's growing demand for clerical workers. They also demonstrated the strength of two features of the prewar order: the overwhelming importance of marriage for women, and the sexual segregation of the labor force.[2]

Although teaching in the primary and secondary schools remained a woman's occupation, the war induced some women to move into better jobs and others to enter the field. Opportunities in the military and in civilian employment lured women away from teaching positions which averaged less than $1,500 a year in 1940 and fell to half that amount in rural areas. In 1942, for example, Alice Dunnigan saw a government advertisement in her Russelville, Kentucky, post office calling for clerical help. Her successful application enabled her to double her salary of $623 per year, which she had earned as a teacher in a segregated school. Educating herself at night at Howard University, she moved up to a professional job in the Office of Price Administration and became chief of the Associated Negro Press's Washington bureau after the war.[3]

Military service and new job opportunities at higher salaries drew even more men away from teaching. Desperate for staff, school boards moved toward more equitable policies in compensation and hiring. By 1950, the number of cities reporting pay differentials based on sex had decreased from 47 to 20 percent. Marriage had handicapped women in 95 percent of the cities in 1941, but in only 59 percent in 1951, and by then only 8 percent absolutely refused to hire married women, in contrast to 58 percent before the war. Women even increased slightly their preponderance in school teaching and occupied almost 80 percent of the positions in 1950. But they lost ground in administrative jobs. In 1950 they comprised less than 10 percent of high-school principals, about the same proportion as they had been in 1900. And, women were even fewer superintendents: of the 360 larger cities in the country, only one had a female superintendent in 1950. The teaching shortage, which continued in the postwar period, provided considerable opportunities for women to secure jobs under somewhat better conditions of work and pay, but it did not alter the male monopoly over administrative positions.[4]

College and university officials shared with school administrators the problem of securing adequate staff during the war. In addition, they faced a crisis of dwindling enrollments as the war threatened to deprive them of the group of young men who had provided 60 percent of the 1.5 million college students in 1940. Their attempts to sustain enrollments consequently benefited women. But the sex ratio on college campuses did not shift as dramatically as would have been expected given the military monopoly on young men. Even in 1944, women did not quite constitute 50 percent of college enrollments. This was so, in part, because the enrollment of women declined, though not so much as that of men. The patriotic and financial lure of defense jobs and a higher marriage and birth rate reduced the number of women in colleges by 25,000 between 1940 and 1944. Barnard tried to keep its young women in school when they were eager to plunge into war work as nurses' aides or ambulance drivers or to use their partial education for work in war plants as engineering aides. Other institutions were not so successful and in fact made it easier for women to exchange studies for jobs. Indiana University, for example, developed a shortened curriculum, three semesters of courses which would prepare women for jobs in special fields such as science, nursing, and civil service where workers were urgently needed.[5]

As female enrollments dropped, military programs enabled institutions of higher education to maintain significant male enrollments. Temporary draft deferments were available to men in science, engineering and medical fields. In addition, the army and navy contracted with colleges and universities for special training programs. So great was the military presence on campus that a Harvard alumnus pronounced his school, which had 4,500 servicemen enrolled in 1942, "one of the foremost military and naval academies in the U.S.," and the President of the University of California at Berkeley called it "a military tent with academic sideshows." During the war more than one million men received college credits through military programs. On many campuses they occupied some or all of the women's residence halls. In 1944, the invasion of France and acceleration of the Pacific war required an expansion of fighting forces and impelled the military to call most of its uniformed students to active duty. It was only then that the male/female ratio of college students approached parity.[6]

Because women were able to stay in college longer, they temporarily surpassed men in first degrees awarded. The numbers of women obtaining degrees at all levels, nonetheless, fell during the war and did not resume the prewar trend of gradual increases until 1947. The war altered somewhat the experiences of collegiate women. Coeducation became even more the norm as the percentage of women enrolled in women's colleges declined from 17.7 percent in 1940 to 12 percent in 1950. Harvard permitted mixed classes in increasing numbers during the war, and in 1947 formally adopted what it called "joint instruction," but it allowed Radcliffe women access to the superior Harvard undergraduate library only on Saturday afternoons. Women in coeducational institutions during the war enjoyed greater opportunities for leadership in such extracurricular activities as student government and publications. And, the wartime emphasis on scientific knowledge altered somewhat women's curricular choices. Higher proportions of women took mathematics and science courses, and, according to one survey, the number of bachelor's degrees in sciences awarded to women increased by 29 percent. Greater numbers of women enrolled in engineering programs, and such major institutions as Columbia University and Rensselaer Polytechnic Institute admitted women to engineering programs for the first time.[7]

The war also provided a boost for women with career aspirations in medicine. In the early years they experienced even greater difficulties getting into medical schools because administrators preferred to train men who could supply the military forces with doctors. But, as the war progressed the growing need for physicians and the dwindling supply of qualified male candidates opened the door to more women applicants. Thus, a woman who had applied unsuccessfully to three New York medical schools in 1943 gained admission in 1944; she credited the wartime shortage of male applicants with providing her the opportunity to become a psychoanalyst. One of the last medical schools to exclude women completely, Harvard admitted twelve women to its 1945 freshman class, deciding that some "very superior women" were preferable to the available supply of "mediocre men." Nationally, women comprised 14.4 percent of all medical school freshmen in 1945. The war also impelled more hospitals to admit women graduates as interns. In just one year female doctors gained acceptance into more than 300 hospitals which had previously refused them.[8]

The acute nursing shortage in the face of mounting wartime needs afforded new opportunities for black women in this field. Before the war only forty-two of the 1,200 nursing schools admitted blacks and most of these were segregated institutions. To increase the supply of nurses, in 1943 Congress passed the Bolton Act, establishing the Cadet Nurse Corps. Students who joined received federal funds for an accelerated course, promising on completion of their education to practice essential nursing for the duration of the war. These funds supported the vast majority of black women in nurses training and particularly benefited the black institutions. At Freedman's Hospital in Washington, D.C., for example, nursing enrollments more than doubled following passage of the Bolton Act. Black students also gained entry for the first time into such large city hospitals as Philadelphia's General and New York's Bellevue. Between 1940 and 1950 the number of minority women nurses doubled, and the number of nursing schools opened to blacks grew to 330.[9]

Most of women's wartime gains in education did not withstand the end of hostilities. The numbers of women at all levels and in most fields continued to increase, but relative to men, their educational status fell below prewar levels. The nation's efforts to compensate those who had risked their lives and sacrificed years in defending it had a profound impact on American higher education and upon the relative positions of men and women. In providing educational support to all veterans who qualified and chose to use it and to the institutions they attended, the GI Bill of Rights sparked a tremendous expansion in higher education. Because most soldiers were men they gained the lion's share in this "democratization of higher education." And, the lingering attitudes about woman's place meant that even as college became more accessible to young people in general, families continued to support the higher education of sons over that of daughters.

As they were discharged from the military, veterans flocked to college campuses, so that at their peak enrollment in 1947, they comprised almost half of the 2.3 million college students, and women just one-third. By 1946, thousands of qualified women were being turned away as colleges found their faculties and facilities strained and most gave preference to veterans. This preference was not surprising given the nation's gratitude to returning soldiers along with the fact that colleges received direct federal subsidies for each veteran enrolled as well as funds to construct housing for veterans. Early in 1946 Cornell University, where women had been in the majority during the war, had cut back their proportion to 20 percent. Wisconsin at first limited the number of out-of-state women it admitted, and later banned almost all non-residents. As other institutions restricted female admissions, representatives at a meeting of the American College Public Relations Association discussed the crisis for women and expressed concern for "the young women of the next five to ten years blocked from their educational heritage." Moreover, the better schools felt the most intense pressures as veterans chose state universities, well-known liberal-arts colleges, and technical schools when their credentials permitted. Of course, women veterans, too, partook of GI educational benefits, but they had constituted under 3 percent of military personnel. When the program ended in 1956, 64,728 women had been among the 2,232,000 veterans educated under the GI Bill, a proportion approximating their representation in World War II service.[10]

The massive enrollments of veterans brought a new group of women to the college campus, or at least to its fringes. Half of the veterans who studied under the GI Bill were married, and their presence introduced a novel feature of American higher education—the married student. "Vetsvilles" appeared on campuses throughout the country, where veterans' families created communities in trailers, Quonset huts, and other temporary dwellings and established their own government units, baby-sitting exchanges, and food cooperatives. The monthly subsistence check, which by

1948 was $105 for a married veteran, was usually insufficient to make ends meet; veterans supplemented them with part-time jobs, savings, loans, and the contributions of their wives. At Stanford University almost two-thirds of veterans' wives had jobs; at Michigan State, nearly one-half. Students' wives performed a growing share of the clerical work in colleges and universities and continued to be a part of academic life after the last veteran had left the campus. The veterans' example made the combination of marriage and education an accepted collegiate pattern in postwar America. The possibility of continuing schooling after marriage increased women's educational opportunities, and was all the more important as women wed earlier than ever before. Yet, men benefited most because the typical married student was male and wives were much more likely to drop out of college than husbands.[11]

The postwar transformation of higher education enlarged the differences between men and women. As enrollments swelled, as college education spread beyond the exceptional or privileged few and became a key to middle-class status, women lost ground. The numbers of college women increased significantly. In 1940, 77,000 women graduated from college; in 1950, 104,000 attained bachelors' and other first-level degrees. But, while women were 40 percent of all graduates in 1940, their proportion had dropped to one in four by 1950. As World War II veterans completed their education, women's share of college degrees rose, but even by 1959, women accounted for just one-third of all graduates. Their share of masters' and doctors' degrees also declined during the 1940s, from 38 to 29 percent and from 13 to 10 percent, respectively.[12]

In some respects the distribution of educational attainment among black men and women took a different form. Since the late nineteenth century, paid employment had been a necessity for high proportions of black women, even when married, so that young women were raised with expectations of having to work outside the home for long periods of their lives. At the same time, the occupational situation for black women created a particular urgency for higher education. The exclusion of black women from most middle-range professional and white collar jobs limited their employment choices to domestic or farm work on the one hand, or teaching on the other. The desire for dignified work formed a powerful incentive for college-level study: by 1940 black women outnumbered men in first-level degrees awarded by black institutions. War temporarily increased this gap, but, aided by the GI Bill, black men returned to college campuses in the postwar period where they outpaced female enrollments by several thousand. At the end of the decade, the 6,467 bachelors' degrees earned by men at black institutions constituted almost half of the 13,108 conferred, and black men had increased their share of masters' degrees to 44 percent.[13]

This near parity in education between black men and women did not obtain at the higher levels. Black men maintained their ascendency in doctoral degrees and in education for the more prestigious professions. In 1949, women comprised less than 10 percent of medical students in black institutions, and just slightly more in law-school enrollments. Black women shared with white women the difficulties attending their efforts to pursue traditionally male fields. At Howard University Law School in the war years Pauli Murray experienced "male condescension . . . never far from the surface," and upon graduating found her opportunities even more limited than those of her male classmates. Moreover, the GI Bill provided some black men access to integrated education outside the South; but, since so few black women served in the military—just 4,000 at their peak strength in the WAC—the effect of the GI Bill was negligible for black women as a group. Whether the sexual division of education paralleled the behavior of whites at the advanced levels or formed a distinct pattern at the bachelor's and master's levels, the educational opportunities of both black men and women remained far below their white counterparts.[14]

Throughout the 1940s women continued to fill two out of every five of the teaching positions at black colleges, but elsewhere the growing numbers of college women had fewer role models. From a peak of 27.7 percent in 1940, women's representation among academic personnel dropped to 24.5 percent in 1950 and declined even further during the ensuing decade. Women's share of faculty positions fell even at the women's colleges which had traditionally employed a disproportionate number of women. The largest women's colleges staffed nearly three-fourths of their faculty positions with women in 1940, but less than 60 percent in 1955. In

1946, the American Association of University Women hailed the appointments of women to head Sweet Briar and Vassar colleges as steps promising reversal of a recent trend to name male presidents to women's colleges. Yet, by 1950 women headed only ten of the nonsectarian women's colleges. Reorganization of student personnel administration on a number of coeducational campuses further diluted the position of women in academia. Deans of women found themselves reporting to a (male) dean of students. In the process they lost direct access to the head of the institution, control over their own budgets, and a voice in policymaking at the top level.[15]

The somewhat greater tendency of women to educate themselves in traditionally male fields lost momentum as peace returned. In the field of medicine, in fact, women lost the slight gains that wartime exigencies had enabled them to achieve. In 1949, women were 12 percent of all medical-school graduates, the class which had begun in 1945 when opportunities for women were at their peak. While 600 women received M.D.s in 1949, only 400 were entering the freshman class. By the mid-1950s women's share of medical-school graduates had fallen to 5 percent, slightly below that of 1941. A survey by the New York Infirmary in 1946 reported 42 percent of hospitals refusing women interns and 35 percent denying them residencies. The war had permitted several hundred women who would not otherwise have had the opportunity to become doctors, but their younger sisters faced the same quotas that had prevailed in the 1920s and 1930s.[16]

A postwar survey of medical students indicated that women faced attitudinal as well as institutional obstacles and that women themselves held self-limiting attitudes. Two-thirds of the 114 male medical students questioned had less confidence in women doctors than in men. While only one-sixth approved of the traditional 5 percent quota on women students, a majority believed that women should be selected more carefully than men. Recognizing discrimination against women in the profession, men thought that individual women should overcome it by superior performance and accommodating personalities rather than by collective action. Female students imposed limitations upon themselves to effect an accommodation with society's norms and practices. A majority of the single students said that they would consider marriage even if that meant abandoning a career. Most of the fifty-seven women

surveyed believed that married women should restrict their practices to avoid making night calls, and almost half felt that if both
husband and wife were physicians it was important for the husband to be more successful.[17]

Encouragement of women to prepare for scientific and engineering careers also faded as the war ended, and those pursuing such
training faced far stiffer competition. Engineering schools doubled
their enrollments in the fall of 1946, but women were fewer than
1,300 of the 200,000 enrolled. A survey of 130 schools revealed
that only half admitted women: where women were admitted,
they usually found only a handful of other women among their
classmates. But it was not simply the postwar pressures on colleges
and universities that deterred women from enlarging their wartime
inroads into male professions. Even where women students did not
face male competition, their inclination to specialize in scientific
fields diminished. At Vassar within ten years after the war, the
proportion of women majoring in chemistry and physics had
decreased to 10 percent from the wartime peak of 21 percent, and
the drop was almost as great in mathematics and the biological
sciences. In the absence of a national demand for women's services
in the sciences, women followed the more traditional patterns
coincident with their sex-role socialization, the advice of a substantial segment of professional educators and counsellors, and the
realities of the labor market.[18]

In the postwar years women made their educational choices
amidst a national debate over the purpose and content of women's
education. Such a discussion was certainly not new: Americans
perennially worried over the efficacy of their educational institutions and disagreed about their appropriate functions. But the
debate reached a particular stridency in the late 1940s as a movement among educators grew to refashion women's education in
order to prepare them better for home and family life. The earliest
proposal to accommodate women more fully to the traditional
sexual order appeared in 1942 in a study of college graduates which
had been conducted during the Depression. The investigators,
Robert G. Foster and Pauline Park Wilson, concluded that their
education had not adequately prepared these women to handle the
various problems they encountered after graduation. Eighty-two
percent reported difficulties with housekeeping caused by lack of

skill, dislike of monotonous tasks, and inadequate opportunity for intellectual and creative pursuits. Consequently, Foster and Wilson recommended courses which provided better preparation for domestic responsibilities and efforts to infuse housekeeping with higher social status. Noting that women's choices of roles were frequently in conflict with "the one which society prescribed for her or the one which her husband and parents assigned to her," they asserted that college should prepare women to shift their roles. Referring to the woman who unhappily sacrificed her profession to childrearing, they criticized her college, which "had prepared her well to FOLLOW her vocation, but neither the college nor her parents had prepared her for GIVING UP her vocation."[19]

The opinions of Foster and Wilson found increasing support in the postwar period. Educators were joined by psychologists who emphasized the differences between the sexes and warned that women's pursuit of intellectual and occupational achievements similar to those of men were not only doomed to failure, but were damaging to women, their families and society. The most blistering indictment of the current curricula for women was made by Lynn White, Jr., President of Mills College, in a speech to the American Association of University Women in 1947. That many in his audience were affronted by his call for a distinctly feminine course of study did not deter him from elaborating on his proposal in a book, *Educating Our Daughters*, published in 1950. On the positive side, White insisted that greater exposure to female professors was important for both men and women students. In addition, he recognized that men had succeeded in creating a value system in which male activities were the most highly rated and urged a new scale of values which would give comparable status to female accomplishments and enhance women's self-respect. But the main thrust of White's argument was to reinforce the sexual division of labor and women's attachment to home and family. Emphasizing sex differences in biological makeup and social roles, White pleaded that women's curricula better enable women "to foster the intellectual and emotional life of her family and community," and to infuse the home with beauty, culture, and gourmet cooking. White conceded the need for colleges to prepare women to earn a living and insisted on the absolute freedom of women to pursue the vocation of their choice, but he failed to comprehend the extent to which a curricular emphasis on preparation for marriage would severely limit that choice.[20]

His critics were quick to point that out. Harold Taylor, President of Sarah Lawrence College, insisted that educating women for marriage and motherhood was to promote rigid, subservient behavior, to fashion women "in terms of the needs and wishes of men, and not in terms of their own fulfillment." White's opponents emphasized the diversity in life patterns among women and demanded above all the right of women to a fully human education which meant curricular choices unprejudiced by an overemphasis on women's domestic roles. They conceded that women graduates were marrying at higher rates than ever before, but pointed to the growing tendency for married women to work outside the home and particularly to the incidence of employment among college-educated wives which was greater than for women who did not go beyond high school. A feminine course of study would ill prepare women for work outside the home and would especially handicap those who sought advanced study for the professions. Even those women who would never use their education for vocational purposes needed a liberal education undiluted by courses in flower arrangement and "the theory and preparation of a well marinated Shish Kebab," advocated by White. Where courses could better prepare students for family living, childrearing and responsible citizenship, they were equally important to men and women. Marriage itself would be jeopardized by a distinct female curriculum and the consequent reduction of a common ground for intellectual companionship.[21]

What the proposals of White and others obscured was the fact that the content of women's education was already different from that of men. Women concentrated their studies in the humanities and social sciences, and in preparing for vocations they overwhelmingly selected training in traditionally female fields such as teaching and social work. The self-limiting strategies of college women were noted by Mildred McAfee Horton, who had returned from her service as Director of the WAVES to preside over Wellesley College. She was disturbed to find that because women expected to marry they assumed they should be content with subordinate positions and they felt that competition for higher-status jobs was unfeminine. Even more alarming to Horton were the implications for all women: these complacent attitudes and low levels of ambition contributed to a general depreciation of women as workers and undermined those women who aspired to high-level careers.[22]

Advice to women students also sought to adapt them to existing social and economic realities. Vocational guidance manuals persistently emphasized fields where women would face little competition from men, and career counseling of women was predicated on the assumption that most would marry and that that relationship would take precedence over career aspirations. Indiana University, for example, defined women's education in terms that linked it with wifehood and motherhood. Although the college bulletin listed "Earner" as one of four roles for which women were to educate themselves, that role was subordinated to marriage: "Those few years when she earned her way in the business or professional world would make her a good sport about the ups and downs of her husband's business." Moreover, the educated woman would enjoy "an occasional opportunity" to return to work. "The electric mixer, the mink muff, the trip to the Derby—all were provided with her extra earnings." The bulletin discouraged women from planning their entire curricula around courses which would equip them for employment and discussed fields of concentration in terms of their compatibility with marriage.[23]

Even the literature which did not assume marriage counseled women to tailor their vocational plans to a male-dominated world rather than to their individual potentialities. Simmons College advised women who wanted to go into advertising to prepare themselves for secretarial work. A successful advertising woman echoed this advice: "Stenography is more important today than it ever was! You simply have to do something to pay your way along as you learn the business . . . to justify your place on the payroll." A YWCA handbook to guide women in curricula planning for careers covered a wide range of vocations, including scientific and technical fields. Yet, it too prescribed a uniquely female pattern, stressing clerical work as entry to better positions and teaching as "the first great profession for the college girl."[24]

For college women seeking the easiest adjustment to the postwar order, the advice to choose fields compatible with marriage and to limit their vocational aspirations was realistic. A survey of 5,000 women who had graduated from liberal-arts colleges between 1946 and 1949 found that two-thirds had married within three to six years after graduation. Only half of the women had been able to find the kind of work to which they had aspired. Women who had chosen traditionally female fields such as teaching, nursing and secretarial work had been largely successful. But less than half of those who sought work in science, psychology, music, personnel work or journalism landed a job in these fields upon graduation. Two-and-one-half times as many women were employed in clerical occupations as had planned to work in this field. Not surprisingly, clerical workers were least satisfied with their jobs.[25]

Between 1940 and 1950 college women did broaden somewhat their participation in the professions. While teaching and nursing had claimed three-fourths of women in the professional category in 1940, these fields accounted for two-thirds in 1950. In journalism women made significant gains, increasing their share of editorial and reporting positions from one-fourth to one-third. In other fields the numbers of women multiplied, but the vocations remained overwhelmingly male. Among engineers, women increased their percentage from 0.3 to 1.2; among lawyers their proportion grew from 2.4 to 3.5; and among dentists, from 1.5 to 2.7. Overall, women's share of professional occupations declined slightly from 42 to 39 percent. Black women experienced a small gain in professional work, relative both to white women and black men, but they were still largely confined to teaching and nursing.[26]

The majority of white women, in fact, were not attending college primarily to prepare for a vocation. Anticipation of marriage and maternity dominated their educational motives. Most college women expected to work until marriage or motherhood, and a minority of these hoped to resume employment after they had raised their families. Nor did women deny the importance of college training for a skill to fall back on should they be deprived of male support. But to a much larger degree than men they were motivated by social or personal reasons. A Vassar student wanted "to be a real partner to the man I marry." Another hoped "to converse with my husband's friends and business acquaintances with a mature and confident manner that can only come from a thorough education." Again racial realities put different pressures on black women. To a survey taken in the early 1950s fully 90 percent responded that they attended college primarily to prepare for a vocation.[27]

Both black and white women believed that preparation for marriage and family responsibilities should be one of the three major purposes of college education. Their greater need to accommodate family duties to paid employment and the difficulties of raising children in a racist society no doubt accounted for black women's belief that college might have done more to prepare them for traditional female roles. Moreover, the discrepancy in educational achievement between black men and women meant that more black women "married down." For these women marital adjustment was more precarious in a society whose norm was for husbands to surpass their wives in educational and occupational status. Indeed, some educators believed that black women felt pressure to restrain their efforts to realize their full potential so as not to threaten their marriages.[28]

Full-time homemakers who regretted that their college education had not better fit them for current roles bore witness to the abrupt transition women had to make from college or paid employment to total domesticity. Surveys of college-educated housewives in the late 1940s and 1950s revealed a sizeable minority who expressed discontent. While a number of these women believed that courses in child psychology, budgeting and the like would have eased their frustrations, virtually all referred to the fatigue, boredom, monotony and mental stagnation that attended their domestic roles. According to one woman who criticized her college education, "Some of my interests and attitudes were so very academic that I didn't take to the routine of a homemaker for quite awhile." Another woman also felt the sharp discontinuity between college and homemaking: "I would much prefer to play a Bach fugue than . . . scrub the kitchen floor. I have needed all my philosophy courses to reconcile myself to accepting the monotony of household chores."[29]

Proponents of a distinctly feminine curriculum had of course been influenced by such expressions and used them as ammunition. Both the women who experienced dissatisfaction and the educators who sought to refashion women's education were responding to a growing contradiction between changing elements of women's behavior and traditional attitudes and practices. More and more women were attending college and they enjoyed greater economic opportunities than ever before. Yet, as popular media celebrated marriage and motherhood, college women were marrying at younger ages and with greater frequency, and they were bearing more children. Lynn White and his cohorts sought to ease this disharmony by sizing down women's education to fit their future marital and maternal roles. They failed to make drastic changes in women's education, but women themselves adapted their behavior so as to sustain their customary roles and responsibilities. They specialized in traditionally feminine fields and they adjusted their employment to fit around their families' needs and interests. They weathered the contradiction between the intellectual and social stimulation of their educational years and the isolation and routine of domesticity, viewing that dissonance as a personal problem or the result of inappropriate education.

The brief promise of greater educational equity which surfaced amidst the imperatives of war vanished as another imperative, the need to compensate those who had defended the nation, increased the distance between women's and men's opportunities. Relative to men, women did lose ground, but in absolute terms they progressed as the numbers enrolled in colleges increased from 600,953 in 1940 to 805,953 in 1950. The democratization of higher education expanded the boundaries of woman's place and afforded to more women a vision of life beyond domesticity and work beyond the routine and subordinate. The persistence of sex-role socialization, economic discrimination, and the family and domestic claims on married women denied most of them realization of these possibilities, but did not prevent all women from feeling the contradiction between the promise and the reality. In the 1940s and 1950s many educators and women themselves sought to ease the tension by adjusting to the world as it was. A later generation would attack the intensifying contradiction by challenging the larger social and economic structures.[30]

NOTES AND REFERENCES

1. Richard Lingeman, *Don't You Know There's a War On? The American Home Front, 1941–1945* (New York: G.P. Putnam's Sons, 1970), pp. 168–69; National Manpower Council, *Womanpower* (New York: Columbia University Press, 1957), p. 168.

2. Ibid., pp. 174–90.

3. D'Ann Campbell, "Wives, Workers and Womanhood: America during World War II," Ph.D. dissertation, University of North Carolina, 1979, pp. 112–14; Lt. Frances S. Miller, "I Deserted to the Navy," *Journal of the American Association of American Women* (hereafter *JAAUW*) (Fall 1945): 12–14; Alice Allison Dunnigan, *A Black Woman's Experience: From Schoolhouse to White House* (Philadelphia: Dorrance and Company, 1974), pp. 186–205.

4. *The Status of Women in the United States, 1953*, Women's Bureau Bulletin No. 249 (Washington, D.C.: Government Printing Office, 1953), pp. 16–17.

5. United States Bureau of the Census, *Statistical Abstracts of the United States, 1952* (Washington, D.C.: Government Printing Office, 1952), p. 123; Virginia Crocheron Gildersleeve, *Many a Good Crusade* (New York: Macmillan, 1954), pp. 260–62; mimeographed pamphlet, "How Indiana University's New Streamlined Curricula for Women Meets Wartime Needs," December 1942, Indiana University Library, Bloomington.

6. John M. Blum, *V Was for Victory: Politics and Culture during World War II* (New York: Harcourt, Brace, Jovanovich, 1976), pp. 141–44; Geoffrey Perrett, *Days of Sadness, Years of Triumph: The American People,*

1939—1945 (New York: Coward, McCann and Geoghegan, 1973), pp. 371—73; "University Deans' Survey," *Journal of the National Association of Deans of Women* (hereafter *JNADW*) 7 (October 1943):39.

7. Office of Education, Federal Security Agency, "Historical Summary of Staff, Enrollments, Degrees and Finances of Institutions of Higher Education," May 1950, Papers of the American Association of University Women, Folder 52, Schlesinger Library, Cambridge, Mass.; Mabel Newcomer, *A Century of Higher Education for Women* (New York: Harper and Brothers, 1959), p. 43; J. A. Lewis, "Harvard Goes Coed, But Incognito," *New York Times Magazine*, May 1, 1949, p. 38; "Women Students," *JAAUW* 39 (Winter 1946):102; *The Outlook for Women in Science*, Women's Bureau Bulletin No. 223-I (Washington, D.C.: Government Printing Office, 1949), p. 27.

8. Mary Roth Walsh, *"Doctors Wanted, No Women Need Apply": Sexual Barriers in the Medical Profession, 1835—1975* (New Haven: Yale University Press, 1977), pp. 224—35; Eli Ginzberg and Alice M. Yohalem, *Educated American Women: Self-Portraits* (New York: Columbia University Press, 1966), pp. 31—32.

9. Mabel K. Staupers, "A Story of Integration," *Women United*, Souvenir Year Book of the National Council of Negro Women, October 1951, p. 58; *Negro Women War Workers*, Women's Bureau Bulletin No. 205 (Washington, D.C.: Government Printing Office, 1945), p. 13; Estelle Massey Riddle, "The Negro Nurse and the War," *Opportunity: Journal of Negro Life* 21 (April 1943):44—45, 92.

10. *Statistical Abstracts of the United States, 1949*, pp. 122—23; Keith W. Olson, *The GI Bill, the Veterans, and the Colleges* (Lexington: University of Kentucky Press, 1974), pp. 35, 43, 45, 89; "Doors Closing for Women Students," *JAAUW* 39 (Spring 1946):167; "Women Students," ibid. 39 (Summer 1946):231—32; Gladys B. Longly, "Certain Educational Guidance Questions Answered," *JNADW* 9 (October 1945):128.

11. Olson, *The GI Bill*, pp. 75—78; Joseph C. Goulden, *The Best Years, 1945—1950* (New York: Atheneum, 1976), pp. 66—84; Kate Hevner Mueller, *Student Personnel Work in Higher Education* (Boston: Houghton Mifflin, 1961), pp. 429—37.

12. National Manpower Council, *Womanpower*, p. 197; *Handbook on Women Workers*, Women's Bureau Bulletin No. 275 (Washington, D.C.: Government Printing Office; 1960), p. 103; *Handbook of Facts on Women Workers*, Women's Bureau Bulletin No. 242 (Washington, D.C.: Government Printing Office, 1952), p. 97.

13. Jeanne L. Noble, *The Negro Woman's College Education* (New York: Columbia University Press, 1956), pp. 28—30; *Statistical Abstracts of the United States, 1952*, p. 124. Statistics on black students in integrated schools are not available.

14. Noble, *The Negro Woman's College Education*, p. 30; "Current Trends and Events of National Importance in Negro Education," *Journal of Negro Education* 19 (Spring 1950):207; Pauli Murray, "Black Women, Racism and the Legal Process in Historical Perspective," November 12, 1979, pp.

9–11, National Archives for Black Women's History, Washington, D.C.

15. *Statistical Abstracts of the United States, 1952*, p. 124; Jessie Bernard, *Academic Women* (University Park: Pennsylvania State University Press, 1964), pp. 40–44; Newcomer, *A Century of Higher Education*, p. 165; editorials, *JAAUW* 39 (Winter 1946):92; (Spring 1946):151; Alice C. Lloyd, "Women in the Postwar College," ibid., p. 133; Hallie Farmer, "Current Trends in Educational Administration: What They Mean for Women," ibid. 42 (Summer 1949):212; *The Status of Women in the United States*, p. 17.

16. Walsh, "Doctors Wanted: No Women Need Apply," pp. 242–46; Marguerite W. Zapoleon, "Women in the Professions," *Journal of Social Issues* 6 (1950):15–16; Howard Whitman, "M.D.—For Men Only," *Woman's Home Companion*, November 1946, p. 32.

17. Josephine J. Williams, "The Woman Physician's Dilemma," *Journal of Social Issues* 6 (1950):38–44.

18. *The Outlook for Women in Architecture and Engineering*, Women's Bureau Bulletin No. 223-V (Washington, D.C.: Government Printing Office, 1949), pp. 23–25; Newcomer, *A Century of Higher Education*, p. 93.

19. Robert G. Foster and Pauline Park Wilson, *Women After College: A Study of the Effectiveness of Their Education* (New York: Columbia University Press, 1942), pp. 48–50, 113, 116, 173, 194–217.

20. Lynn White, Jr., "The Reorientation of Women's Higher Education," Address at the AAUW National Convention, April 15, 1947, Records of the Women's Bureau, 58-A-850, Box 6, National Archives. See also White, *Educating Our Daughters* (New York: Harper and Brothers, 1950); Ferdinand Lundberg and Marynia Farnham, *Modern Woman: The Lost Sex* (New York: Harper and Brothers, 1947); Margaret Habein, "Problems in Women's Education," *JNADW* 13 (March 1950):117–23.

21. Newcomer, *A Century of Higher Education*, pp. 31, 172–75; Katharine Elizabeth McBride, "What Is Women's Education?" *Annals of the American Academy of Political and Social Science* 251 (May 1947):142–52; Marguerite J. Fisher, "Educating Women for—What?" *Independent Woman* 29 (August 1950):231–32, 256. The most extensive response to advocates of a feminine education is Mirra Komarovsky, *Women in the Modern World: Their Education and Their Dilemmas* (Boston: Little, Brown and Co., 1953).

22. Rachel Conrad Nason to Frieda Miller, May 23, 1947, Records of the Women's Bureau, 58-A-850, Box 6.

23. "What Makes an Educated Woman?" *Indiana University Bulletin* 43 (May 15, 1945).

24. Simmons College Bulletin, *Advertising as a Vocation for Women* 42 (January 1949); Speech by Dorothy Dignan, April 4, 1949, pp. 9–10, Papers of the Advertising Women of New York, Box 1, Schlesinger Library; Josephine H. Gerth, *Highways to Jobs for Women: How to Pick College Courses for Your Career* (New York: Woman's Press, 1948), pp. 24–39, 45.

25. Robert Shosteck, *Five Thousand Women College Graduates Report:*

Findings of a National Survey of the Social and Economic Status of Women Graduates of Liberal Arts Colleges of 1946–1949 (Washington, D.C.: B'nai B'rith Vocational Service Bureau, 1953), pp. 2–5, 37–39.

26. *Changes in Women's Occupations, 1940–1950*, Women's Bureau Bulletin No. 253 (Washington, D.C.: Government Printing Office, 1954), pp. 3, 10–11, 31–32, 50–57.

27. Shosteck, *Five Thousand Women College Graduates*, p. 2; Newcomer, *A Century of Higher Education*, pp. 65–67; Komarovsky, *Women in the Modern World*, pp. 92–99; David Riesman, "Some Continuities and Discontinuities in the Education of Women," Records of the Committee on Women's Education, EC 35, Schlesinger Library; Noble, *The Negro Woman's College Education*, pp. 46–47, 116–17.

28. Ibid., pp. 51, 124–25, 135.

29. Komarovsky, *Woman in the Modern World*, pp. 100–65; Ernest Havemann and Patricia Salter West, *They Went to College: The College Graduate in America Today* (New York: Harcourt Brace and Co., 1952), pp. 64–68.

30. Frank Stricker, "Cookbooks and Law Books: The Hidden History of Career Women in Twentieth Century America," *Journal of Social History* 10 (Fall 1976):10–13, 19 n75.

Japanese Americans awaiting evacuation bus
at Centerville, California, 1942
Courtesy of the National Archives

Chapter Seven

Women Under the Law

The 1940s brought the most serious attention to women's status under the law since the days of the women's suffrage campaign. Twenty years after the 19th Amendment had given women the most basic right of citizenship, they found themselves subject to numerous state and federal laws which denied them rights and opportunities available to men. The atmosphere of the 1940s facilitated discussion of these discriminations. The nation's need for womanpower enlarged popular and official sensitivity to women's legal disabilities. Propaganda's depiction of the war as a struggle for freedom and democracy sharpened the disparity between American ideals and the reality of sex discrimination. Economic recovery provided a more hospitable climate for organizations representing women's interests; those energies which had been so largely channeled to resisting intensified discrimination during the Depression could now be redirected along more positive lines. Finally, the employment of women in the military along with the influx of millions of women into the labor force belied to a certain degree the conception of women as dependent beings, a fiction which justified their unequal treatment under the law. Although no legal revolution transformed women's position in the 1940s, by the end of that decade their status under the law as citizens, married women, and workers had made significant progress.

For 7 million nonwhite women the legal disabilities of gender were compounded by discriminatory laws based on race. The 19th Amendment, which had granted suffrage to women, had little meaning for most of them, who along with men of color were virtually disfranchised. Those born in China and Japan were ineligible for citizenship no matter how long they had lived in the United States. New Mexico and Arizona withheld voting rights from all Native Americans within their borders. Southern states, where three-fourths of the black population lived, circumvented the voting protections of the 15th Amendment by a variety of legal and extralegal means. Less than 2 percent of the southern black population voted in 1940. One barrier to their exercise of the franchise fell in 1944 when the Supreme Court ruled the white primary unconstitutional. But the others remained; by 1952, 87 percent of southern black women and 65 percent of men had never voted.[1]

Barred from the voting booth, southern blacks were also constrained by law from comingling with whites in almost all institutions. In the North, segregation in public places usually resulted from residential segregation which was itself bolstered by zoning laws, restrictive covenants, and policies of the Federal Housing Administration. In the South, state statutes and municipal ordinances arrayed the full force of the law behind separation of the races. Seventeen states and the District of Columbia required separate primary and high schools. Black schools usually received lower funding. Consequently, their equipment was poorer, their teachers were paid less, and their curricula were inferior, a situation that was paralleled at the college level. Blacks could not use public libraries or recreational facilities; where separate institutions were provided they were almost always inferior. Twenty states had compulsory segregation laws which separated blacks from whites in transportation, hotels, restaurants, and places of amusement.[2]

Black women made little progress against the statutory foundations of their second-class citizenship. Supreme Court decisions eroded to a small extent segregation and discrimination in higher education, housing, interstate transportation and the system of justice, but the machinery of segregation from cradle to grave remained intact throughout most of the South. The most important benefits of the 1940s for black women resulted from geographical mobility, heightened expectations, and increasing consciousness of racial discrimination. Politically active black women were aware of and worked against the legal disabilities they suffered as women. Their major efforts, however, were associated with those of black men in a new movement for civil rights that would begin to bear significant fruit in the next decade.

Japanese-American women suffered the most devastating denial of rights during the war years. The attack on Pearl Harbor inflamed long-standing prejudice and resulted in the internment of 110,000 Japanese Americans in concentration camps. These included 50,000 women, 40 percent of whom were Issei, born in Japan and ineligible for citizenship by federal law. The majority were Nisei, children of Japanese, but citizens by reason of their birth in the United States. Japanese Americans were concentrated on the West Coast, and they alone of all ethnic groups were deemed threats solely because of their ancestry.

The government first arrested hundreds of men as "dangerous" enemy aliens. To those women who suffered the loss of husbands and fathers were added thousands who stood helpless and frightened while FBI agents searched their homes for weapons, radio transmitters, and cameras. But the worst blow came in February 1942 when President Roosevelt ordered the removal of all Japanese Americans from the western parts of Washington, Oregon, and California, where most of them lived. Families could take only those items which they could carry. Skeptical of government provisions to store possessions at owners' risk, many families succumbed to pressure to sell their belongings at a pittance. A Nisei music teacher sold her valuable piano for $30 while her brother disposed of his produce stand at a severe loss. Although they had little choice, some women devised a means of resistance to predators who sought profit from their misfortune. One whose husband had already been arrested was given forty-eight hours in which to move. Offered $17.50 by a secondhand dealer for a precious set of family porcelain, she, "with tears streaming down her cheeks . . . stood there smashing cups and bowls and platters until the whole set lay in scattered blue and white fragments across the wooden floor."[3]

Japanese Americans were moved to relocation camps in desolate areas bounded by barbed wire and guarded by armed sentries. As many as eight people lived in rooms no larger than twenty by twenty-five feet. These "homes" were designed primarily for sleeping: there was no water, kitchen, or privacy except by partitioning of areas with sheets and blankets. In each block, 250 individuals shared toilet and washing facilities and ate communal meals in mess halls. In such a setting traditional family relationships fragmented. The father's role as breadwinner was usurped by the government. Women no longer met the daily material needs of their husbands and children. Cramped living conditions inhibited families from spending much time together. Families frequently stopped eating together as children sought companionship of their peers. The difference in citizenship status between Issei parents and their Nisei children further diluted parental authority.[4]

Within the confinement of concentration camps, some Japanese-American women found their traditional existence altered in ways not totally negative. Before evacuation they had worked outside the home at rates higher than their white counterparts. Issei women had labored with their husbands on family farms, in small family businesses, or in service occupations. Internment provided some respite from the dual burden of work outside the home combined with domestic duties and offered them opportunities to learn English or to take other classes. All internees could volunteer to work in the camps: men and women earned equally meager rates of $16 to $19 per month for forty-eight hour weeks. Yet, some were able to do work more commensurate with their education and skills that racial prejudice had denied them before evacuation. One young Nisei woman found hospital work "immensely" more satisfying than her previous employment in the fields and in a family-owned pool hall. Another woman who had worked in a cannery was able to use her skills as a dietitian in the Manzanar camp.[5]

These opportunities could not compensate for the psychological and economic devastation sustained by most Japanese Americans. While conservative estimates placed their losses at $400 million, Congress appropriated just $38 million to settle all evacuee claims. In 1952, although it restricted Japanese immigrants to 185 per year, Congress removed the total exclusion of Japanese from immigration and naturalization. This, too, offered small consolation to those whose race alone made them victims of a program which disrupted their lives and violated their most basic rights.[6]

For the vast majority of American women, gender rather than race formed the legal basis for their second-class citizenship. Virtually all of these legal disabilities derived from state laws, among which there was endless variety. The greatest discrimination women faced as citizens was their ineligibility for jury service. In 1940, twenty-four states banned women from serving on juries, and only half of those which admitted women did so on the same basis as they treated men. Securing their right to jury duty depended upon women's ability to persuade state legislatures since an 1879 Supreme Court decision had specifically held that states could exclude women without violating their constitutional rights.[7]

Married women faced a variety of laws which treated them differently from, and sometimes subordinated them to, their husbands. In almost every state husbands determined their wives' domicile. Reflecting the double standard of sexual morality, several states allowed a husband, but not a wife, to sue for divorce on grounds of the wife's unchaste conduct before marriage. A few states gave the husband, but none the wife, superior rights to children's custody, earnings, or guardianship. Five states prevented a woman from disposing of her own real property without her husband's consent. Community-property states recognized coordinate status of husband and wife in ownership of property, yet gave husbands general control over its management. Various jurisdictions imposed restrictions on a married woman's right to conduct business, to act as a trustee, executor, or administrator, or to control her earnings produced by work within the home. In harmony with the conventional division of labor within the family, most states obligated husbands to support their wives.[8]

The third area in which women experienced the differential impact of the law was in their role as workers. Many states had minimum wage laws applying only to women and children. Maximum hours statutes rarely imposed the same limitations on men and women, and women alone were prohibited from night work. More than half the states absolutely banned certain kinds of work considered hazardous for women. Other statutory requirements applicable to women only included employers' responsibility to provide seats, minimum periods for meals and rest, and specific restroom facilities, and the prohibition of certain kinds of lifting. Beginning with a few laws in the late nineteenth century, over the next sixty years state legislatures had gradually expanded this protective labor legislation so that it comprised hundreds of laws by the 1940s.[9]

Public attention to women's status under the law turned on the question of which statutes were actually disadvantageous to women and what was the best means to eliminate the legal disabilities. Shortly after women achieved the vote, the smaller, more militant wing of the suffrage movement, represented by the National Woman's party, adopted as its goal the passage of a new amendment which would eliminate all legal distinctions based on sex. The NWP viewed suffrage as just one step along the way to sexual equality and promoted an equal rights amendment as the most expedient way to revise all of the laws which treated men and women differently. For many years the NWP waged a lonely battle. The vast majority of politically active women opposed the amendment and worked vigorously against it. Introduced in Congress in 1923, it received favorable reports by judiciary subcommittees in 1936 and 1937, but by 1940 it had not yet gained serious attention from either house.

Debate between opponents and supporters of the amendment reflected pragmatic and tactical differences as well as conflicting conceptions of women's nature and their appropriate roles. NWP members and the allies they had gained when groups like the National Federation of Business and Professional Women and the National Association of Women Lawyers voted endorsement, stressed the similarities between men and women, and insisted that equality demanded identical treatment under the law. They believed that sex-differentiated legislation insulted women, damaged their self-respect by lumping them together with children, and created real economic hardships. Married women could not act as fully independent beings, and women workers suffered from protective legislation which denied them access to more remunerative, higher-status jobs. Among the numerous examples they cited was a Connecticut law preventing waitresses from serving after 10 P.M., when tips were best, and an Ohio law which banned women from operating motion-picture projectors. Noting that protective laws did not apply to all women workers, amendment supporters imputed selfish motives to male advocates of such legislation: "Their hearts bleed for women working at night when the pay is better, but we do not hear any protestations regarding charwomen who nightly clean offices all over the land." A constitutional guarantee through an equal rights amendment, they argued, was the surest way to eliminate the host of legal distinctions which maintained women's inferior position.[10]

Opponents of the amendment were represented by the Women's Bureau of the Department of Labor, the National Women's Trade Union League, the American Association of University Women, the National Consumers' League, and the National League of Women Voters, offspring of the mainstream women's suffrage organization. These groups concurred in the need to eliminate injustices such as the ban on jury service and discriminations against married women. But they spoke much more of the advantages women enjoyed under existing laws which the amendment would wipe out. Above all, they argued that women's distinct physical nature and their roles as wives and mothers required differential treatment. Because women bore and raised children they needed the laws which gave husbands primary responsibility for family support. Women's maternal roles, along with their weaker physical constitutions, necessitated laws which regulated the conditions of their employment. Antiamendment forces charged their opponents with placing their own privileged aspirations ahead of the interests of poorer women forced into the labor market by material necessity. While their allies in the legal community predicted judicial chaos, women's organizations insisted that women stood to lose much more than they might gain by a blanket amendment. Those laws which actually harmed women, they insisted, should be attacked on a state-by-state basis.[11]

The issue of protective legislation occupied center stage in the equal rights amendment controversy. Major organizations like the NWTUL, the NLWV, and the NCL had, in their programs to advance the status of women, devoted great attention to the unwholesome conditions attached to the labor of blue-collar women. Because most of these workers were not unionized, they were unable to protect themselves through collective bargaining. When amendment proponents argued that necessary labor legislation could be made to apply to both sexes, opponents pointed to the difficulties involved in such an approach. Labor unions supported protective legislation for women, but they believed that male workers should rely on their collective power to improve working conditions and wages. Even stronger barriers to legislative protection of male workers lay in judicial doctrine and precedent. Since the early twentieth century, courts had found such legislation a violation of the right of contract between employers and employees, but had upheld statutes applying only to women by reason of their physical differences and maternal roles. Acknowledging the desirability of extending protective laws to male workers, opponents of the amendment invoked judicial history and insisted that single-sex laws were better than none at all, which would be the case should the amendment pass.[12]

A number of developments in the early 1940s improved the position of amendment advocates. A 1941 Supreme Court decision upholding federal wage and hours legislation which treated the sexes identically suggested that other labor legislation which applied equally to men and women might survive judicial scrutiny. The election of several new women to the House and one to the Senate provided the amendment its first female support in Congress. But it was the war-induced changes in women's behavior that most invigorated the cause of amendment supporters. They pointed out that war production needs had made several states suspend laws regulating women's employment, without harm to women workers. Women's service in the military and their exposure to combat conditions in the nursing corps provided even more striking examples of women's endurance under strenuous conditions. Amendment supporters also invoked the avowed war aims of the United States. If the nation was fighting for freedom and democracy, "Surely we will not refuse to our own that which we purchase for strangers with the blood of our sons." Their male allies in Congress were responsive to such appeals. Women's tremendous contributions to the war effort earned them equal opportunities: to refuse them their rights was "a stain on our flag."[13]

The momentum generated by World War II increased the ranks of amendment supporters and impelled serious congressional consideration. Though not endorsing the proposed amendment per se, the Republican party in 1940 and the Democrats in 1944 adopted platform planks in support of constitutional equality. Organizational support was augmented when the General Federation of Women's Clubs and the National Education Association

voted endorsement. In 1945, the new president, Harry S Truman, reaffirmed the nod he had given the amendment while still a
senator. How seriously he took the issue was questionable, given
the context of his initial endorsement: "Nearly every man has his
wife on a pedestal anyway, and this will only make the legal aspects
of the situation more satisfactory. . . ." Judiciary Committees in
both houses of Congress voted favorably on the amendment in
1942, but it was not until after the war that the Senate engaged in
the first formal debate. In 1946, it voted thirty-eight to thirty-five
in favor, but that majority fell short of the two-thirds necessary to
submit a constitutional amendment to the states.[14]

The amendment's progress induced its opponents to redouble
their efforts. In 1944, more than a dozen labor and women's
organizations met with the Secretary of Labor and Director of the
Women's Bureau to form a coalition, the National Committee to
Defeat the Un-Equal Rights Amendment. Moving quickly beyond mere negativism, it soon changed its name to the National
Committee on the Status of Women. Continuing to lobby against
the amendment, the committee also worked against what it considered the most glaring discriminations against women. In drafting
its own federal bill as an alternative to the amendment, the NCSW
displayed its continuing assumption that the law must honor basic
sex differences. That bill prohibited sex discrimination in federal
law and administration, except where it was justified by differences in physical makeup, biological or social function; it established a Commission on the Legal Status of Women to investigate
and make recommendations for additional legislation; and, it urged
the states to follow suit.[15]

In the midst of the postwar debate over equal rights, a Supreme
Court decision illustrated the power of prevailing judicial doctrine
to restrict women's opportunities. In 1948, the Court upheld
Michigan's law prohibiting women from employment as bartenders. Enacted in 1945, the statute prevented women from obtaining
licenses unless they were wives or daughters of male tavern owners. The plaintiffs, two women who owned bars and their daughters whom they employed, argued that the law violated their rights
under the equal protection clause of the 14th Amendment.
Twenty-four other women who owned or tended bars swore
affidavits describing the economic hardship they suffered under

the law and demonstrating that they had fixed drinks without detriment to themselves or their customers. Despite these claims and the failure of defendants to show any deleterious effects of women tending bar, both the district court and the Supreme Court assumed that female bartenders might give rise to "social and moral problems." The district court was not concerned that the law allowed women to serve drinks but not to make them, conjecturing that the legislature "deemed it necessary to have male control in the establishment but that it was not necessary to regulate the routine tasks of the waitresses. . . ." Nor did it bother the Supreme Court that the exemption for female relatives of male bar owners did not require their presence on the premises: the simple fact of male ownership "minimizes hazards that may confront a barmaid without such protecting oversight."[16]

The *Goesaert* case, though extreme in nature, demonstrated the extent to which women could be victims of protection. Indeed, Michigan's law coincided with a national effort by the International Union of Hotel and Restaurant Employees and Bartenders to exclude women from the union and from bartending, practices it had temporarily abandoned during the wartime labor shortage. At its 1949 convention, the union claimed success in seventeen states and encouraged current drives to pass exclusionary legislation in several more. Union men asserted the need to protect "the morals of American womanhood," and the need to placate antiliquor forces, but some were frank to admit their interest in eliminating female competition for jobs. Supreme Court Justice Felix Frankfurter refused to "give ear to the suggestion that the real impulse behind this legislation was an unchivalrous desire of male bartenders to try to monopolize the calling," even though the three dissenting judges expressed disbelief that the law had been motivated by "solicitude for the moral and physical well-being of women." That economic motivations preceded gallantry was evident in the failure to apply the proscription against female waitresses, whose jobs were presumably more dangerous since no barrier separated them from their patrons. These less-skilled and lower-paying female jobs, of course, held little attraction for men.[17]

The *Goesaert* decision reflected the prevailing judicial reluctance to scrutinize economic regulation or to substitute its opinion for that of legislatures. And, it illustrated how tenacious was the judicial view of women as creatures warranting specific protection and supervision. Neither court considered seriously whether a woman's right to procure a job should be weighed against the state's authority to regulate labor and business and to promote the welfare of its citizens. Justice Frankfurter wrote the majority opinion for the Supreme Court. This former counsel to the National Consumers' League, longtime advocate of protective legislation, and opponent of the equal rights amendment saw nothing in "the vast changes in the social and legal position of women" to "preclude the states from drawing a sharp line between the sexes." Nor had Frankfurter's previous career as advocate of the underdog sensitized him to the gravity of sex discrimination. The justice took obvious amusement in sprinkling his opinion with references to "barmaids" and to "the historic calling" of "the alewife, sprightly and ribald. . . ."[18]

Ammunition provided by the *Goesaert* case failed to help supporters of the equal rights amendment. Each side of the equal rights controversy remained unalterably opposed to the other's proposal, and the decade ended in stalemate. In 1950, the Senate defeated the Women's Status bill. Its passage of the equal rights amendment, sixty-three to nineteen, was a hollow victory for the NWP and its allies, for the Senate approved a rider to safeguard all the "rights, benefits, or exemptions now or hereafter conferred by law upon persons of the female sex." Despite the stalemate, the intensified discussion of equal rights had beneficent effects on women's legal status. The momentum generated in the war years sustained the small NWP and facilitated its survival into the 1960s, when it contributed to the origins of a new women's movement, to federal legislation prohibiting sex discrimination in employment, and to congressional passage of the equal rights amendment.[19]

In the short run, too, the controversy over the amendment helped to erode some of women's legal disabilities, despite the fact that it divided and dispersed the energies of collective womanhood. Brightening prospects for passage of the amendment led to increased media attention thereby heightening public consciousness about differential treatment under the law. Those same prospects gave impetus to amendment opponents to bolster their tactical position by enlarging their efforts to improve women's status through other means. Largely unsuccessful at the national level, women's groups on both sides of the amendment issue achieved significant gains through revision of state laws and constitutions.

The major goal at the federal level, one supported by both groups, was passage of an equal pay bill. Their position braced by women's performance in defense industries and encouraged by the National War Labor Board's favorable rulings, women's organizations coalesced behind a bill to prohibit wage discrimination by private employers in interstate commerce. Labor unions joined the coalition in an effort to maintain prevailing wages and to prevent employers from displacing men with cheaper female labor. But, although both the House and Senate committees on Education and Labor reported the bill favorably in 1946, and in subsequent years, Congress failed to act on the measure.[20]

A number of elements in the postwar situation foreclosed the possibilities for federal equal pay legislation. Employers' organizations had never supported it, and although they testified on behalf of the principle, they fought its enforcement by law. In addition, the postwar wave of strikes and the election of more conservative members to Congress had reduced legislative sympathy for the goals of organized labor, a development manifested in the antilabor Taft-Hartley Act of 1947. Moreover, equal pay proponents lost the support of half of organized labor when the American Federation of Labor failed to testify for the bill in 1948 and 1950. While the AFL continued to voice support of equal pay and many of its members endorsed the bill, the AFL Executive Council feared that such legislation would encourage women "to depend upon legislation instead of accepting personal responsibility for promotion of their welfare by joining a union and personally contributing to effort for progress." Unmentioned was the fact that the prewar stratification of the labor market by sex had been reestablished and the threat of women undercutting wages and taking men's jobs had diminished.[21]

Inability to obtain congressional action made women dependent on state legislatures. Before the war, only Michigan and Montana had equal pay bills, both enacted at the close of World War I. The second global conflict prompted legislation in Illinois, Massachusetts, New York, and Washington, and six more states followed suit in the next five years. While women's organizations in Pennsylvania obtained an equal pay law without the support of organized labor, in most states union efforts were crucial. The campaign in Washington, for example, was directed by a coalition of labor unions which were primarily interested in protecting the wage levels and jobs of men. In its first year of operation, women workers filed sixty-five complaints, winning equal wages in each of them. In addition to the twelve more general equal pay laws, teachers were specifically protected against salary discrimination in fifteen states and the District of Columbia. By 1950, the incidence of sex differentials in teachers' salaries had been reduced to less than 10 percent. State equal pay laws did not apply to all industries, varied in enforcement provision, and failed to attack historical differentials between "men's" and "women's" jobs. But they did afford some protection to some women and helped to publicize and to legitimate the principle of equal pay.[22]

In safeguarding their rights under the law, women could point to just one quite modest victory at the federal level. Early in the decade women's independence under the law was threatened by the Treasury Department's attempt to close what it considered to be income-tax loopholes. Because married couples living in community-property states could reduce their tax burden by filing separate returns, thereby being assessed in lower brackets, Treasury officials proposed that joint filing be mandatory in all states. Defenders of women's rights immediately grasped this proposal as a step backwards to the ancient common-law doctrine that a married woman had no independent identity under the law, but was subsumed under the person of her husband. In 1941 the vast majority of Americans were not subject to income tax, so the proposed legislation would affect only a limited group. Nonetheless, women's organizations from the Daughters of the American Revolution to the National Women's Trade Union League were adamant in their defense of the principle of married women's legal independence, and they also pointed out that the proposed law would deter married women from employment at the precise time that defense industries needed additional workers. Opponents even suggested that the regulation would discourage marriage and encourage immorality as couples would evade the higher tax rate by "living in sin." With support from lawyers and religious leaders, women's groups succeeded in thwarting this minor but symbolic assault on women's status as independent persons.[23]

In their efforts to win eligibility for jury service throughout the nation, women received a slight nod from federal judges and a rebuff from Congress. In 1941, half of the states barred women from jury service, and federal law provided for women jurors only in federal courts meeting in states where women were eligible. A 1946 Supreme Court decision gave new support to women's right to federal jury service by overturning an indictment on the ground that women had been systematically excluded from grand jury panels. Since California law rendered women eligible for state juries, the Court declared, they could not be barred from federal juries convening in that state. The Court's reasoning, however, stressed sex differences rather than women's rights as citizens to jury service: "a community made up exclusively of one sex is different from a community composed of both . . . a flavor, a distinct quality is lost if either sex is excluded." Women's organizations cited the *Ballard* decision in their campaign for a law to make women eligible for federal jury service throughout the country. They were supported by a committee of federal judges who in 1942 had recommended that federal jury service for women be uniform and not dependent upon the laws of individual states. Although Congress considered such legislation in 1947, it failed to act for another ten years.[24]

Women enjoyed greater success at the state level, where, again, their efforts were abetted by the wartime manpower shortage, women's greater participation in the public sphere, and heightened awareness of discrimination. Women still had to counter opposition on the grounds that they were too delicate, emotional, or ill-informed, that women should not be drawn away from domestic responsibilities, or that new facilities necessary to accommodate women were too costly. In Massachusetts, it required a state referendum to prod legislators into action. Nonetheless, during the 1940s thirteen states made women eligible for jury service; the eight holdouts were all southern or southwestern states. Sex distinctions continued even in states which permitted women to serve. Only twenty states made jury duty compulsory for women on the same terms as men; the others allowed women to decline solely on the basis of their sex or forced them to take the initiative in placing their names on jury lists. Women in New York had been serving on juries since the 1930s but their efforts to get mandatory service enacted were rebuffed by the state senate throughout the decade. In 1948 the State Supreme Court invalidated the section of

Arizona's law making women's jury service optional, but other states retained their nonmandatory provisions for women. By 1950, although women had won recognition of their ability to serve on juries, the majority of state legislatures remained wedded to the assumption that women's paramount duties as wives and mothers precluded their service under conditions identical to those of men.[25]

A number of states removed other legal restrictions on women. A campaign organized by Florida members of the National Woman's party, the National Association of Women Lawyers, and the Federation of Business and Professional Women's Clubs achieved a law in 1943 which eliminated the ancient common-law disabilities of married women. Additional southern states joined Florida in modernizing their laws to empower women to engage in business, convey their property, make contracts, and enjoy their earnings without interference by their husbands or by special court procedures. New Jersey legislation banned discrimination against married women in holding public office or employment, and North Carolina and West Virginia outlawed such discrimination against teachers. Single as well as married women benefited when Oklahoma ended its exclusion of women from the state's highest offices and when Wisconsin repealed its ban against women as employees of the legislature.[26]

Women's gains under the law during the 1940s represented in most instances near-final steps in a process which had been underway for decades. The drive for married women's independent status was a century old and those states which enacted reforms were simply catching up with the rest of the nation. Women's organizations regarded women's right to public office and employment and to jury service as logical concomitants to their right to vote, and they had sought these reforms since the 1920s. Conditions of war abetted their efforts and speeded their achievements. The restrictions on married women's economic freedom created public inconvenience and uncertainty when their husbands were absent. And, the occupation of men in the military or in defense industry made it reasonable to increase the pool of potential jurors.

The greatest effect of the war, however, was the attention it focused on two more dramatic issues, equal pay and the proposed equal rights amendment. Women's employment in male jobs promoted efforts for equal pay legislation by groups committed to female equality as well as by those concerned with protecting the jobs and wages of men. This conjunction of interests moved eleven state legislatures, but it had neither the power nor the durability to obtain national equal pay legislation. Women's response to the war-induced requirement to cross sex-role boundaries also inspired proponents of the equal rights amendment and garnered them additional support. Although Congress failed to pass the amendment, increased public discussion spun off into piecemeal improvements in women's legal status in the states and provided nourishment to sustain supporters for another two decades. The extent of women's legal gains in the 1940s depended in part on changing social norms, but it also reflected both the strengths and weaknesses of women themselves as a political force.

NOTES AND REFERENCES

1. United States President's Committee on Civil Rights, *To Secure These Rights* (Washington, D.C.: Government Printing Office, 1947), pp. 32–33, 35–40; Gunnar Myrdal, *An American Dilemma: The Negro Problem and Modern Democracy* (New York: Harper and Bros., 1944), pp. 474–86; Sandra Baxter and Marjorie Lansing, *Women and Politics: The Invisible Majority* (Ann Arbor: University of Michigan Press, 1980), p. 78.

2. Myrdal, *An American Dilemma*, pp. 622–39; United States President's Committee, *To Secure These Rights*, pp. 62–65, 67–70, 74–78.

3. Roger Daniels, *Concentration Camps U.S.A.: Japanese Americans and World War II* (New York: Holt, Rinehart and Winston, 1972), pp. 1–90; Dorothy Swaine Thomas, *The Salvage* (Berkeley: University of California Press, 1952), p. 494; Jeanne Wakutsuki Houston and James D. Houston, *Farewell to Manzanar* (Boston: Houghton Mifflin, 1973), pp. 12–13.

4. Ibid., pp. 10–35; Dorothy Swaine Thomas and Richard S. Nishimoto, *The Spoilage* (Berkeley: University of California Press, 1960), pp. 28–40; Daniels, *Concentration Camps U.S.A.*, pp. 109–10; Daisuke Kitagawa, *Issei and Nisei: The Internment Years* (New York: The Seabury Press, 1967), pp. 84–88.

5. Evelyn Nakano Glenn, "The Dialectics of Wage Work: Japanese-American Women and Domestic Service, 1905–1940," *Feminist Studies* 6 (Fall 1980):439–40, 459–61; Thomas, *The Salvage*, pp. 377–78, 596; Thomas and Nishimoto, *The Spoilage*, pp. 35–39; Kitagawa, *Issei and Nisei*, pp. 89–92; Houston and Houston, *Farewell to Manzanar*, pp. 5, 10, 33–34.

6. Daniels, *Concentration Camps U.S.A.*, pp. 168–70.

7. Matilda Fenberg, "Jury Service for Women," *Women Lawyers Journal* 33 (Spring 1947):45–48; Dorothy Crook, "Women in the Eyes of the Law," *Independent Woman* 20 (July 1941):209; Barbara Allen Babcock, Ann E. Freedman, Eleanor Holmes Norton, and Susan C. Ross, *Sex Discrimination and the Law: Causes and Remedies* (Boston: Little, Brown and Co., 1975), p. 103.

8. "Sex Discrimination and the Constitution," *Stanford Law Review* 2 (July 1950):692, 696, 702, 712; Address of Emma Guffey Miller to the American Association of University Women, February 10, 1945, Miller Papers, Folder 44, Schlesinger Library; Crook, "Women in the Eyes of the Law," pp. 209, 220–21.

9. "Sex Discrimination and the Constitution," pp. 713–18.

10. William H. Chafe, *The American Woman: Her Changing Social, Economic, and Political Roles, 1920–1970* (New York: Oxford University Press, 1972), pp. 112–32; Address of Emma Guffey Miller, February 10, 1945; *Equal Rights* 32 (March–April 1946):15, and 36 (March–April 1950):10; "The National Woman's Party Explains Its Proposal for An Equal Rights Amendment," *Congressional Digest* 22 (April 1943):102–16.

11. American Forum of the Air, "Should the Equal Rights Amendment Be Adopted?" August 19, 1942 (Washington, D.C.: American Forum of the Air, 1942), pp. 5–8; Chafe, *The American Woman*, pp. 112–32; National Committee to Defeat the Un-Equal Rights Amendment, "These Lawyers and Legal Scholars Oppose the So-Called Equal Rights Amendment," n.d., Records of the Women's Bureau, 55-A-556, Box 10; "Brief of the UAW-CIO Opposing the Proposed Equal Rights Amendment," n.d., pp. 2–11, United Automobile Workers, Research Department, Box 7, Wayne State Labor History Archives, Detroit.

12. Judith A. Baer, *The Chains of Protection: The Judicial Response to Women's Labor Legislation* (Westport, Conn.: Greenwood Press, 1978), pp. 14–106; Chafe, *The American Woman*, pp. 112–32.

13. Rebekah S. Greathouse, "The Effect of Constitutional Equality on Working Women," *American Economic Review* 34 (March 1944):227–36; Jane Norman Smith to Alice Paul, December 7, 1942, Smith Papers, Folder 119, Schlesinger Library; "Should Congress Approve the Proposed Equal Rights Amendment?" *Congressional Digest* 22 (April 1943): 107–12.

14. Louise Dudley Kelly, "The Politics of the Equal Rights Amendment, 1944–1953," unpublished paper, 1980, pp. 6–11; "President Reaffirms Stand on Amendment," *Equal Rights* 31 (September–October 1945):1.

15. National Committee on the Status of Women in the United States, Second Report, January 1946–April 1947, Records of the National Consumers League, File C-16, Library of Congress; Joseph P. Chamberlain et al., "Proposed Statement in Regard to Women's Bill, H.R. 2007 and S. J. Res. 67, 80th Congress," April 14, 1947, ibid.

16. Babcock et al., *Sex Discrimination and the Law*, pp. 93–96; Baer, *The Chains of Protection*, pp. 111–21.

17. Babcock et al., *Sex Discrimination and the Law*, pp. 93–96, 280–81; Edith Carroll, "Barmaids Come Back," *New York Times Magazine*, March 18, 1945, p. 27; *New York Times*, December 21, 1948, p. 52.

18. Baer, *The Chains of Protection*, pp. 110, 116–21; Leo Kanowitz, *Women and the Law: An Unfinished Revolution* (Albuquerque: University of New Mexico Press, 1969), pp. 33–34, 179–81; Babcock et al., *Sex Discrimination and the Law*, pp. 37–41, 94–95.

19. *Equal Rights* 36 (January–February 1950):1; Leila J. Rupp, "American Feminism in the Postwar Period," in Gary Reichard and Robert Bremner, eds., *Reshaping America: Society and Institutions, 1945–1960* (Columbus: Ohio State University Press, forthcoming).

20. Alice K. Leopold, "Federal Equal Pay Legislation," *Labor Law Journal* 6 (January 1955):7–9.

21. Ibid., pp. 9, 14, 21; Florence C. Thorne to Matthew Woll, May 11, 1951, Papers of the American Federation of Labor, Series 8, File A, Box 44, State Historical Society of Wisconsin, Madison; unsigned memo, n.d., ibid.

22. Women's Bureau, "Movement for Equal Pay Legislation in the United States," May 1, 1950, pp. 2–3, Selma Borchardt Papers, Labor History Archives, Wayne State; *New York Times*, July 9, 1947, p. 24; Karen Anderson, "The Impact of World War II on the Puget Sound Area on the Status of Women and the Family," Ph.D. dissertation, University of Washington, 1975, pp. 70–71; Mary Anderson to Helen Adele Maguire, June 5, 1944, Records of the Women's Bureau, 55-A-556, Box 10; Leopold, "Federal Equal Pay Legislation," p. 22; Women's Bureau, "Working Paper on Equal Pay," September 1951, p. 8, John Edelman Collection, Labor History Archives, Wayne State, Box 29.

23. D. W. Smithburg to George Pettee, August 4, 1942, p. 6, Records of the Women's Bureau, 54-A-78, Box 8; Citizens Information Service Against Mandatory Joint Income Tax Returns, "A Petition to Our Representatives in Congress Concerning Mandatory Joint Income Tax Returns for Husbands and Wives," n.d., Papers of the American Association of University Women, Schlesinger Library, Folder 38; *New York Times*, March 26, 1942, June 29, 1942.

24. Marguerite J. Fisher, "The Status of Juror Service for Women," *Independent Woman* 26 (November 1947):332; Fenberg, "Jury Service for Women," pp. 45–46; Babcock et al., *Sex Discrimination and the Law*, pp. 103–104.

25. *The Legal Status of Women in the United States of America*, Women's Bureau Bulletin 157 (Washington, D.C.: Government Printing Office, 1953), pp. 99–100; *New York Times*, March 25, 1945, p. 32; April 20, 1945, p. 34; January 12, 1947, IV, p. 6; March 24, 1950, p. 20; Gertrude Samuels, "The Verdict on Women Jurors," *New York Times Magazine*, May 7, 1950, pp. 22, 25–29.

26. "Married Women in Florida," *Equal Rights* 29 (May 1943):41; Marjorie Varner, "A Great Victory Won," ibid. (June 1943):48; Women's Bureau, United States Department of Labor, "Facts on Women Workers," February 21, 1946, pp. 1–2.

Margaret Chase Smith, Frances P. Bolton, Margaret Hickey, and Emily
Taft Douglas discuss "Public Affairs and the Woman Citizen" at the 1946
convention of the Federation of Business and Professional Women's Clubs
Courtesy of Manuscripts Collection, University of Missouri—St Louis

Chapter Eight

Women in the Political Arena

In many respects the political behavior of women in the 1940s paralleled that of men. Similar concerns motivated them as voters, party activists, members of pressure groups, and office-holders, and in these capacities women, like men, displayed a wide range of political views and objectives. Two elements of women's political participation distinguished them from men: their small numbers in high-level party and public offices; and their collective efforts to advance the position of their own sex. World War II and the economic recovery it generated gave a temporary boost to women's political fortunes as the absence of men increased women's value in the public realm, and as the need for women's contributions to the war effort gave saliency to issues concerning their status.

Having enjoyed the franchise for but a single generation, women continued to lag behind men in voter turnout. Scattered data for the 1930s indicated a female participation rate of less than 50 percent. In 1948, when the first national surveys were taken, women's turnout was 56 percent of eligible voters contrasted to 69 percent for men, and by 1952 the gap had narrowed to 62 and 72 percent, respectively. The disfranchisement of most southern blacks resulted in extremely low voting rates for both men and women; even by 1952, 87 percent of southern black women, and 65 percent of men, had never voted. As was the case with men, greater voter participation was related to higher levels of education and income. Similarly, women were motivated by party loyalty and a sense of civic duty to the same extent as men, but women displayed lesser confidence in their own competence and ability to influence the political process. Moreover, women tended to be more dependent upon men, especially their husbands, for political information. These differences reflected social norms which assigned men leadership in matters of public affairs as well as the short amount of time that women had had to become habituated to political participation.[1]

Their own organizations afforded women autonomous and more active vehicles for engagement in the political process. Along with a multitude of women's clubs which were apolitical or whose objectives had little to do with the status of women, there existed a number of national organizations which placed women's equity issues at the top or high on their public policy agendas. These groups represented only a minority of women, but they covered a broad spectrum of class, race, economic participation, and educational background. Professional women were represented by specific organizations like the National Women Lawyers Association and the American Medical Women's Association, as well as by the larger American Association of University Women (AAUW) and National Federation of Business and Professional Women's Clubs (BPW). The National Council of Negro Women (NCNW), a federation of eighteen national organizations and fourteen local councils, spoke for black women, while the National Women's Trade Union League (NWTUL) voiced the concerns of women in industrial and service occupations. These organizations functioned as traditional pressure groups, designing publicity campaigns to influence public opinion, petitioning legislators and executive officials, testifying before legislative committees, and forming coalitions among themselves and with other groups.[2]

Women's organizations also provided a training ground for women in politics. By the 1940s, the League of Women Voters (LWV) had virtually abandoned issues concerning women's status, but it and groups like the AAUW and BPW prepared women for office-holding. Within these organizations women became familiar with political issues, enjoyed opportunities for leadership and public visibility, and gained self-confidence in a supportive environment. The limitation of this mode of political education was that these groups also tended to isolate women from the mainstream of party politics. The LWV especially prided itself in its independence from electoral politics. It prohibited officers from partisan activity and could not mobilize its members to work for women candidates. Cool to the efforts of other women's groups to get women appointed to government positions, the league's president wrote in 1946 that it was not a feminist organization, but took the position that the best qualified, regardless of sex, should be appointed. More realistic about the chances of qualified women, by the mid-1940s the AAUW and BPW recognized the limitations of a policy of neutrality in electoral politics and voted to allow endorsement and active support for women candidates.[3]

Other limitations diluted the political force of those women's organizations directed to elevating the status of their sex. Capitalizing on the exigencies of war, organizations like the BPW, the AAUW, NCNW, and NWTUL were united in their determination to expand female participation in the public sphere and to improve the conditions of such participation. But they displayed sharp differences in ordering priorities and defining the appropriate means to those ends. While gender sometimes served as a common organizing principle, more frequently considerations of class and race stood in the way of a united womanhood. The white, middle-class insularity of more privileged women resulted in their failure to recognize the immediate material needs of blue-collar women and in their insensitivity to the weight of racial oppression on their black sisters.

Women's organizations displayed considerable solidarity in working for the expansion of economic opportunities. They pressured employers and government officials to provide for the training and full utilization of women in war production and to safeguard women's gains in the reconversion period. They bridged disagreement over the equal rights amendment and protective legislation to form coalitions on the state and national levels to campaign for equal pay legislation. Although the protective legislation dispute did not create an irrevocable breach among women's organizations, it did disperse women's collective energies, and it reflected the extent to which economic differences divided women.[4]

Both the AAUW and the BPW neglected opportunities to form stronger links with blue-collar women. Although the AAUW fought the equal rights amendment, its Committee on the Legal and Economic Status of Women rejected a member's proposal that the association seek closer ties with industrial women's groups by concerning itself with female union membership. The AAUW's general director displayed a similar myopic vision when she voiced concern at a Women's Bureau conference on women workers that too little attention was being paid to professional and business women. Margaret Hickey, president of the BPW, did urge her organization to reach out to production workers, noting that some clubs had members in defense plants, and the organization's journal wrote favorably about unions and female labor leaders. But the BPW resisted the principle of unionization of office workers and continued to press for the equal rights amendment. From the point of view of Rose Schneiderman, President of the National Women's Trade Union League, "higher salaried women too often allow their concern over the special discriminations against women in their group to obscure the more fundamental problem which millions of working men and women face," that of finding jobs with decent conditions. Elizabeth Christman, one of the three representatives of blue-collar women on the Women's Advisory Committee to the War Manpower Commission, expressed a similar perspective. Commenting on the committee's recommendations for women in the postwar period, she objected to the report's emphasis on professional women.[5]

Race as well as class differences distinguished the perspectives these organizations brought to the issue of child care. A high priority for the AAUW, more than sixty of its branches were involved in establishing centers as early as 1942, and the organization was an active advocate for a federal program. It defined the issue, however, as a community rather than a woman's problem and emphasized professionalism in child-care services over all else. The AAUW vigorously—although unsuccessfully—supported transfer of jurisdiction over the federal program from the Federal Works Agency, an emergency agency whose primary function was administration of government-financed construction, to the Children's Bureau and Office of Education and their state counterparts. While liberals supported such a move because it promised a high-quality program administered by experts in child development, proponents of the transfer ignored black women's concern over racial discrimination. Alpha Kappa Alpha (AKA), a national affiliate of the NCNW, objected vehemently to the proposed legislation reorganizing the federal child-care program. Its representative pointed to the positive record of the Federal Works Agency in distributing funds equitably, arguing that the records of both the Children's Bureau and the Office of Education were "full of instances of injustices to Negroes and a lack of concern for their welfare." To black women the primary imperative of securing services for parents and children of their race overshadowed the question of which agencies could provide the best quality services.[6]

The NWTUL remained neutral in the jurisdictional debate, but its blue-collar constituency ensured a perspective on child care which embraced the problems of mother as well as the interests of the child. Unlike elite women who often addressed the issue in terms of child neglect, union women consistently emphasized working mothers' anxiety over the security of their children and defended child-care programs as essential for both "the welfare of the child and the peace of mind of the mother." Moreover, blue-collar women were well aware that their middle-class counterparts tended to view working mothers with disapproval and to suspect them of child neglect. The propensity of privileged women to advocate child care more as a means of social control than as a way to solve women's problems and promote female opportunities foreclosed the possibility of a united female front around the most basic contradiction between women's traditional responsibilities and their participation in the public sphere.[7]

Class and race differences also characterized the approach of women's organizations to the issue of female participation in the military service. Leaders in the drive for equal status in the armed services, the AAUW and BPW looked upon women's opportunity for military service as an essential step toward the recognition of their competence and right to equal participation in the war effort. The NWTUL lent its support to equal status in the military but did not campaign actively for it. Black women were not among the early advocates of the women's services, but once they were created both the NCNW and AKA consistently pressured the navy to admit blacks into the WAVES and demanded the end of segregation and discrimination in the WAC. The AAUW and BPW ignored military discrimination against black women while they concentrated on opening the United States Medical Corps to women physicians. Impervious to the wholesale discrimination against their black sisters, white women sought the expansion of professional opportunities for a few privileged women and elimination of the insulting aspersions cast upon women by the military's exclusion of female doctors.[8]

Like their male counterparts, privileged white women also displayed considerable indifference to racial inequities which claimed priority among black women's organizations. Mary McLeod Bethune, civil rights leader and founder of the NCNW, sought alliances with white women's organizations, but often had to make a special effort to see that black women were not forgotten when joint meetings of women's groups were held. Responding to the initiative of the NCNW in 1944, a coalition of women's groups formed the Co-ordinating Committee for Building Better Race Relations. Middle-class women's organizations with a feminist orientation were absent from the committee, which was comprised of women's religious groups, the YWCA, and the NWTUL. The NWTUL consistently advocated bills to eliminate lynching, abolish the poll tax, and establish a permanent Fair Employment Practices Commission—three cardinal items on the agendas of AKA and the NCNW. The AAUW endorsed a permanent FEPC in its 1945 platform, but this was the extent of white women's efforts to transcend racial barriers. Indeed, publicity concerning the discriminatory practices of local affiliates forced both the AAUW and BPW to disavow exclusionary membership policies.[9] The pressure-group activity of a vocal minority of women was unique in its attention to critical aspects of women's second-class status, but that activism was limited by divisions along the lines of class, occupation, and race similar to those which organized men's political interests.

Collective womanhood achieved its greatest unity around the goal of expanding women's power by securing their appointment to government positions. A coalition of more than a dozen women's groups, the Committee on Women in World Affairs was founded in 1942 by educators Mary Wooley and Emily Hickman to push for female appointees to international organizations and conferences. Women who worked in government agencies alerted the committee when appointments were to be made; the committee in turn solicited names and organized letter-writing campaigns to appropriate officials. The CWWA was particularly effective in crossing racial lines, soliciting a representative of the National Council of Negro Women for its executive board and recommending black women for government appointments.[10]

A second coalition grew out of a 1944 White House Conference on Women in Policy-Making, called by the AAUW, the BPW, the General Federation of Women's Clubs, and the National Education Association, and attended by representatives of seventy-five women's organizations. The work of its continuing committee was similar to that of the CWWA, but it promoted women for national as well as international positions and spun off into parallel activities on the state and local levels. In addition, there was a less formal network of women in Washington, most of whom were active in the other coalitions, and many of whom worked in federal agencies. Each woman had responsibility for monitoring a few agencies, and the group also worked with the Women's Division of the Democratic National Committee to press directly on the White House for women appointees. Women themselves conceded that the results of these activities were not spectacular, but they were able to preserve the gains made by women during the Roosevelt administration, gains which seemed threatened in the immediate postwar years, and they won a modest expansion of opportunities for women in the federal government.[11]

As elected officials, women also enjoyed a small advance as members of state legislatures in the 1940s. The number of women elected to statehouses grew from 144 in 1941 to 228 in 1945, the most rapid increase since the early postsuffrage years. A slight decline immediately after the war was followed by the election of 249 women in 1950. The overall percentage of women in state legislatures remained small, and in some there were none at all. But in a few, particularly in those states which had large legislatures and consequently smaller districts, women's representation approached one-fourth of the total.[12]

The modest advance of women into state legislatures was not replicated at the national level. Eight or nine women had served in each Congress during the 1930s, and in the following decade from eight to eleven held office at any one time. There was, however, a qualitative change. Before the 1940s more than one-third of the congresswomen had been appointed or elected to fill unexpired terms, often those of their deceased husbands. A few of these women, such as Edith Nourse Rogers (R.-Mass.), developed political careers of their own, gaining reelection and substantial political influence, but most were not returned to Congress. After 1940, more women won election or reelection on their own. Of the twenty-eight female legislators between 1916 and 1940, only ten served more than one term. From 1940 to 1950, twenty-two women entered Congress for the first time, and twelve of these served at least two terms. Increasing longevity expanded women's influence and won them appointments to important committees.[13]

While these congresswomen represented diverse political views, almost all of them worked and voted for legislative goals of the major women's organizations. Most had served apprenticeships in party work, but a number of them had also gained political experience and a sensitivity to women's issues through their membership in women's organizations. The activities of New York Democrat Caroline O'Day had included the suffrage movement, the League of Women Voters, and the Women's International League for Peace and Freedom. Chase Going Woodhouse (D.-Conn.) and Emily Taft Douglas (D.-Ill.) had held offices in their states' LWV. Woodhouse had taught economics at Smith and Connecticut College for Women and was a founder of the Institute for Women's Professional Relations, established to advance women's career opportunities. Republican Margaret Chase Smith, who represented Maine in the House from 1940 to 1948 and in the Senate thereafter, had been president of her state's Federation of Business and Professional Women and a member of the national board. Clare Boothe Luce (R.-Conn.), best known as an author and playwright, had cut her political teeth as the assistant to Alva Belmont, president of the National Woman's party.[14]

A feminist consciousness among other congresswomen grew from different experiences and was frequently sharpened by encounters with male associates in their parties and in Congress. Mary T. Norton, the "Dean of Congresswomen," who represented New Jersey from 1924 to 1950, had experienced hostility to women workers as a secretary in the early 1900s. Chosen by boss

Frank Hague to pioneer in organizing women for the Democratic party, Norton confronted male hostility; she came to appreciate deeply the struggles of the suffragists and frequently recalled their courage to female audiences. In Congress she rebuked a colleague for referring condescendingly to her as "the lady," and she believed that important legislation had been "stolen" from her House Labor Committee because a woman chaired it.[15]

Helen Gahagan Douglas (D.-Cal.) averred that, "as far as being a woman in Congress, the mere fact that I am a woman has made no difference at all." But most female legislators did discover in the overwhelmingly masculine atmosphere of Congress that their gender set them apart and occasioned treatment ranging from hostility to patronization and trivialization. Even Douglas recognized the specific problems of female legislators in combining their official duties with their traditional familial roles. Margaret Chase Smith explicitly rejected the label "feminist," yet she spoke of the "old prejudice of men against women [in politics] that comes out in vigorous resistance." When Smith decided to run for a Senate seat in 1948, she was rebuffed by party leaders, one of whom said, "The little lady has simply stepped out of her class." She proved him wrong by outpolling both the governor and a former-governor in the Republican primary. Such experiences sharpened in female legislators a consciousness of sexism and inspired their efforts to elevate women's status.[16]

Thus, virtually every congresswoman sponsored at least one piece of legislation designed to remove discriminations against women or to advance their opportunities Edith Nourse Rogers shepherded the military legislation through the House, and Margaret Chase Smith worked to equalize conditions of service for the WAVES and to obtain more equitable status for women in the peacetime military. Frances P. Bolton (R.-Ohio) also supported women's participation in the military and even urged that they be subject to the draft, opposing distinctions between the sexes in privileges, opportunities, and duties. In addition, Bolton sponsored the legislation for the Cadet Nurse Corps, which provided federal support for the training of more than 100,000 nurses.[17]

As were other political women, congresswomen were also divided over the proposed equal rights amendment, which received its first endorsement from women legislators in the 1940s. Republican women were more likely to support it, and Smith, Rogers, Luce, and Katharine St. George were especially outspoken advocates. Most Democratic congresswomen, whose party tradition included support for protective legislation, opposed the amendment but promoted the Women's Status bill, designed to attack sex discrimination by other means. On other women's issues, the female component of Congress reached near unanimity. Women of both parties sponsored the equal pay bills, and most congresswomen fought to safeguard the Women's Bureau from budget cuts. With a lone exception, they went as one body before the House Appropriations Committee to speak on behalf of funds for day-care centers. These congresswomen with a consciousness of sexual inequality served as mouthpieces for feminist-oriented women's organizations and ensured consideration of legislation in women's interest. But their small numbers made achievements dependent upon support from male colleagues.[18]

The paucity of women in elective office was due only in part to their recent entrance into the political arena. Women's eligibility for voting and office-holding had thus far left unshaken the cultural norms which defined politics as masculine and which socialized women into passive, nurturant roles. But, if custom inhibited political aspirations among women, those who did aspire confronted public, and especially male, resistance. Public opinion polls taken in November 1945 found only a minority of men and women responding favorably to questions concerning women in politics, but women were more supportive than men. Thirty-eight percent of women and 26 percent of men believed that women were not sufficiently represented in important government positions; 37 percent of women and 29 percent of men indicated that they would vote for a female presidential candidate; and 43 percent of women and 33 percent of men supported the appointment of a woman to the cabinet.[19]

Resistance to women in high-level office did not prevent them from being active in party politics. They did much of the work at the local level and, especially in urban areas, often constituted the majority of canvassers, election clerks, and inspectors. Women also enjoyed opportunities for political development and a measure of autonomy within the Women's Divisions of both major parties. Although dependent upon the national committees for their budgets, these units enabled women to plan and direct their own activities. In addition to establishing the Women's Divisions, both parties had provided women equal representation on the national committees since 1924, and by the 1940s in all but eight states women enjoyed equal representation on at least some state and local committees. The wartime shortage of men increased the value of women not only as campaign workers but also as local and state committee members. Within the Democratic party, the number of women who chaired county committees increased from twelve to more than 100 between 1940 and 1944.[20]

Moreover, party leaders recognized in 1944 that women now comprised the majority of potential voters and took steps to magnify the visibility and influence of women within the party structures. Both parties broke precedent in their national conventions when women gave major addresses at evening sessions, Congresswoman Luce for the Republicans and Gladys Tillett, head of the Women's Division, and Helen Gahagan Douglas for the Democrats. In addition, women enjoyed equal representation on the Platform and Resolutions Committee of both parties for the first time. As delegates, however, they fared less well. Of more than 1,000 seats, women held fewer than 15 percent. While Republican women increased their representation slightly, from 87 in 1932 to 99 in 1944 and 112 in 1948, Democratic women lost ground as their number of delegates decreased from 208 in 1932 to 174 in 1944 and 137 in 1948.[21]

The poor showing of women in the ranks of delegates was symbolic of the extent to which habit and prejudice stunted women's growth in party affairs. They themselves recognized the reluctance of men to share power. One-third of the national committeewomen of both parties responded vigorously to a 1944 survey that their influence was nominal. India Edwards, who directed the Democratic Women's Division in the late 1940s, found still prevalent among male leaders the notion that a woman's place was in the home, "except, of course, just before election when 'the little woman' is rewarded for her interest in politics by being allowed to tramp the sidewalks" in search of potential supporters. Edwards recalled how Edward J. Flynn, national committeeman from New York and chairman of the Democratic National Committee in the early 1940s, defined the ideal female politician: "She is a lady, she presides gracefully at meetings, she can introduce the President properly, she never differs with my opinion, and she can be counted on to make fat contributions. . . ." When J. Howard McGrath, Chairman of the Democratic National Committee, stressed the importance of women's ballots in the 1948 elections, Eleanor Roosevelt noted this as a typical example of the deference paid to women's vote during election campaigns. But, in between, she wrote, "the ideas that women might have on how women are best organized, and how their interests are best kept alive in political questions, are a matter of very little concern to the men officials of either political party."[22]

Opportunities for black women to wield political power were even more circumscribed. The first black woman elected to a state legislature, Democrat Crystal Fauset, served only briefly in the Pennsylvania Assembly in 1939. Irene McCoy Gaines exercised leadership in local Republican party politics and presided over the Chicago Council of Negro Organizations, but lost her bid for the Illinois legislature in 1940. Black women often combined three forms of political activism—as members of women's groups, political parties, and civil rights organizations. Daisy E. Lampkin, a cofounder of the NCNW and Republican party functionary, served as national field secretary for the National Association for the Advancement of Colored People from 1935 to 1947 and was credited for building its largest membership in history. These and other black women held offices in both major parties, but always in units concerned with "Colored" voters. Mary McLeod Bethune was unique both in having access to key officials in the Roosevelt administration and in holding a position of prominence and serious respect among male leaders of civil rights organizations.[23]

Women in the Democratic party perceived a sharp difference in the political climate when Harry S Truman succeeded Franklin Roosevelt in 1945. In Roosevelt they had found a leader with years of experience in New York politics where reform-minded women had played prominent roles. Eleanor Roosevelt had consistently promoted women and her efforts along with those of Molly Dewson who headed the Women's Division had brought women into positions of influence within the New Deal and the Democratic party structure. The new president's political background, on the other hand, was one in which women's presence had been negligible, and his wife exhibited little interest in politics or in women. Truman respected the political skills of India Edwards, and she found him receptive to her efforts to advance women and their interests. But while he occasionally stood firmly behind women when opposition arose, he was generally unwilling to exert his power over recalcitrant officials and party leaders. Moreover, his inclination to trivialize women's concerns was evident in a letter he wrote to Emma Guffey Miller, prominent Pennsylvania politician. In response to her serious plea for consideration of the equal rights amendment, Truman flippantly replied that "it has been my experience that there is no equality—men are just slaves and I suppose they will always continue to be."[24]

Women party activists like Edwards and Miller had relatively narrow ground on which to advance the position of women. They could and did appeal to leaders on the basis of women's voting power, but women did not vote as a bloc, and such claims resulted in little more than window dressing during campaign periods. Women were dependent upon the good will of male politicians, and their concern for their parties' fortunes made them unwilling to criticize publicly the parties' inadequacies in areas of importance to women. The dilemma was illustrated when Edwards met the press in 1949. Because the exclusively male Gridiron dinner was in progress, all the reporters were women. Questioned about the absence of women in key positions in the Truman administration, Edwards insisted that they had real influence. Tenaciously clinging to her defense of Truman as May Craig and Doris Fleeson pressed harder, Edwards finally resorted to blaming women themselves for their lack of advancement. They were "petty," she said, "immature," "inexperienced," and lacked the facility for dealing with political matters on an impersonal level.[25]

Edwards's loyalty to the Truman administration, even at the occasional expense of the women she represented, failed to protect their influence in the Democratic party. The selection of a new party chairman in 1951 was made without consulting the national committeewomen, who first learned about it in the newspapers. After the Democratic defeat in 1952, party leaders abolished the Women's Division, again without conferring with women. In part an economy measure, the reorganization was portrayed as an advance for women, by "integrating" them into the total party structure. In practice it redistributed women's activities among units controlled by men, took away the *Democratic Digest*, a magazine which women had been publishing since 1922, and deprived them of an independent base within the party. Within a few months, the Republican party effected a similar reorganization.[26]

Along with opposition or indifference from party leaders, women's political fortunes also fell victim to the anti-Communist hysteria which suffused the country after the war. While Red-baiting harmed the political careers of liberal men as well as women, for the latter it contributed yet another handicap to the already formidable ones associated with gender. The smear tactics of Richard Nixon against Helen Gahagan Douglas in 1950 received the most media attention, but Margaret Chase Smith, Helen Mankin of Georgia, and Sarah T. Hughes of Texas faced similar charges. Smith overcame them in her 1948 Senate race, but Mankin and Hughes lost their bids for congressional seats in 1946.[27]

Nor were women in appointed positions immune to accusations that they were Communist-sympathizers. Dorothy Kenyon, a lawyer, social reformer, and women's rights activist from New York, had served three years as the United States representative to the United Nations Commission on the Status of Women when in 1950 Senator Joseph McCarthy accused her of being a fellow traveler. The first person to appear before the Senate subcommittee which investigated McCarthy's charges, Kenyon denied them, was defended by numerous public figures, and cleared by the subcommittee, but she received no more political appointments. The second woman named by McCarthy, Esther Caukin Brunauer, was also cleared, but her career in international affairs ended when the State Department dismissed her. In addition, the Senate held up confirmation of Anna M. Rosenberg for Assistant Secretary of Defense and of Kathryn McHale for the Subversives Control Board while committees investigated disloyalty charges. One objection to McHale was that as Executive Director of the American Association of University Women she had defended Kenyon and Brunauer, both of whom had worked for the association.[28]

The Red Scare had a chilling effect on women's organizations as well as on individual women. The National Council of Negro Women was particularly vulnerable to Red-baiting. In 1949 its board of directors debated the question of cooperating with groups charged as Communist-front organizations. By 1951 (after Bethune had retired from the presidency), the board was endeavoring "to prove our patriotism" by instructing members and affiliates to shun alliances with any individuals or organizations on the attorney general's list of subversives. Moreover, the crisis atmosphere which attended the Cold War dissuaded women's organizations from insisting on the primacy of women's claims to equality when issues of national security seemed more critical. Although women had sought to avoid the appearance of pursuing selfish interests during World War II, the fact that that crisis had required an unprecedented mobilization of women encouraged women's groups to take a more aggressive stance on behalf of feminist goals. Even when the Cold War broke out into military conflict, the limited nature of the Korean conflict precluded a similar response. Margaret Hickey, president of the Business and Professional Women and government advisor on women during World War II, had sounded the death knell on the "old, selfish, strident feminism" in 1945. In the atmosphere of the Korean War, she called for a "new feminism" which emphasized women's responsibilities as citizens rather than women's rights.[29]

The expansion of women's political activity as voters, party workers, and office-holders in the 1940s was part of a gradual development which had taken on momentum when women won the franchise. Its pace briefly quickened when the need for womanpower during World War II increased the importance of women's public roles, focused greater public attention on sexual inequities, and inspired women's organizations to press more forcefully for the advancement of women. In the postwar period, that momentum faltered, a victim of a national situation no longer dependent upon extraordinary contributions from women in the public sphere; a new administration less sensitive and sympathetic to women's capabilities and aspirations; the Cold War and attendant Red Scare; the continuing reluctance of men to share power with women; and the inability of women's organizations to bridge class and racial divisions and to mobilize more than a minority behind their objectives. That latter failure testified to the powerful claim of family roles over most of American womanhood.

NOTES AND REFERENCES

1. Harold F. Gosnell, *Democracy: The Threshold of Freedom* (New York: The Ronald Press, 1948), pp. 57–58, 299; Martin Gruberg, *Women in American Politics: An Assessment and Sourcebook* (Oshkosh, Wisc.: Academia Press, 1968), p. 9; Marjorie Lansing, "The American Woman: Voter and Activist," in Jane S. Jacquette, ed., *Women in Politics* (New York: John Wiley and Sons, 1974), p. 8; Sandra Baxter and Marjorie Lansing, *Women and Politics: The Invisible Majority* (Ann Arbor: University of Michigan Press, 1980), p. 78; Angus Campbell, Philip E. Converse, Warren E. Miller, and Donald Stokes, *The American Voter* (New York: John Wiley and Sons, 1960), pp. 484, 489–92.

2. Susan M. Hartmann, "Women's Organizations during World War II: The Interaction of Class, Race, and Feminism," in Mary Kelley, ed., *Woman's Being, Woman's Place: Female Identity and Vocation in American History* (Boston: G. K. Hall, 1980), pp. 313–14.

3. Percy Maxim Lee, "Why Not More Women in Public Office?" *National Municipal Review* 43 (June 1954):307–308; Baxter and Lansing, *Women and Politics*, pp. 119–20; Anna Lord Strauss to Mrs. LaFell Dickinson, December 23, 1946, Papers of the National League of Women Voters, Box 695, Library of Congress; M. Eunice Hilton, "If We Want Women in Public Office . . . ," *Independent Woman* 27 (March 1948):83; American Association of University Women, General Director's Letter 14 (June 1947), Schlesinger Library.

4. Hartmann, "Women's Organizations during World War II," pp. 315–16, 318–19; Report of the Equal Pay Committee Meeting, September 10, 1945, Papers of Mary Anderson, folder 58, Schlesinger Library,

Radcliffe College; *New York Times* December 29, 1943, p. 20, October 17, 1944, p. 17.

5. Hartmann, "Women's Organizations during World War II," p. 319.

6. Ibid., pp. 320–21.

7. Ibid., p. 321.

8. Ibid., pp. 317–18.

9. Florence K. Norman to Organizational Presidents, January 31, 1941, Papers of the National Council of Negro Women, Series 2, National Archives for Black Women's History, Washington, D.C.; Report of the Executive Secretary, January 1944, ibid., Series 3; NCNW, News Release, January 17, 1947, ibid., Series 5; Hartmann, "Women's Organizations during World War II," p. 318.

10. A substantial amount of material concerning the CWWA (originally the Committee on the Participation of Women in Post War Planning) is in the papers of Lucy Somerville Howorth, Schlesinger Library. The relationship between the NCNW and CWWA is documented in the papers of the NCNW, Series 2.

11. Lucy Somerville Howorth, "Women Step Forward," September 27, 1944, Howorth Papers, Box 9; Howorth, "A Program of Action," January 25, 1947, Papers of the American Association of University Women, folder 33, Schlesinger Library; Background and Facts on Roster of Qualified Women, January 22, 1945, Papers of the American Association of University Women, Status of Women Historical File, AAUW Archives, Washington, D.C.; Women's Bureau, "Progress for Women in the United States, 1947–1949," August 1949, pp. 17–23, Papers of the AAUW, Schlesinger Library; Howorth, Memo to Accompany File of Women in World Affairs, 1958, Howorth Papers, Box 7; Howorth, Memo to Accompany Three Clippings, 1958, ibid., Box 6. For an excellent study of the women's network in the New Deal, see Susan Ware, *Beyond Suffrage: Women in the New Deal* (Cambridge, Mass.: Harvard University Press, 1981).

12. Emmy F. Werner, "Women in the State Legislatures," *Western Political Quarterly* 21 (March 1968):40–50; Virginia Rishel, "More Women in Government?" *Journal of the American Association of University Women* 42 (Fall 1948):21; Bernice T. Van Der Vries, "Women in Government," *State Government* 21 (June 1948):127.

13. Emmy F. Werner, "Women in Congress: 1917–1964," *Western Political Quarterly* 19 (March 1966):16–30; Rudolf Engelbarts, *Women in the United States Congress, 1917–1972* (Littleton, Colo.: Libraries Unlimited, Inc., 1974), pp. 44–45; Louise M. Young, *Understanding Politics: A Practical Guide for Women* (New York: Pellegrini and Cudahy, 1950), pp. 188, 199–200; Hope Chamberlin, *A Minority of Members: Women in the U.S. Congress* (New York: New American Library, 1974), pp. 367–75. See also Diane D. Kincaid, "Over His Dead Body: A Positive Perspective on Widows in the U.S. Congress," *Western Political Quarterly* 31 (March 1978):96–104.

14. Chamberlin, *A Minority of Members*, pp. 113, 166, 171–72, 181, 195; "Her Nomination a Victory for Us All," *Independent Woman* 27 (August 1948):225; Stephen Shadegg, *Clare Boothe Luce, A Biography* (New York: Simon and Schuster, 1970), pp. 31–33, 36–37.

15. Mary T. Norton, Autobiography Manuscript, pp. 17–18, Norton Papers, Special Collections Department, Alexander Library, Rutgers University; Gary Mitchell, "Women Standing for Women: The Early Political Career of Mary T. Norton," *New Jersey History* 96 (Spring-Summer 1978):27–30; Eleanor Roosevelt and Lorena A. Hickok, *Ladies of Courage* (New York: G. P. Putnam's Sons, 1954), p. 154; *New York Times*, June 7, 1943, p. 10.

16. Address of Helen Gahagan Douglas, "Women's Status in a Changing World," February 20, 1950, Norton Papers, Box 5; Margaret Chase Smith with William C. Lewis, Jr., *Declaration of Conscience* (New York: Doubleday and Co., 1972), p. 85; Margaret Chase Smith, "A Challenge to Women," *Independent Woman* 28 (April 1949):102; Chamberlin, *A Minority of Members*, pp. 146–49.

17. Ibid., p. 61; Smith, *Declaration of Conscience*, pp. 85–97; Frances P. Bolton, "Women Should Be Drafted," *American Magazine* 147 (June 1949):47, 132–33; Roosevelt and Hickok, *Ladies of Courage*, p. 173.

18. "The Honorable Katharine St. George," *Equal Rights* 34 (March–April 1948):23; "Sniping at the Equal Rights Amendment," *Independent Woman* 26 (February 1947):88; Norton, Autobiography Manuscript, pp. 193–94.

19. George H. Gallup, *The Gallup Poll: Public Opinion, 1935–1971, Volume I, 1935–1948* (New York: Random House, 1972), p. 548; Berenice A. Carroll, "Political Science, Part I: American Politics and Political Behavior," *Signs* 5 (Winter 1979):289–306 assesses recent studies of women's political activities and aspirations and criticizes the "blame the victim" approach to women's low level of high public office-holding. See also Jeane J. Kirkpatrick, *Political Woman* (New York: Basic Books, Inc., 1974), pp. 8–20, 215–40, and Baxter and Lansing, *Women and Politics*.

20. Arnold W. Green and Eleanor Melnick, "What Has Happened to the Feminist Movement?" in Alvin W. Gouldner, ed., *Studies in Leadership: Leadership and Democratic Action* (New York: Harper and Brothers, 1950), p. 281; Roosevelt and Hickok, *Ladies of Courage*, pp. 11–21; Marguerite J. Fisher, "Women in the Political Parties," *Annals of the American Academy of Political and Social Science* 251 (May 1947):87–89, 93; "Women Draw Big Supporting Roles in Election-Year Political Drama," *Newsweek* 33 (June 19, 1944):46.

21. Ibid., p. 45; Fisher, "Women in the Political Parties," pp. 91–92; Young, *Understanding Politics*, pp. 85–86.

22. Fisher, "Women in the Political Parties," pp. 87–89; India Edwards, "Your First Step to Full-Time Citizenship," *Independent Woman* 26 (February 1947):34; India Edwards, *Pulling No Punches: Memoirs of a Woman in Politics* (New York: G. P. Putnam's Sons, 1977), p. 161.

23. See Barbara Sicherman and Carol Hurd Green, eds., *Notable American Women: The Modern Period* (Cambridge, Mass.: Harvard University Press, 1980) for biographical essays on Fauset, Gaines, Lampkin, and Bethune; Jeanne Noble, *Beautiful, Also Are the Souls of My Black Sisters: A History of the Black Woman in America* (Englewood Cliffs, N.J.: Prentice-Hall, 1978), pp. 140–41.

24. Joseph P. Lash, *Eleanor and Franklin* (New York: W. W. Norton, 1971), pp. 387–92; Doris Fleeson, "Influence of Women Seen Nil in Washington Events Today," *Washington Star*, October 4, 1945; Edwards, *Pulling No Punches*, pp. 171, 270; Edwards, Oral History Interview, January 16, 1969, pp. 83–88, Harry S Truman Library, Independence, Mo.; Truman to Emma Guffey Miller, August 12, 1950, Truman Papers, Official File 120-A, Truman Library.

25. Transcript of "Meet the Press," December 10, 1949, Oral History T95, Archives of the National Federation of Business and Professional Women's Clubs, Washington, D.C.

26. Roosevelt and Hickok, *Ladies of Courage*, pp. 22–31; Edwards, *Pulling No Punches*, pp. 203–204, 269.

27. Ingrid Winther Scobie, "Helen Gahagan Douglas and Her 1950 Senate Race with Richard M. Nixon," *Southern California Quarterly* 58 (Spring 1976):113–26; Smith, *Declaration of Conscience*, pp. 105–12; Anna Holden, "Race and Politics: Congressional Elections in the Fifth District of Georgia, 1946 to 1952," M.A. thesis, University of North Carolina, 1955, pp. 33–76; Sarah T. Hughes to Lucy Somerville Howorth, July 30, 1946, Howorth Papers, Box 13.

28. *New York Times*, November 20, 1950, pp. 1, 16, December 6, 1950, p. 28, December 8, 1950, p. 19, December 15, 1950, p. 24; Robert Griffith, *The Politics of Fear: Joseph R. McCarthy and the Senate* (Lexington: University Press of Kentucky, 1970), pp. 67–71; Betty Miller Unterberger, "Esther Delia Caukin Brunauer," and Susan M. Hartmann, "Dorothy Kenyon," in Sicherman and Green, *Notable American Women*, pp. 114–15, 395–97.

29. National Council of Negro Women, Minutes of the Executive Committee, January 23, 1949, pp. 19–20, Papers of the NCNW, Series 3; ibid., September 15, 1951; Lucy Somerville Howorth, "Women's Responsibility in World Affairs," *Journal of the American Association of University Women* 37 (Summer 1944):196–97; Proceedings, "Women's Organizations Mobilize," October 6, 1950, Howorth Papers, Box 7.

Military wedding at the Post Chapel, Fort Hamilton, New York,
April 13, 1944
Courtesy of Culver Pictures, New York

Chapter Nine

The Unshaken Claim of Family

The expansion of women's public roles in the 1940s did not diminish their attachment to traditional private roles. On the contrary, throughout the 1940s more women married than ever before. They formed families at younger ages, and they produced a birth rate higher than it had been for two decades. World War II promoted more marriages, but in some respects it added to the material and emotional strains of family and domestic life. The economic boom sustained the rush to the altar and the delivery room. The physical risks and demands of housekeeping, childbearing and childrearing were reduced by medical and technological innovations, but higher standards of wifehood and motherhood intensified the psychological stress for women who aspired to a feminine ideal more exacting than it had been in the past.

Even during the war, the new public images of women designed to evoke their contributions to the national effort did not subsume the ageless ideal of woman as wife and mother. In fact, the media's pleas to women to assume novel responsibilities emphasized that such activities were not only compatible with traditional femininity, but they indeed increased women's ability to find husbands, manage their homes, and raise their children more effectively. Hollywood projected images of treacherous, sensual, and evil women along with heroines at work as teachers, editors, welders, executives, congresswomen, lawyers, and psychiatrists. Yet romance remained central for these professional women, and the most popular films which had major female characters glorified women's domestic roles.[1]

Throughout the 1940s the popular culture continued to "propagandize for romance," and to uphold marriage as the key to female happiness, while psychologists insisted that women could enjoy mental health only through dependence upon a man. Even those writers who took issue with such assertions accepted the centrality of marriage in women's lives. President Harry S Truman articulated this priority in 1948 when he addressed a Women's Bureau conference marking the 100th anniversary of the first American women's rights convention. Conference organizers had adopted the title "The American Woman, Her Changing Role: Worker, Homemaker, Citizen," but Truman insisted on reversing the order in his remarks, placing "homemaker" first.[2]

In the 1940s marriage became the central feature of women's lives even more than it had in the past. The marriage rate in 1940 was 105 per 1,000 women aged seventeen to twenty-nine, well above the rate of 89.1 for the "normal" years of 1925–1929. Between 1940 and 1943, according to Census Bureau estimates, more than a million more families were formed than would have been expected in normal times. The marriage boom in part represented weddings which had been postponed during the economic crisis of the 1930s. Even more so, it reflected the influence of war. Especially before draft policies became clear and before fathers were drafted, marriage offered to some men the hope of deferment. Moreover, many couples were moved by the imminence of separation to formalize relationships earlier than they might normally have done. As Karen Anderson has observed, young women's awareness of the male deficit and their consequent concern about marital prospects imparted even more urgency to the search for a husband. And, while dependents' benefits were modest, the government did provide a measure of economic support for soldiers' wives and children.[3]

Although the marriage rate declined somewhat during the years of greatest military mobilization, it remained above prewar levels. In 1946 it peaked at 148, and averaged 121 during the postwar years. By 1950 the proportion of women fourteen years and older who were married had reached 66.1 percent, up from 59.5 in 1940. The difficult conditions of the Depression and war years made family life more attractive, and the relative economic prosperity of the postwar period made marriage financially possible. GI benefits, which were available to 40 percent of the male population in the twenty to twenty-four age group, provided an especially important financial cushion. Further reducing the economic uncertainties of family formation was the increasing propensity of wives to work outside the home, at least until the advent of the first child. These developments also encouraged people to marry at younger ages. The median age at first marriage for women reached an unprecedented low, falling from 21.5 to 20.3 during the 1940s, while that for men dropped even more, from 24.3 to 22.7.[4]

Younger and hastier marriages also contributed to a rising divorce rate. As the return of soldiers produced a record high of 2.3 million marriages in 1946, it also resulted in 600,000 divorces, a record number. In 1947, one of every twenty-nine World War II veterans under forty-five who had ever married was divorced, but that was true for only one in sixty comparable nonveterans. The greater incidence of divorce among veterans represented in part the dissolution of marriages into which couples had rushed before the man was shipped off to military duty. They reflected as well the inability of men and women to accommodate their relationships to the new roles and independence each had experienced during the wartime separation. The divorce rate leveled off after 1946, but by 1950 it stood at about 25 percent of the number of marriages, well above the prewar level. Yet, the increasing incidence and acceptance of divorce did not mean a rejection of marriage: most of those who divorced promptly remarried.[5]

In some respects the conditions of wifehood were more attractive by the late 1940s than they had been for earlier generations. Rising incomes during the early years of the decade did little to ease the burdens of housekeeping, for the casualties of war included stoves, refrigerators, electric sweepers, and aluminum, stainless-steel, and copper utensils. These shortages, along with scarcities of housing, food, and clothing, made all the old tasks more time-consuming, while housewives were urged to assume such new ones as raising Victory Gardens or volunteering for the Red Cross. The postwar economic recovery lightened domestic labor for most wives, and brought them more comfortable homes. Yet, as the physical conditions of homemaking improved, women were subject to cultural pressures which made wifehood and maternity just as time-consuming and more psychologically stressful.[6]

Providing adequate housing remained a national problem throughout the 1940s. The housing crisis which had begun during the Depression when construction ground to a virtual halt was exacerbated by the war. Some federally financed housing was built in war-impacted areas, but the general diversion of funds, materials, and labor into military production, combined with the marriage boom, increased the national housing deficit. At the end of the war 5 million families were looking for a home: meanwhile they were living "doubled up" with other families, in basements, coal sheds and boxcars. One newspaper carried an ad for a large icebox which "could be fixed up to live in." Women, of course, bore the brunt of poor housing because they spent more time at home and were responsible for much of its upkeep. Although nearly 5 million new units were built from 1946 to 1950, by the end of the decade more than 2.5 million families were still doubled up, and twice as many lived in slum dwellings.[7]

Little progress was made in housing for poor families, but those with some means enjoyed the opportunity to move into more comfortable and attractive dwellings. The GI Bill underwrote home mortgages for more than 1 million veterans by the end of 1947; in all, 4 million veterans and their families eventually benefited from the government's guarantee of low-interest loans on $13 billion worth of property. Home ownership became the norm as the percentage of owner-occupied dwellings rose from 43.6 in 1940 to 55 in 1950. The revival of the construction industry provided more families with basic amenities: for example, the proportion of homes with electricity grew from 79 to 94 percent. As was the case with electricity, the dramatic changes in plumbing had occurred before the 1940s, but here, too, millions of families enjoyed modern conveniences for the first time. The proportion of dwellings with private toilets increased from 60 to 71 percent, and those with private baths or showers from 56 to 70.[8]

Most of the new homes were built in the suburbs, where nearly half of the nation's population increase occurred. Suburban living was not new, for since the nineteenth century affluent families had escaped urban grime and congestion by moving out to the country-side. In the late 1940s however, the development of large-scale, prefabricated construction along with government support for the housing industry opened suburbia to working-class and lower-middle-class families. Massive migration to the suburbs did not become a reality until the 1950s. By then a variety of critics were decrying the architectural monotony, the lack of community in-stitutions, the cultural drabness, and the behavioral conformity suburbs imposed upon their residents. For some full-time home-makers, the move to the new subdivisions occasioned boredom and loneliness as they were cut off from the kinship networks which characterized central cities and no longer enjoyed easy access to commercial and cultural diversions. Women more than men regis-tered dissatisfaction with particular aspects of suburban living, but the overwhelming majority of women and their families viewed the conveniences and status associated with their exodus from the city in highly positive terms.[9]

Among those conveniences were kitchens designed and equipped to lighten and brighten women's household work. The application of technological innovations to the home had begun to transform housekeeping early in the century, but Depression and war had slowed the pace of this development. Once the economy had converted to civilian goods production, most housewives had access to new products and machines which reduced the physical drudgery of their daily routines. In 1950, seven out of ten homes had electric washing machines, nearly 15 million more than had had them in 1940. The percentage of all households owning refrig-erators leaped from 45 to 80 during the decade. Nearly three-fourths of all homes were equipped with electric or gas stoves, and more than half had vacuum cleaners. Electric dishwashers, auto-matic clothes driers, garbage disposals, blenders, and home freez-ers all appeared in the 1940s but remained beyond the reach of the vast majority of women. Other products were more accessible. The use of more easily laundered synthetic fibers in clothing doubled during the decade. Although 44 percent of all families reported some canning of fruits and vegetables in 1947, the transfer from home to commercial food processing continued. Per-capita consumption of canned baby food, for example, increased almost seven-fold; families ate less fresh and more canned or frozen fruit in 1950 than they had in 1940.[10]

Acquisition of new appliances and products may have lightened the homemaker's physical load, but they did not reduce the amount of time nonemployed women spent in housework, which remained at fifty-one to fifty-six hours per week from the 1920s to the 1960s. A 1948 survey of urban, white, homeowning women found that even though most of them possessed washing machines, refrigerators, electric sweepers, and gas or electric ranges, just one in five enjoyed as many as three hours of leisure a day, while the majority had two hours or less. The development of processed foods and kitchen appliances did enable women to spend less time preparing and cleaning up after meals, but time saved here was shifted to other activities like child care, shopping, and decorating. Despite the technological changes that dramatically reduced the manual effort in doing laundry, the amount of time women devoted to this task increased as families' wardrobes expanded and as linens and clothing were changed more frequently. A housewife in 1946 compared the modern woman's domestic responsibilities with those of her grandmother and concluded, "We are not . . . using laborsaving devices to decrease labor, but only to increase standards." While the modern woman's labor was less strenuous, she worked harder because she was expected to keep her family cleaner and better fed, her house tidier and more attractively decorated, herself younger- and lovelier-looking, and her children better adjusted emotionally.[11]

The media played a significant role in encouraging women to conform to more exacting norms of domestic maintenance. As early as the 1920s advertisers of food and household products sought to promote consumption by appealing to women's pride, guilt, and need to feel valued. Women's magazines, too, established ever-higher standards as they featured experts' advice which urged women to develop new skills as nutritionists, consumers, decorators, and childrearers. Yet such appeals did not produce the same effect on employed and nonemployed homemakers. A study made in the 1940s conformed with other research in finding that wage-earning wives devoted thirty-four hours a week to housekeeping, while full-time homemakers spent fifty-six. The difference was not due simply to the wage-earner's ability to purchase labor-saving devices, nor to her ability to get her husband to share domestic chores. Rather, household work tended to fill the amount of time available. Full-time homemakers did have greater opportunity to meet the higher expectations of housewifery, but, as JoAnn Vanek has argued, they also had compelling reasons to keep busy. Especially as greater numbers of wives contributed to their families' well-being through paid employment, full-time housewives needed to emphasize to themselves and others the value of their contributions by spending long hours at their domestic work.[12]

Wives of returning soldiers carried an additional domestic responsibility, that of easing their husbands' adjustment to civilian life. Psychiatrists, military doctors, sociologists, and servicemen themselves cautioned Americans not to ignore the social aspects of demobilization and assigned women the primary role in ensuring the veterans' satisfactory readjustment. Women were, above all, to be sensitive and responsive, to adjust their own needs and desires to those of their men. Sociologist Willard Waller, for example, advised women to accept "more than the wife's usual responsibility for her marriage," to offer "lavish—and undemanding—affection," and to expect "no immediate return." The independence and self-confidence experienced by women during the war posed especially critical problems. Wives were reminded that soldiers wanted "feminine" women who would display "tenderness, admiration, or at least submissiveness." A marriage counselor urged women to "let him know you are tired of living alone, that you want him now to take charge." Even the advice which recognized the importance of employment to women suggested that women give up their jobs if keeping them threatened marital reconstruction. The extent to which wives heeded these admonitions, of course, eludes the historian's grasp. But these writings did represent the views of a significant body of opinion leaders, many of whom were veterans themselves or clinicians dealing with military personnel. While these authorities did not ignore the veterans' own responsibility for their social adjustment, they did reinforce the norm which focused responsibility for marital success upon women. That success, moreover, required conformity to such traditional ideals of womanhood as dependence, submissiveness, and self-abnegation.[13]

More exacting models of motherhood along with a sharp increase in the birth rate expanded women's childrearing responsibilities. During the Depression the birth rate had hovered around

18 to 19 per 1,000 population, the lowest in the nation's history. The effect of war on reproduction was felt quickly. In 1941 the birth rate reached 20.4, but most births were recorded in April and in July, approximately nine months after the Selective Service Act, which initially exempted fathers, was first introduced and then passed by Congress. By 1943 it had climbed to 22.7. A subsequent decline during the last two years of the war, when more couples were separated, was followed by another rise, and the birth rate fluctuated around 25 for the rest of the decade. A small increase in reproduction among women in their thirties indicated births which had been postponed during the economic crisis. But the greatest increase occurred among younger women, resulting from their greater tendency to marry, their younger age at marriage, and, consequently, their earlier beginning of child-bearing. Moreover, the sharpest increase in birth rate occurred in metropolitan areas among the most highly educated women. The baby boom did not signify a return to very large families. There was a substantial increase in the proportion of women bearing their third child, and the rate of fourth births moved up somewhat. But at the fifth and higher levels, the century-old decline continued through the 1940s.[14]

While there were no major breakthroughs in contraceptive technique, access of American women to more effective means of controlling their fertility continued to increase. By 1940, physicians could furnish contraceptive information to their patients in all states but Massachusetts and Connecticut. In the early 1940s there were more than 800 contraceptive clinics, and seven southern states provided family planning services through their public health programs. Devout Catholics had a better chance at controlling fertility since 1930 when Pope Pius XI had sanctioned the rhythm method under certain circumstances and since improved medical information more accurately pinpointed the fertile period. Moreover, condom usage became more popular, due in part to the government's efforts to protect servicemen from venereal disease during World War II. The Planned Parenthood Federation of America capitalized on wartime exigencies by propagandizing birth control in terms of its contribution to national health and strength and to women's ability to undertake war work. That a popular consensus had formed around the desirability of contraception was indicated by public-opinion polls which reported a majority of Americans favoring government clinics to provide birth-control information to married couples.[15]

These attitudes conformed to actual practice. Studies made in 1938–39 and in 1941 revealed that among white, urban women with at least an elementary-school education and a relatively comfortable standard of living, 83 to 89 percent used contraception. A more comprehensive survey of white women in 1955 found similar proportions of users. In all socioeconomic groups, except for the 6 percent with the least income and education, a majority of white women attempted to control their fertility. Black women were much less likely to employ contraception. Poverty and lack of education denied many of them access to information and materials. Cultural norms along with realistic suspicions about the motivations of white birth-control advocates further inhibited their use. When researchers surveyed 357 black women in rural Maryland in 1950–51 they found that just one in five practiced birth control. But almost 10 percent had been sterilized, a practice routinely prescribed by local doctors after a sixth pregnancy. In the early 1940s black organizations cooperated with the Planned Parenthood Federation in campaigns to make contraception available to black families. These efforts and the Maryland finding that contraception was attempted by one-third of the younger women promised increasing control over fertility for minority women.[16]

The little research available indicates that couples were using more effective forms of contraception. Douching became less popular as a contraceptive device, and condoms, diaphragms, and the rhythm method gained in usage. But none of these practices was failproof, and the rhythm method was much less effective than appliance methods. Thus, women continued to have unwanted pregnancies. Of the wives who used contraceptives in the 1955 survey, one in four reported at least one accidental pregnancy, and 16 percent of all wives said that their most recent pregnancy was unwanted. Both the accident rate and the rate of unwanted pregnancies climbed with the number of children already born; half of the women reported that their fourth pregnancy was accidental, and nearly 30 percent said their fourth one was unwanted.[17]

When contraception failed or was not used, a large minority of women resorted to abortion as they had always done. Because all states outlawed abortion, except to preserve the life, and occasionally the health, of the mother, most abortions were illegal. No adequate statistics on abortion existed, but medical experts estimated the number of illegal abortions to be from 300,000 to 1 million per year, or between 10 and 25 percent of births.

During the 1940s Alfred C. Kinsey and his associates at the Institute for Sex Research interviewed more than 5,000 women about their sexual and reproductive lives. The sample was highly skewed in favor of economically comfortable, urban, highly educated and younger women; between 20 and 25 percent of these women who had ever married reported that they had had criminal abortions. Interviews with a smaller group of black women, skewed in a manner similar to the white sample, found that black women with less than high-school educations had a lower incidence of abortion than their white counterparts, but that the rates of college-educated blacks were similar to those of white women. Increasing concern about abortion was manifested in a conference called by the National Committee on Maternal Health in 1942. The medical and legal experts who participated registered alarm at the inclination of women to terminate their pregnancies, focusing their concern on the physical and mental health of women rather than on fetal life. Convinced of the need to control abortion, they recognized the ineffectiveness of legal means and sought to attack the problem with public discussion and education.[18]

Later in the decade, physicians moved to reduce the incidence of therapeutic abortion—the one form of abortion over which they did exercise direct power. By the late 1940s virtually all hospitals reporting indicated that they had significantly cut the rate of therapeutic abortions. This was due in part to medical and surgical advances which enabled women with physical diseases to deliver safely. But especially as psychiatric problems gained a larger share of total indications, the decline in therapeutic abortions represented a specific effort on the part of doctors to deny hospital abortions to women who wanted and needed them. Two doctors at the University of Iowa Hospital, for example, lamented the presence of "economic pressure, social factors, and convenience" in requests for abortions. Criticizing the tendency to employ "medical means to solve a social problem," they urged physicians to apply "strict medical principles" in deciding whether to approve

abortions. They cautioned doctors about recommending termina-
tion even in cases where continuing a pregnancy might shorten the
mother's life.[19]

In many hospitals control over a woman's ability to terminate
her pregnancy passed from her physician, usually in consultation
with another specialist, to newly established hospital abortion
committees. Reporting on the California Hospital's institution of
such a board in 1948, a staff doctor announced approvingly that the
committee had rejected half the cases it reviewed. By the early
1950s other hospitals were reporting similar drastic reductions
in abortion rates. Poor and nonwhite women experienced even
greater difficulty in obtaining therapeutic abortions as the disparity between ward and private patients receiving abortions grew.[20]

Doctors sometimes cited fear of criminal prosecution as the
reason for the more stringent approach to therapeutic abortion.
Yet most courts accepted physicians' professional judgments and
placed the burden on prosecutors to prove that an abortion was not
necessary. What physicians seemed to fear more was that their
hospitals might acquire a reputation for a liberal abortion policy.
Describing the substitution of an abortion board for the traditional
two-doctor approval system at Mount Sinai Hospital, Dr. Alan
Guttmacher remarked that "those of us who have charge of an
obstetrical service do not want its prominence to stem from its
great leniency toward abortion." The head of Obstetrical and
Gynecological Service at another New York hospital, Columbia-
Presbyterian, indicated an even harsher motivation. Criticizing
the psychiatric indication as a "subterfuge," he suggested "the
control of the number of abortions, as, to some extent, a technique
of social control" over sexual behavior.[21]

Underlying physicians' attitudes about abortion was the perva-
sive conviction that woman's destiny lay in childbearing. In the
words of one doctor, "There is no other experience in life on any
level that will provide the same sense of fulfillment, of happiness,
of complete pervading contentment." If women did not recognize
this, then doctors must help them to see its truth. A woman who
"cannot tolerate pregnancy, or is in intense conflict about it," was
immature, in the view of a Columbia University psychiatrist. Her
"psychopathology" should be treated with psychotherapy rather
than abortion which was likely to produce even more severe emo-

tional disturbance. Linking his hospital's declining abortion rate to the establishment of a committee to rule on all requests, a University of Virginia psychiatrist maintained that if a woman did not want a child, "it is up to the committee to find out why and to do something . . . " The remedies included "education" of the woman and her husband, psychotherapy and shock treatment. Although the therapeutic abortion rate had never been exceedingly high—one for every 150 live births, according to a 1945 obstetrics text—by the late 1940s women found it even more difficult to obtain a hospital abortion.[22]

In seeking to limit the incidence of abortion, doctors continued to emphasize women's well-being over fetal life. But their assumption that abortion must result in psychological trauma reflected Freudian stereotypes about woman's purpose rather than women's actual experience. Among the women in the Kinsey sample reporting on the consequences of their abortions, three in four (and 82 percent of married women) indicated no unfavorable effects at all. Less than one in ten reported emotional problems and even fewer experienced severe physical consequences. Certainly the relatively privileged position of the women in this sample afforded them access to more skilled practitioners, and poor women undoubtedly suffered greater physical harm from illegal abortions. Yet no matter how great a woman's material resources, her decision to terminate a pregnancy required her to violate a law as well as a social norm. That so many did so with so few emotional complications indicated their determination to define and meet their own needs even when that required defiance of law and of the "wisdom" of experts.[23]

Women who carried pregnancies to term enjoyed deliveries which were safer to them and their babies. Maternal mortality took an especially sharp plunge in the 1940s, from 37.6 per 10,000 live births to 8.3. That drop was due in part to the increasing incidence of hospital delivery. Three in five women delivered their babies in hospitals in 1940, but by 1950 close to 90 percent did so. The impersonality, isolation, and loss of control associated with hospital birth along with the higher risk of infection and increased possibility of harmful intervention in some ways made childbirth more difficult emotionally and physically. But hospital birth also gave women access to life- and health-saving practices. Two new medical procedures were especially critical in reducing maternal mortality: the use of penicillin and other antibiotics decreased the dangers of puerperal fever, and the development of blood plasma and transfusion techniques lowered the risk of death from hemorrhaging. Infant mortality also declined, though not as precipitously. Antibiotics and immunization brought down infant deaths from 47 per 1,000 live births in 1940 to 31.3 in 1949.[24]

Changes in the use of anesthetics were also beneficial to mothers and babies. By the 1940s doctors began to replace twilight sleep with spinal anesthesia, which was safer and allowed women to remain conscious. Some women dispensed with drugs entirely as natural childbirth, pioneered in the 1930s by London obstetrician Grantly Dick-Read, gained favor in the United States. By overcoming fear, and thus tension and pain, and by learning exercises to strengthen their muscles and control their breathing, women could exercise more control over childbirth, deliver healthier babies, and enjoy speedier recoveries. While some doctors readily cooperated with women's requests to forego anesthesia and even encouraged patients to undertake natural childbirth, the majority objected to the inconvenience and loss of control it occasioned for them. Yet the popularity of Dick-Read's *Childbirth Without Fear*, first published in the United States in 1944, indicated a growing interest among middle-class women. Its effects, however, were not uniformly beneficial. With its emphasis on the exultation of delivery, natural childbirth encouraged the glorification and mystification of motherhood as woman's primary means of fulfillment. Although Dick-Read and his American followers recommended that anesthesia be administered to women who wanted or needed it, natural childbirth established expectations that some women could not fulfill. Women who needed drugs or who failed to experience birth as an ecstatic high too easily regarded themselves as failures.[25]

More accessible to less-privileged women was a new federal program which helped to reduce the risks of childbearing. Motivated by concern over the morale of married servicemen, in 1943 Congress authorized the Emergency Maternity and Infant Care (EMIC) program. Under this program the federal government bore the entire cost of medical care for wives of enlisted men in the four lowest grades and for their infants up to the age of one year.

By the end of 1946, an estimated 1 million babies had been born under EMIC, representing one out of every seven births. EMIC enabled many women to receive medical care beyond the means of their own financial resources, and especially to benefit from hospital services. In Mississippi, for example, only 30 percent of total births occurred in hospitals, but under the EMIC program more than 70 percent of the beneficiaries delivered in hospitals.[26]

For minority women whose husbands were not in the military, childbearing continued to pose considerably higher risks. Although maternal mortality for nonwhites declined from 77.3 to 22.2, it remained three times the rate for white women. In 1950 more than one of every four minority women gave birth without having a doctor present and just 58 percent delivered in hospitals. Infant deaths showed a similar racial disparity. Nonwhite infant mortality fell from 73.8 to 44.5, in contrast to the white rate, which dropped from 43.2 to 26.8. The lack of adequate medical care took its toll on native Americans as well as on blacks. Among Arizona Indians infant mortality was 135.7.[27]

Mothers who listened to experts found their roles as caregivers more demanding and emotionally taxing. Earlier standards of child care had focused on strict scheduling of infant activities and avoidance of excessive maternal attention. The highly popular *Infant Care*, first published by the Children's Bureau in 1914, advised mothers that a stringent regimen for the child was as important in conserving the strength and peace of mind of the mother as it was in establishing discipline, order, and good habits in the child. While the behaviorist approach to childrearing forged by John B. Watson in the 1920s reinforced the importance of regularity, denial, and some maternal distance, its tone presaged the worry- and guilt-producing approach which would dominate child care two decades later. Missing from Watson's advice was any concern for the mother's well-being; instead women were warned that their mistakes could wreck their children's future. "Mother love," wrote Watson, was "a dangerous instrument."[28]

Social commentators and psychologists in the 1940s charged that women had failed to heed such threats. In 1942 Philip Wylie coined the term "momism" to describe overprotective, overindulgent mothers. In *Generation of Vipers*, amidst churchmen, scientists, educators, doctors, public officials, and businessmen, women took their share of the blame for what Wylie considered the current moral decay. Women's overt loving care and self-sacrifice for their families masked an egotism, vanity, and power-hunger which sapped their children's ability to grow into independent adults. The large numbers of men unfit for military service added further to the attacks on mothers. More than 1.8 million men were rejected and another half million were discharged from the army alone, all for emotional disorders. Dr. Edward A. Strecker, psychiatric consultant to the military, diagnosed these men as "immature," and found "in the vast majority of case histories, a 'mom' is at fault." In *Their Mothers' Sons*, published in 1946, Strecker charged these women with failing to cut "the emotional apron string," thereby stunting their children's psychological growth and condemning them to mental illness.[29]

Strecker took pains to exonerate individual mothers. He linked "momism" to women's own inadequate upbringing, to their husbands' shirking of responsibilities, and to a social system which both encouraged women to devote their lives to children and failed to provide them avenues for satisfaction outside the home. Yet such a distribution of the blame could do little to allay the anxieties of mothers trying to figure out just how much maternal care resulted in smothering. The contradictions in Strecker's book made it impossible for mothers to find the narrow way between neglect and oversolicitation. While he warned against excessive involvement in their children's lives, he also criticized mothers who paid too much attention to their own appearance as well as "pseudo-intellectuals" who were always taking courses. Moreover, while Strecker rooted emotional immaturity in the practices of self-sacrificing mothers, he criticized "moms" for too readily seeking divorce, while praising good mothers who were willing to "tolerate difficult and unsatisfactory marriages for a long time," for the sake of their children.[30]

The internal contradictions of childrearing experts were compounded by a general shift in dominant theory which took place in the 1940s as the behaviorist approach gave way to permissiveness. One mother witnessed the change in her own practices. Serving a new vegetable one evening, she recognized that she expected the oldest child to eat it all, the middle one to taste it, and the youngest "could do whatever he wanted." Promulgated by pediatrician and researcher Arnold Gesell, permissiveness began to invade new editions of the Children's Bureau's *Infant Care* in 1942 and was popularized by Dr. Benjamin Spock, whose *Baby and Child Care* first appeared in 1946. In place of the behaviorist method's strict scheduling, women were to let the child take the lead; mothers were to watch the child closely and respond to its signals for physical and emotional attention. Each activity of the child was a learning experience fraught with implications for its psychological development. Consequently, the mother must constantly watch the child, fine-tuning her behavior to that of the child, ever-so-delicately constructing situations most conducive to the child's own discovery of appropriate behavior.[31]

Older schools of child-training had placed women at the center; permissiveness required self-denial of women, as the mother became "secondary to the infant care 'experts' and the baby's demands." Women were to subordinate their own needs for rest, for fulfilling other domestic responsibilities, for pursuing nonfamilial interests, and to do so "with a deep sense of satisfaction and happiness." As Nancy Pottishman Weiss has pointed out, although *Baby and Child Care* was ostensibly intended to reassure, it in fact undermined women's self-confidence "by allusions to the physician's veto power, reminders of the pitfalls of improper child care, and orchestrations of daily events in a mother's life." While it magnified the importance of the mother's attention to the child's daily development, Dr. Spock's "Bible" also echoed Wylie's and Strecker's cautions against smothering and spoiling. Moreover, women had to cope with the conflict between ideals of permissive motherhood and the standards expected from them in other familial roles. The child's ability to develop self-reliance depended upon its freedom to explore and experiment, but such freedom made it more difficult for women to fulfill the ideal of keeping a neat, clean, attractive home. Children required constant maternal attention, but women were also to nurture relationships of intimacy and companionship with their husbands, a standard which called for parental privacy and attention to each other.[32]

The actual behavior of middle-class women indicated conformity to the precepts of the new childrearing orthodoxy. Investigations of childcare practices produced some conflicting findings, but most studies reported that middle-class mothers were more lenient, less punitive, and imposed fewer restrictions and demands upon their children. These differences reflected more than middle-class mothers' greater faith in and access to the advice of experts. Permissiveness required more attention and energy from the mother, and economically pressed women may have found strictness the only way to deal with their more demanding domestic duties. To the extent that they recognized the limits of class mobility, working-class mothers practiced a mode of child-training that would facilitate their children's adjustment to future roles. For strictness and discipline prepared working-class children for the subordinate places in which most would find themselves as they moved beyond the home into the authoritarian environments of school and work.[33]

Despite the increasing popularity of marriage, women headed nearly 15 percent of all households in 1950, and about one in ten of all children lived with their mothers only. Black women bore the economic hardships of sole parenthood at twice the rate of white women. In 1950, 17.6 percent of black families were headed by a woman, while 8.5 percent of white families were so constituted. Death, divorce, and separation accounted for most of the situations in which women without husbands raised children. However, during the Forties women demonstrated an increasing tendency to have children outside of marriage, as the rate of births to single women doubled during the decade. In 1940, single women bore children at the rate of 7.1 per 1,000 women aged fifteen to forty-four; by 1950 the rate had reached 14.1.[34]

Single women were also more likely to live on their own or with nonrelatives, thereby enjoying greater independence. Yet, most Americans viewed marriage as the exclusive road to happiness. Presented with three alternatives, three-fourths of young women polled in 1943 preferred marriage and domesticity. Eighteen percent wished to combine marriage with a career, but less than one in ten considered a successful career as a single woman to be a desirable alternative. That most Americans sought marriage is not surprising, but that only 9 percent believed a single person could be happy indicated the power of the marital imperative. Women who failed to conform lived under a social stigma greater than that which had marked their forebearers. As David Riesman pointed out, in the nineteenth century the failure to marry was thought of "as a social disadvantage and sometimes a personal tragedy but not necessarily as a quasi-perversion." Among earlier generations of highly educated women, large numbers had chosen careers over marriage. Despite the hand-wringing of social commentators over this cream of womanhood's failure to reproduce, these women had enjoyed the satisfactions of work and of close relationships with other women. By the 1940s, college women no longer viewed careers as desirable alternatives to marriage, and close relationships among women had become increasingly suspect.[35]

The suspicion, of course, was that these relationships had a sexual component. In the 1940s, as in earlier and later decades, fiction writers portrayed lesbian characters as sick, tormented, and threats to "innocent" women; only a few dealt with lesbian relationships in a sympathetic, positive light. Moreover, the weight of expert opinion continued to define homosexuality in pathological terms. Neither fiction nor most social-science literature reflected the reality of lesbians' lives. Among the women interviewed by Kinsey and his associates during the 1940s, one in four reported sexual attraction to other women, between 3 and 12 percent of the single women were lesbians, and those with the most extensive same-sex experience reported high levels of comfort with their sexual orientation.

The war-induced mobility and general weakening of social controls undoubtedly increased women's opportunity to discover and act upon their sexuality. Lesbians in Buffalo, New York, for example, recalled that the war altered the social atmosphere in ways which made their lives easier. The need for women to take the places of absent men increased the incidence and acceptability of women in public places. Women had more money to spend and enjoyed greater freedom of movement, congregation, and opportunity to meet other woman-identified women. As it became more customary for women to be out alone and to socialize with other women, the social lives of lesbians became less overtly deviant and consequently less vulnerable to public hostility or ridicule. There was little change, however, in societal norms which condemned women who lived outside of heterosexual structures. Although laws against homosexuality were rarely enforced against lesbians, cultural opprobrium was nearly as great as it was for male homosexuals. American society had never tolerated homosexuality, but the premium placed upon marriage and traditional family life in the postwar years demanded even greater personal resources from those women whose primary identification was with other women, regardless of the sexual content of their relationships.[36]

Wifehood and motherhood had always claimed supremacy among American women's aspirations and the norms of society itself. What Betty Friedan called "the feminine mystique" was no more than a slightly revised version of the nineteenth century model which centered women's purpose and responsibility in the home. The blows dealt to family life by the material deprivation of the 1930s and the dislocations and anxieties of the war years enhanced the attractions of domestic privacy. While a significant minority of women continued to struggle for sheer survival, for most women the economic resurgence increased the possibilities for marriage and motherhood and enabled women to perform domestic roles with greater ease and comfort. In several respects, however, the pressures on women increased. More and more were combining marriage with work in the absence of any institutional or ideological changes that would diminish the tension between private and public claims. Higher and sometimes conflicting standards of housekeeping, wifehood, and maternity intensified psychological stresses. And the exaltation of customary family life separated even further from the mainstream those women who could not or would not conform to the imperatives of heterosexuality, marriage, and traditional domestic life.

NOTES AND REFERENCES

1. Leila J. Rupp, *Mobilizing Women for War: German and American Propaganda, 1939–1945* (Princeton: Princeton University Press, 1979), pp. 137–66; See Chapter 10 for treatment of women in the popular culture.

2. Bernice Milburn Moore, *Women After the War* (New York: Young Women's Christian Association, 1945), p. 9; William H. Chafe, *The American Woman: Her Changing Social, Economic and Political Roles, 1920–1970* (New York: Oxford University Press, 1972), pp. 200–16; *Report on the 1948 Women's Bureau Conference, The American Woman, Her Changing Role: Worker, Homemaker, Citizen*, Women's Bureau Bulletin 224 (Washington, D.C.: Government Printing Office, 1948), p. 1.

3. J. Frederic Dewhurst and Associates, *America's Needs and Resources: A New Survey* (New York: The Twentieth Century Fund, 1955), pp. 55–56; Jean Lipman-Blumen, "A Crisis Framework Applied to Macro-Sociological Family Changes: Marriage, Divorce, and Occupational Trends Associated with World War II," *Journal of Marriage and the Family* 37 (November 1975):893–94; Philip M. Hauser, "Population and Vital Phenomena," *American Journal of Sociology* 48 (November 1942):313; Karen Anderson, *Wartime Women: Sex Roles, Family Relations, and the Status of Women during World War II* (Westport, Conn.: Greenwood Press, 1981), pp. 76–77.

4. Dewhurst et al., *America's Needs and Resources*, pp. 55–57; Richard A. Easterlin, *Population, Labor Force, and Long Swings in Economic Growth: The American Experience* (New York: National Bureau of Economic Research, 1968), p. 117; Kingsley Davis, "The Early Marriage Trend," *What's New: Contemporary Comment No. 4* (Fall 1958):4.

5. Dewhurst et al., *America's Needs and Resources*, p. 57; Lipman-Blumen, "A Crisis Framework," pp. 896–97; Paul H. Landis, "Sequential Marriage," *Journal of Home Economics* 42 (October 1950):625–28.

6. Jean Joyce, "Farewell to Homemaking as Usual," ibid. 35 (June 1943):353–55.

7. Richard O. Davies, *Housing Reform during the Truman Administration* (Columbia: University of Missouri Press, 1966), pp. 40–41, 103, 117.

8. Ibid.; United States Bureau of the Census, *Statistical Abstracts of the United States: 1952* (hereafter *SA: 1952*) (Washington, D.C.: Government Printing Office, 1952), pp. 738, 740.

9. Geoffrey Perrett, *A Dream of Greatness: The American People, 1945–1963* (New York: Coward, McCann and Geoghegan, 1979), pp. 70–72; Herbert J. Gans, *The Levittowners: Ways of Life and Politics in a New Suburban Community* (New York: Vintage Books, 1967), pp. xv–xvii, 220–45.

10. Dewhurst et al., *America's Needs and Resources*, pp. 139–40, 182–84, 239–42; *SA: 1952*, pp. 89, 818.

11. JoAnn Vanek, "Time Spent in Housework," *Scientific American* (November 1974):116–21; J. Roy Leevy, "Leisure Time of the American Housewife," *Sociology and Social Research* 35 (November–December 1950): 97–105; Evelyn Ardis Whitman, "I'm Tired of Grandma!" pp. 217–24 in Elizabeth Bragdon, ed., *Women Today: Their Conflicts, Their Frustrations and Their Fulfillments* (New York: Bobbs-Merrill, 1953).

12. Ruth Schwartz Cowan, "The 'Industrial Revolution' in the Home: Household Technology and Social Change in the 20th Century," *Technology and Culture* 17 (January 1976):1-23; Vanek, "Time Spent in Housework," pp. 118–21; Elizabeth Sweeney Herbert, "When the Homemaker Goes to Work," *Journal of Home Economics* 44 (April 1952):258–59. With somewhat different emphases, Betty Friedan discussed the factors of advertising, higher standards, and Parkinson's law in accounting for time spent in housework. See *The Feminine Mystique* (New York: Dell Publishing Company, 1963), pp. 197–246.

13. Susan M. Hartmann, "Prescriptions for Penelope: Literature on Women's Obligations to Returning World War II Veterans," *Women's Studies* 5 (1978):223–39.

14. Hauser, "Population and Vital Phenomena," p. 312; Wilson H. Grabill, Clyde V. Kiser and Pascal K. Whelpton, *The Fertility of American Women* (New York: John Wiley and Sons, 1958), pp. 25–41, 381–92; Easterlin, *Population, Labor Force and Long Swings in Economic Growth*, pp. 105–10.

15. Gunnar Myrdal, *An American Dilemma: The Negro Problem and American Democracy* (New York: Harper and Brothers, 1944), pp. 178–81; David M. Kennedy, *Birth Control in America: The Career of Margaret Sanger* (New Haven: Yale University Press, 1970), pp. 150–51, 245–55; Ronald Freedman, Pascal K. Whelpton, and Arthur A. Campbell, *Family Planning, Sterility and Population Growth* (New York: McGraw-Hill, 1959), pp.

61−62, 100−53; Linda Gordon, *Woman's Body, Woman's Right: A Social History of Birth Control in America* (New York: Grossman Publishers, 1976), pp. 329−30, 348−59; George H. Gallup, *The Gallup Poll: Public Opinion, 1935−1971* (New York: Random House, 1972), pp. 42, 204, 631. The Gallup poll showed a drop in approval from 77 percent in 1940 to 64 percent in 1947, which may reflect polling errors as well as changing economic conditions.

16. John Winchell Riley and Matilda White, "The Use of Various Methods of Contraception," *American Sociological Review* 5 (December 1940):891−95; Freeman et al., *Family Planning*, pp. 61, 103, 407; Myrdal, *An American Dilemma*, pp. 178−81, 1227, fn 67; Christopher Tietze and Sarah Lewit, "Patterns of Family Limitation in a Rural Negro Community," *American Sociological Review* 18 (October 1953):563−64. For activities of the Planned Parenthood Federation and black organizations see Mary Church Terrell Papers, Boxes 12 and 13, Library of Congress; and Papers of the National Council of Negro Women, Series, 5, National Archives for Black Women's History, Washington, D.C.

17. Freeman et al., *Family Planning*, pp. 73−75, 175−78.

18. Mary S. Calderone, ed., *Abortion in the United States: A Conference Sponsored by the Planned Parenthood Federation of America* (New York: Harper and Brothers, 1958), pp. 54, 180; Paul H. Gebhard, Wardell B. Pomeroy, Clyde E. Martin, and Cornelia V. Christenson, *Pregnancy, Birth and Abortion* (New York: Harper and Brothers, 1958), pp. 15−20, 93−94, 166; *The Abortion Problem: Proceedings of the Conference Held Under the Auspices of the National Committee on Maternal Health* (Baltimore: The Williams and Wilkins Co., 1944), pp. 23, 28.

19. Calderone, ed., *Abortion in the United States*, pp. 38, 72, 78−84; Keith P. Russell, "Changing Indications for Therapeutic Abortions," *Journal of the American Medical Association* 151 (January 10, 1953):108−11; David C. Wilson, "The Abortion Problem in the General Hospital," p. 191 in Harold Rosen, ed., *Therapeutic Abortion* (New York: The Julian Press, 1954); J. G. Moore and J. H. Randall, "Trends in Therapeutic Abortion," *American Journal of Obstetrics and Gynecology* 63 (January 1952): 31, 38−40.

20. Keith P. Russell, "Therapeutic Abortion in a General Hospital," *American Journal of Obstetrics and Gynecology* 62 (August 1951):435, 437− 38; Wilson, "The Abortion Problem," pp. 190−93; Lawrence Lader, *Abortion* (Boston: Beacon Press, 1966), pp. 24−30; Calderone, *Abortion in the United States*, pp. 115, 139, 170.

21. Ibid., pp. 34−36, 40, 92, 95, 108.

22. Ibid., p. 112; Wilson, "The Abortion Problem," pp. 196−97; May E. Romm, "Psychoanalytic Considerations," in Rosen, *Therapeutic Abortion*, p. 210.

23. Pomeroy et al., *Pregnancy, Birth and Abortion*, pp. 205−12.

24. Sam Shapiro, Edward R. Schlesinger, and Robert E. L. Nesbitt, Jr., *Infant, Perinatal, Maternal and Childhood Mortality in the United States*

(Cambridge, Mass.: Harvard University Press, 1968), pp. 146, 248, 329; "Welcome, Strangers," *Newsweek* 35 (January 23, 1950):49; *SA:1952*, p. 68; Richard C. Wertz and Dorothy C. Wertz, *Lying-In: A History of Childbirth in America* (New York: The Free Press, 1977), pp. 164−73.

25. Ibid., pp. 178−92; Frederick W. Goodrich, Jr., and Herbert Thoms, "A Clinical Study of Natural Childbirth," *American Journal of Obstetrics and Gynecology* 56 (November 1948):875−83.

26. Martha M. Eliot and Lillian R. Freedman, "Four Years of the EMIC Program," *Yale Journal of Biology and Medicine* 19 (March 1947): 621−35.

27. Shapiro et al., *Infant, Perinatal, Maternal and Childhood Mortality*, pp. 248, 274−75; "Welcome Strangers," pp. 49−50.

28. Nancy Pottishman Weiss, "Mother, the Invention of Necessity: Dr. Benjamin Spock's *Baby and Child Care*," *American Quarterly* 29 (Winter 1977):519−31.

29. Philip Wylie, *A Generation of Vipers* (New York: Rinehart and Co., 1942), pp. 46−51, 184−204; Edward A. Strecker, *Their Mother's Sons: The Psychiatrist Examines an American Problem* (Philadelphia: J. B. Lippincott, 1946).

30. Ibid., pp. 30, 45, 62−63, 70−73, 160−74, 212.

31. Arnold Gesell and Frances L. Ilg, *Infant and Child Care in the Culture of Today: The Guidance and Development in Home and Nursery School* (New York: Harper and Brothers, 1943), pp. 4−5, 49−51; Martha Wolfenstein, "Fun Morality: An Analysis of Recent American Child-Training Literature," *Journal of Social Issues* 7 (1951):15−25; Weiss, "Mother, the Invention of Necessity," pp. 531−34.

32. Clark E. Vincent, "Trends in Infant Care Ideas," *Child Development* 22 (September 1951):197−209; Sibylle Escalona, "A Commentary upon Some Recent Changes in Child-Rearing Practices," ibid. 20 (September 1949):160; Weiss, "Mother, the Invention of Necessity," p. 534; Dorothy Barclay, "What's Wrong with the Family?" *New York Times Magazine*, September 16, 1951, p. 52.

33. Eleanor E. Macoby, Patricia Gibbs, and the Staff of the Laboratory of Human Development, Harvard University, "Methods of Child-Rearing in Two Social Classes," pp. 380−96 in William E. Martin and Celia Burns Stendler, eds., *Readings in Child Development* (New York: Harcourt, Brace, 1954); Robert R. Sears, Eleanor E. Macoby, and Harry Levin, *Patterns of Child Rearing* (Evanston, Ill.: Row, Peterson and Co., 1957), pp. 420−47. For different conclusions about class differences in childrearing, see Allison Davis and Robert Havighurst, "Social Class and Color Differences in Child Rearing," *American Sociological Review* 11 (December 1946): 698−710.

34. *SA:1952*, p. 46; Paul C. Glick, *American Families* (New York: John Wiley and Sons, 1957), pp. 41−42; LaFrances Rodgers-Rose, "Some Demographic Characteristics of the Black Woman: 1940 to 1975," p. 37 in Rose, ed., *The Black Woman* (Beverly Hills: Sage Publications, 1980);

Abbott L. Ferris, *Indicators of Trends in the Status of American Women* (New York: Russell Sage Foundation, 1971), p. 351.

35. Heather L. Ross and Isabel V. Sawhill, *Time of Transition: The Growth of Families Headed by Women* (Washington, D.C.: The Urban Institute, 1975), pp. 13, 189; D'Ann Campbell, "Wives, Workers, and Womanhood: America During World War II," Ph.D. dissertation, University of North Carolina, 1979, p. 225; Peter Gabriel Filene, *Him/Her Self: Sex Roles in Modern America* (New York: New American Library, 1976), p. 172; David Riesman, "Some Continuities and Discontinuities in the Education of Women," n.d., p. 12, Dewey Memorial Lecture, Bennington College, Records of the Committee on Women's Education, File EC 35, Schlesinger Library, Radcliffe College. Lillian Faderman has analyzed the declining acceptability of close female relationships in *Surpassing the Love of Man: Romantic Friendship and Love between Women from the Renaissance to the Present* (New York: William Morrow, 1981).

36. Madeline Davis, "Multiple Images: A Study of the Lesbian Character in the Fiction and Non-Fiction of the 1940s," unpublished paper, 1979; Alfred C. Kinsey, Wardell B. Pomeroy, Clyde E. Martin and Paul H. Gebhard, *Sexual Behavior in the Human Female* (Philadelphia: W. B. Saunders, 1953), pp. 446–501; Madeline Davis, Liz Kennedy, and Avra Michelson, "The Buffalo Lesbian Community during the 1950's," paper presented at the Fifth Berkshire Conference on the History of Women, Vassar College, June 1981.

The first Wonder Woman strip, 1941 (Wonder Woman is a registered trademark of DC Comics and is used with permission. Copyright 1948. Copyright renewed 1968. DC Comics Inc.)

Chapter Ten

Models of Womanhood
in the Popular Culture

Popular culture in the 1940s expressed and confirmed women's new experiences, particularly those changes in women's lives wrought by war. Especially in the early years of the decade, media images of women were expansive, widening the range of acceptable female behavior, providing positive examples of unconventional women, and blurring traditional gender distinctions. Yet even these new models were rooted in a context which sustained the centrality of women's domestic lives and their relationships with men. As women used their leisure hours to read, to listen to the radio, to watch movies, or to attend to their personal appearance, they were reminded that appealing to men and fulfilling their domestic and familial responsibilities demanded their primary commitment. Moreover, as the war ended, the range of appropriate female behavior portrayed in the popular culture narrowed, in step with the contraction of their actual opportunities in public life. Those fictional women who did step outside of their conventional feminine roles were less frequently depicted as positive models, but instead carried cautionary, even threatening messages to their audiences.

Comic strips were among the most popular conveyors of cultural heroes and heroines. Seventy million Americans read the daily comic pages in newspapers, and sales of comic books grew from 12

million copies each month in 1942 to more than 60 million in 1946.
More than 80 percent of boys and girls aged six to seventeen read
comic books regularly during the war. Both the daily strips and the
comic books were quick to reflect the new situations created by
World War II. As Joe Palooka, Skeezix, and Dick Tracy enlisted in
the war effort, so did their female counterparts. Tillie the Toiler
became a Wac; Fritzie Ritz took a war job; and Winnie Winkel
marrried a GI. "Blondie," "Bringing Up Father," and other popular strips of the domestic comedy genre provided lessons in coping
with home-front problems and encouraged their audiences to conserve scarce goods and buy war bonds.[1]

Other feature strips of the 1940s carried images of womanhood
beyond those of worker, wife, and mother and gave women a
direct role in defeating Axis enemies. Of all the media, comics
offered the most daring female characters. When adventure serials
first came to dominate the genre in the 1930s, women appeared as
girl friends or companions of the hero; they offered a decorative
effect, and as "damsels in distress" provided challenges for the
protagonist. But the adventure strips increasingly depicted these
characters as assertive women, with sufficient courage and re-
sourcefulness to rescue the likes of Buck Rogers and Flash Gordon.
A few heroines even had their own features. Newspaper reporter
and private eye Constance Kurridge, for example, during the
1930s and into the 1940s performed the same feats against evil
forces throughout the world and space as did the male heroes. Pilot
"Flyin' Jennie" also had her own feature from 1939 to the death of
her creator in 1946.[2]

Powerful female protagonists appeared in the characters of
Sheena, Queen of the Jungle; Mary Marvel, long-lost twin of Captain Marvel; and Miss Fury, created by one of the few women
cartoonists, Tarpe Mills, as the female counterpart to Batman. But
the most imaginative creation of all was William Marston's "Wonder Woman," which first appeared in 1941. Wonder Woman came
to America from the Amazon utopia of Paradise Island, "that
enlightened land of women," her mission "to save the world from
the hatred and wars of men in a man-made world." Wonder
Woman was "as lovely as Aphrodite—as wise as Athena—with the
speed of Mercury and the strength of Hercules." Youthful readers

saw not only a woman who was intelligent, strong, and coura-
geous, but they also observed a powerful advocate for all women.
Asserting that she could never love "a dominant man who is
stronger than I am," Wonder Woman promoted the ideal of equality in male-female relationships. She inspired in her female associates self-respect and self-reliance and exemplified the possibilities
and power of female cooperation.[3]

Movies claimed an equally large share of the public's fantasy life.
Hollywood did lose some male stars to the military, but escaped
the restrictions placed on other industries and maintained production at near peacetime levels. Weekly attendance averaged nearly
100 million individuals and in some localities theaters stayed open
around the clock. Women comprised two-thirds of the wartime
audience, and movies provided models of women who, like their
counterparts in real life, undertook male responsibilities and
learned to survive on their own.[4]

The screen validated and encouraged women's military participation and defense work. Betty Hutton played twin sisters in the
comedy *Here Come the Waves* (1945); Lana Turner was the heiress
who joined the WAC in *Keep Your Powder Dry* (1945). The most
popular of the films with military heroines, *So Proudly We Hail*
(1943), depicted the struggles and bravery of army nurses on
Bataan. Women war workers appeared on the screen even more
frequently. *Swing Shift Maisie* (1943) featured Ann Sothern as an
aircraft worker; *Government Girl* (1944) represented the tens of
thousands of young women who flocked into federal jobs during
the war; in *Meet the People* (1944) Lucille Ball played the rich
woman who did her part to speed victory in a defense plant. Less
directly connected with the war effort were screen heroines at
work as business executives, novelists, psychiatrists, journalists,
public officials, and advertising executives.[5]

While providing models of women in professional careers and
examples of women's patriotic contributions through military service and war work, movies also communicated the ability of wom-
en to get along without men and to sustain one another. In 1942,
Americans flocked to see William Wyler's *Mrs. Miniver*, in which
the British housewife played by Oscar-winning Greer Garson
demonstrated that homemakers could summon previously un-

known strengths to safeguard their families' welfare and contribute to the national defense. David O. Selznick's *Since You Went Away*, box-office hit of 1944, featured Claudette Colbert as the American housewife coping with home-front problems, guiding her daughters through their own crises, and taking a job as shipyard welder while her husband fought the war. *Tender Comrade* (1943) likewise combined the themes of women's war work, female solidarity, and self-sufficiency. Its four heroines joined forces to rent a house, coordinate employment with domestic chores, and support each other through anxiety, loneliness, and bereavement. Although the heroines' relationships with men figured prominently in these films, the men themselves were distant, and the movies highlighted women's strengths and capabilities.[6]

The war failed to evoke such positive screen models for black women. The single character role available to black actresses continued to be that of the "mammy" popularized by Louise Beavers and Hattie McDaniel in the 1930s. These fictional women who served white families were usually sturdy, compassionate, resourceful, and sometimes cantankerous individuals. For example, McDaniel, who had won an Academy Award for her role in the 1939 production of *Gone With the Wind*, played Fidelia, the maid in *Since You Went Away*. Because the husbandless Hilton family could no longer afford her wages, she took a war job but kept both her room and her prewar role with the Hiltons. Fidelia portrayed strength as she supported family members through difficult times, and she showed an independent streak in her scolding and chiding of them. Yet, as Melva Joyce Baker has concluded, her most assertive scenes were intended primarily for humor, and the overall image was that of "a devoted and accepted member of the family group who had no other ambitions for herself." Movie stereotypes of black women reflected neither the realities of domestic service nor the changes occurring in black women's lives. The "mammy" tradition was carried on by Ethel Waters into the 1950s, but a new image began to appear on the screen in the 1940s.[7]

Donald Bogle has termed this alternative role the "bourgeois diva." Exemplified by singer Lena Horne, dancer and choreographer Katherine Dunham, and jazz pianist Hazel Scott, the bourgeois diva was usually light-skinned, lacked the "rough ethnic edges" of her predecessors, and matched more closely the characteristics of the dominant white culture. These new stars began their careers in night clubs and concert halls, and it was in their capacity as entertainers that they broke into the movies. Thus, although Lena Horne played in eleven movies during the 1940s, in all but two her role was that of performer. Cast as entertainers rather than in character roles, the scenes of these black actresses were not integral to the plot and could be cut out for screenings before southern audiences. As Horne recalled, "They did not make me into a maid, but they didn't make me anything else either. I became a butterfly pinned to a column singing away in Movie-land."[8]

In its imitation of white norms of beauty, its potential for exploiting the sexuality of these stars, and its failure to allow them roles more compatible with the realities of women's lives, the new stereotype represented only a small improvement in popular models of black womanhood. Yet, it did provide an alternative to the "mammy" image. Moreover, Horne, Dunham, and Scott used their popularity in public protest against segregation and discrimination. Dunham announced to a Louisville, Kentucky, audience that she would not perform there again because "the management refuses to let people like us sit by people like you." When Horne, entertaining at a military base, found German prisoners of war seated in front of black GI's, she walked off the stage to perform directly before the black troops. The new stars not only held out the possibility that black women could be other than servants, but also provided models for resistance to racism.[9]

Other forms of popular leisure provided nontraditional activities for women as well as unconventional models for their audiences. In previous decades the emphasis in women's athletics had been on participation, not competition. The female physical education experts who controlled women's athletics objected to the exploitation, individualism, commercialism, and stress on winning which characterized men's sports and promoted recreation for women which favored intramural over intervarsity play and cooperation over rivalry. Consequently women's prominence in athletics was limited to individuals who excelled in the more feminine sports of tennis, golf, and swimming. Babe Didrikson offered a more dynamic model: as Olympic track and field champion in 1932 she had demonstrated power, speed, and competitive drive uncharacteristic of most women athletes. In the 1940s she transformed women's golf into an attacking game and established it on solid footing as a professional sport. Associated Press in 1950 named her Woman Athlete of the Half-Century.[10]

While Didrikson offered a different image of the athletic woman, team sports for women got a boost from the exigencies of war. Industrial recreation reflected the increase in women workers as corporations sponsored more women's teams than ever before. The *American Industrial Manpower* publication reported on women's teams in basketball, softball, bowling, field hockey, and volleyball. Its advertising testified to women's increased participation by featuring pictures of women using archery, tennis, softball, and casting equipment. While the war expanded athletic opportunities for women workers, transportation shortages sidelined a group of professionals. The All-American World's Champion Basketball Club, begun in 1936, sat out the war, but when they returned in 1947, 2 million fans paid to watch them play. Known as the Red Heads for the red wigs they wore, they played local men's teams throughout the country. Their Globetrotters style of play lent a comic air to the competition, but the Red Heads demonstrated that basketball skills were not the exclusive province of men.[11]

Other women were doing the same for baseball. As 4,000 baseball players were called into military service, and only nine of the forty-one minor leagues survived the wartime manpower shortage and travel restrictions, the war gave women their first serious professional team sport. Fearing the curtailment of major-league baseball, Philip K. Wrigley, owner of the Chicago Cubs, organized the All-American Girls' Baseball League in 1943. The league never expanded beyond the Midwest, but at its peak in 1948 it fielded ten teams and attracted nearly 1 million fans. By then the rules had evolved so that it was virtually identical to the "national pastime" played by men. While players did not command salaries comparable to male professionals, they did enjoy the chance to do what they loved, to receive public attention and admiration and to earn good money—$40 to $100 per week in addition to expenses.[12]

As was the case when women undertook other masculine callings, both press reporters and league officials placed a great deal of stress on femininity. Player profiles in publicity releases highlighted domestic skills like sewing and baking and pointed out such feminine physical features as smallness, blond hair, "saucy" noses, and "gorgeous" smiles. Headlines reiterated the intentions of publicity agents as they proclaimed, "Femininity to Be Featured in New Sport Unit," and "Tom-Boy Tactics Out-of-Bounds." League officials uniformed their players in skirts and insisted they be accompanied by chaperones on the road. Charm courses were a regular feature of spring training, and women could be fired for smoking or drinking in public or for cutting their hair too short. Making a team and remaining on it required a high level of skill, but it also demanded conformity to what the league considered "the highest ideals of womanhood." Although it survived the war for a few years, without the captive audiences created by wartime conditions, women's baseball lost out in competition with other commercial recreation and the rise of television, and the league died in 1954.[13]

Although the appearance of femininity continued to claim high priority in the designing of women's apparel, the dominant fashion modes of the war years symbolized women's increased freedom and mobility and their departure from conventional feminine roles. As exigencies of war pressed upon the garment industry, women's clothing became more simplified, comfortable, and less overtly sexual. Even before the war domestic designers had challenged Parisian haute couture, but the wartime moratorium on the French fashion business gave free reign to Americans like Claire McCardell, who had been promoting styles that were more relaxed, less confining, and easier to maintain.[14]

Convenience and safety for women workers also required more practical and functional outfits. Women donned coveralls, slacks, and comfortable shoes for factory work and the public became accustomed to the sight of women in "masculine" clothes. Hair styles remained long, but safety on the job dictated new arrangements. In response to the concern for industrial safety, movie actress Veronica Lake, who had popularized the peek-a-boo style with hair covering half her face, adopted the upswept coiffure. The upswept style, along with turbans, snoods, and bandannas, appealed to women beyond the factory gates and became generally popular.[15]

Military requirements exerted a third influence on clothing styles as the war machine devoured raw materials formerly used for apparel. Because of the embargo on Japanese products, silk

became scarce as early as 1941. Full military mobilization eliminated other materials as metal was processed into guns instead of
zippers, nylon was diverted into parachutes, and rubber was
banned in the manufacture of girdles. In addition, the government
restricted the use of fabric and leather in order to conserve these
materials and to prevent radical changes in style, thereby discour-
aging the discarding of good, but outmoded, clothing. Promoted
by fashion retailer Stanley Marcus as "patriotic chic," the government regulations limited the width and length of skirts and banned
excessive ruffles and pleats. Stylists had been moving toward
slimmer lines, straighter cuts, and knee-length skirts in the late
1930s, but wartime necessity standardized and stabilized the simplified and rather Spartan look.[16]

Because of rationing, shortages, and a decline in quality, the war
in some ways made wardrobe assembling more difficult for wom-
en. But at the same time they did not have to worry about dramatically changing styles, and they had fewer choices to make. The
need to conserve dye-stuffs decreased the range of colors available
in fabrics, and shoe colors were limited to black, white, brown,
and tan. Moreover, the shorter skirt lengths were compatible with
lower-heeled, more comfortable shoes to which women turned as
scarce transportation necessitated more walking and as shoes were
rationed to two pairs per person by 1944. The continuing emphasis
on women's appearance in women's magazines and other popular
media indicated that both women and men assigned great importance to female attractiveness. But the war altered the norm,
contributing to a dominant style that provided women greater
mobility, comfort, and convenience and that diminished features
of women's adornment which sharply differentiated them from
men.[17]

In contrast to comics, movies, recreation, and fashion, the radio
soap opera only faintly reflected the war-induced changes in wom-
en's experiences. Daytime serials represented a considerable portion of the homemaker's media consumption. Originating in the
early 1930s, the new genre quickly seized the lion's share of
daytime programming; by 1941 a woman's serial was on at least
one network between the hours of 10 and 5:30, and listeners could
choose from among fifty-four serials. The multitude of programs
conformed to a singular formula. Set in the midst of middle-class,

small-city life, they carried multiple plots which focused on women, their private lives and problems. Although the spotlight was on domesticity and private relationships, stories revolved around extraordinary events and experiences including crimes, accidents, amnesia, disease, illegitimacy, missing persons, and mistaken identities. The central characters were women, strong, virtuous, and long-suffering, while the fictional men were generally weak, villainous, or absent.[18]

The expendability of male characters in the serial formula facilitated the most common intrusion of the war into the soap operas, men's departure for military service. Thus, the heroine of "Young Widder Brown" was engaged to a doctor in the medical corps; in "Backstage Wife" Mary Noble's husband joined the coast guard; the husband in "The Right to Happiness" was wounded in combat; and Ma Perkins's son met death as an infantryman. Because soap heroines often took care of men and helped them with their problems, the serials also easily accommodated the theme of the returning veteran. The plot in "Rosemary," for example, involved the Dawson family's taking in a disturbed veteran to rehabilitate him.[19]

To other wartime phenomena, however, the serials were relatively immune. No leading female characters volunteered for military service. Only a few, such as Stella Dallas, Kitty Foyle, and Sally Farrell of "Front-Page Farrell," took jobs in defense industries. Written for the woman who was at home, not at work, the soaps reassured her about the importance of her situation. While two popular serials, "The Romance of Helen Trent" and "Portia Faces Life," featured, respectively, a Hollywood designer and a lawyer, their relationships with men overshadowed their professional careers. Soap-opera heroines reflected the popular acceptance of paid employment for unmarried girls, widows, or abandoned women, but they even more powerfully promoted marriage as woman's finest career. Even during the war, the serials remained, for the most part, impervious to alternative visions of womanhood.[20]

If soap operas fixed women in the private domain, they also emphasized women's strengths and celebrated female values. Ma Perkins, a widow who ran a lumberyard, devoted her major efforts to solving the recurring crises in the lives of individuals and her community. Mary Noble in "Backstage Wife" held her marriage together despite the problems caused by a jealous, unstable husband. Stella Dallas represented the sacrificial mother, but she displayed great courage and ingenuity in rescuing her daughter from a variety of precarious situations and evil forces. In the serials women were often victims, but they were typically the stronger, nobler, and more resourceful of the sexes. Soap operas validated both the practical and psychological contributions of housewives; they conveyed the message that the traditional female activities of helping others and attending to relationships were more important than the masculine standards that stressed success in the public world. While the daytime dramas confined women to conventional roles, they gave those roles some power, virtue and significance.[21]

Although soap operas remained the most firmly attached to traditional models of womanhood, the themes of femininity and domesticity accompanied or underlay the portrayals of new images in other forms of popular culture. Women adapted their appearances to the wartime look, which deemphasized physical differences between the sexes, but they did not completely abandon adornments symbolizing femininity. While some adjusted to the disappearance of silk and nylon by going barelegged, others used leg makeup and some even painted on a seam line. Women emphasized their lips by favoring dark red colors. The focus on breasts did not peak until later, but the sweatergirl look, popularized by Lana Turner and other movie stars, had its origins in the war years, and women competed in Sweater Girl contests as early as 1943.[22]

In newspapers and magazines servicemen read about women's new accomplishments in formerly male provinces. Nonetheless, a significant portion of the media available to GIs stressed not only women's traditional femininity, but also their sexuality. Cartoonist Milton Caniff's contribution to the war effort was the creation of Miss Lace, star of "Male Call," whose purpose was to bolster soldiers' morale. According to Caniff, "Male Call" was "a girl strip, as racy as is permissible . . . designed to appeal specially to the forlorn fellow in the foxhole." Scantily clad, Miss Lace appeared in a variety of situations with military personnel, including one in which soldiers spied on her as she sunbathed in the nude. Criticized by civilian religious leaders and some military chaplains,

Caniff was defended by others for "the clever and tasteful way in which you treat the fighting man's frank and animal interest in the opposite sex."[23]

Real-life sex symbols pervaded the GI's quarters in the form of the pin-up, which Hollywood press agents sent to servicemen in campaigns to promote young actresses. The most popular were Betty Grable and Rita Hayworth, while Lena Horne served as their counterpart for black soldiers. Both Grable and Hayworth were photographed in enticing poses which exuded sexuality. Grable's pin-up was taken from behind and featured the star, in a tight bathing suit, smiling over her shoulder, while Hayworth, clad in a nightgown which highlighted her breasts, knelt on an unmade bed. By 1946 the emphasis on women's physicality had reached the screen in Howard Hughes's *The Outlaw*. Withheld from public viewing for three years, the film featured Jane Russell's bosom, well-defined in a specially designed brassiere and deliberately photographed to be as revealing as possible. By the 1950s, woman as sex object would obliterate the variety of images which had graced the screen during the war years. Symbolic of this shift was Marilyn Monroe, whose career took off after she was photographed in her defense-plant job for an article on women workers in *Yank*, a serviceman's magazine. By the 1950s she would epitomize the screen's obsession with women's bodies.[24]

Women's magazines sustained other conventional stereotypes throughout the war years. While they highlighted women's expanded public roles, they continued to remind women of the importance of a feminine appearance. A *McCall's* article featured women workers: "You'll like this girl. She does a man's work in the ground crew, servicing airplanes, but she hasn't lost any of her feminine sweetness and charm." Advertisers carried the glamour theme to its greatest lengths. A Linit laundry starch ad promoting women's employment in farm work insisted that although the work was hard, "a woman can do anything if she knows she looks beautiful doing it." A Tangee ad conceded that lipstick could not win the war; "But it symbolizes one of the reasons why we are fighting . . . the precious right of women to be feminine and lovely." And a hand-cream manufacturer informed readers, "Barbara is romantically lovely with her . . . white, flowerlike skin—but she's also *today's* American Girl, energetically at work six days a week in a big war plant . . . "[25]

As glamour dominated magazines' wartime messages to young, single women, domesticity reigned in their approach to married women. Women's periodicals often spoke approvingly of wives' employment, but to that approval was attached the condition that domestic claims deserved priority. In 1943 *McCall's* reported on a survey revealing that women "very emphatically" believed that "woman's place is in the home." Another article featured a husband's support for his wife's defense work. His argument, that "there will be a better mutual understanding when women return to their homes," emphasized both the assumption that women's employment was temporary and the belief that the greatest benefit of paid work was not to the woman but to the marital relationship. Imagery of the domestic woman was pronounced in advertisements which sought to sustain demand for items banned during the war. General Electric predicted that women would welcome their return "to the old housekeeping routine" because it would be transformed by new appliances. The Eureka Vacuum Cleaner Company praised its women on the assembly line, but promised that at war's end, "like you, Mrs. America, Eureka will put aside its uniform and return to the ways of peace . . . building household appliances."[26]

The persistence of conventional norms of womanhood was also evident in magazine fiction. In a survey of popular periodicals from 1905 to 1955, Donald Makosky found that female characters were more likely to hold jobs in the 1945 sample than in any other decade's mid-year. Even then, however, their primary motivation was patriotism, and they found greater fulfillment in marriage than in employment. Moreover, the 1945 stories represented "the strongest assault on feminine careerism" of all the years sampled. Although the fiction in 1945 and 1955 demonstrated a more permissive attitude toward working wives, that tolerance extended primarily toward those without children and those who worked at home or in their husband's businesses. Women executives who chose marriage over career were portrayed positively, while several of those who combined career and family were condemned for paying insufficient attention to husbands and children.[27]

Even the movies, notable for their approving reflection of women's military service, paid employment, and self-sufficiency, at the same time conveyed more conventional norms for female behavior and attributes. While *Since You Went Away* documented the new responsibilities and accomplishments of the American wife and mother, it was clear that the heroine accepted her roles as family head and defense-plant worker only as an essential expedient which she would gratefully relinquish when the war ended and her husband returned. Wartime films like *Tender Comrade* praised the ability of women to survive without men, but woman's being was still defined with reference to men. Even in the popular films with military heroines, women were competent and brave, but as Melva Joyce Baker has noted, they were doing "women's work," and "the 'meaning' or 'purpose' in their lives came from their liaisons with men—not from an attachment to their work." Romance, of course, was a staple of Hollywood; yet, while popular films contained plenty of heroes in whose lives women were absent or incidental, for heroines capturing or pleasing men was central.[28]

Along with models of admirable women meeting new challenges Hollywood also projected less positive images. Career women were implicitly criticized for their coldness and ambition, while their fates suggested the incompatibility of professional success with marriage. Ingrid Bergman, the psychiatrist in *Spellbound* (1945), saved Gregory Peck with her professional skill and persistence, but she was dependent upon him to awaken her sexually. In *Together Again* (1944), the mayor played by Irene Dunne resisted the admonition that her position would diminish her appeal to men with the response, "Women can live perfectly well without men." But in the end she sacrificed her office to marriage. Joan Crawford appeared as a successful businesswoman in *Mildred Pierce* (1945). Yet her ambition was motivated by her obsessive quest for her daughter's love, not by a drive for independence and self-satisfaction. Thus, the movie condemned two kinds of women under attack by some experts in real life—the sacrificial mother and the career woman. Katharine Hepburn's roles as journalist in *Woman of the Year* (1941) and as lawyer in *Adam's Rib* (1949) were exceptional for their depiction of a successful professional who could also achieve a satisfying and equitable relationship with a man.[29]

In the middle and late 1940s, movie audiences were increasingly treated to female images which emphasized treachery or helplessness. Especially popular during the decade was the *film noir*, that haunting, pessimistic genre which focused on the dark side of life, on the corrupt and irrational side of human nature, and provided an apt vehicle for the stereotype of the evil woman. *Double Indemnity* (1944), for example, featured Barbara Stanwyck manipulating insurance agent Fred MacMurray into a plot to kill her husband. Rita Hayworth similarly combined guile with sensuality as she destroyed her man in Orson Welles's *The Lady from Shanghai* (1947). *Dark Mirror* (1946) contained the added twist of female competition as the psychotic Olivia de Havilland prepared to murder her twin sister, and a psychiatrist noted, "All women are rivals fundamentally . . . "[30]

The woman as victim was another increasingly popular film image of the later 1940s. In George Cukor's *Gaslight* (1944), the susceptible Ingrid Bergman was driven mad by her scheming husband, and in Alfred Hitchcock's *Notorious* (1946) she played victim to her Nazi husband. Barbara Stanwyck was the terrorized, bed-ridden wife in *Sorry Wrong Number* (1948). In sharp contrast to the war-theme films, which stressed female competence, these movies emphasized women's helplessness, their lack of self-confidence, and what sometimes appeared as their downright stupidity. No specific year demarcated a shift from affirmative to hostile imagery of women, and films with admirable heroines often appeared simultaneously with those portraying evil or helpless women. Yet, by the late 1940s, women found significantly fewer screen models for female strength, self-sufficiency, and satisfying experiences beyond domestic and romantic life.[31]

Like the movies, popular comic features of the postwar era presented a less encouraging, narrower range of female models. One exception was "Grandma," which debuted in 1947 and portrayed an older woman, energetic, feisty, and young in spirit. Although "Wonder Woman" survived in the hands of new writers after William Marston's death in 1947, her feminist characteristics were less in evidence and she became more dependent upon men. Female rivalry was highlighted by teen-agers Betty and Veronica, who spent most of their time in the feature "Archie" competing for the hero's attentions. While the heroine of the widely read "Brenda

Starr" pursued a career as reporter, romantic intrigue claimed a considerable share of the gorgeous character's attention. And the women in Milton Caniff's "Steve Canyon" carried on in the "Miss Lace" tradition, feeding male fantasies with an array of alluring "villainesses, camp followers and ingenues." With the increasing popularity of soap-opera strips and humor features, images of womanhood lacked the variety and the examples of female independence, assertiveness and courage which had characterized the comic strips of the early 1940s.[32]

Postwar clothing styles projected an image which both exaggerated women's specifically female features and enveloped them in garments which were restrictive and impractical. The French designer most responsible for this "New Look" was the hitherto relatively unknown Christian Dior. His intentions were explicit. In his view, women "looked and dressed like Amazons. But I designed clothes for flowerlike women, clothes with rounded shoulders, full feminine busts, and willowy waists above enormous spreading skirts." He even had his models pad their brassieres "to give prominence to this most feminine attribute," and his designs frequently built in padding for the hips and bust. Introduced in Paris in 1947, the New Look was greeted with some initial resistance and then acceptance by American women.[33]

Women seemed to object most to the longer hem length. A *Seventeen* reader called the new styles "monstrous": "We teenagers are modern and don't want drooping hemlines." Women in Dallas, Texas, sought to retain the more moderate skirt length by forming a "Little Below the Knee Club." And, when Dior visited Chicago, women picketed his appearance carrying posters which proclaimed, "Down with the New Look." When polled in the summer of 1947 a majority of women said they did not like the new style, but would wear it anyway.[34]

Women's magazines quickly took up and promoted the New Look to readers who would buy their copies of the radically altered style off the racks. In August 1947, *Seventeen* reported that "the new feeling . . . is being carried over even into teen clothes." The *Ladies Home Journal* conceded that Dior's creations were "as yet too extreme for American wear," but instructed its readers to "study them well—they show the trends," and offered suggestions for adding borders and insertions to older clothes to bring them up to date. Its fashion expert also pointed out that longer, fuller skirts required a new shoe style: "Heels are high, toes slim and pointed." The *Ladies Home Journal* echoed Dior's intentions: "These higher heels, longer skirts, smaller waistlines and shoulders make you feel different, decorative, appealing."[35]

In later years the New Look was modified and somewhat relaxed. Even at its height of popularity women did not have to limit their clothing to the dominant style. In fact, the more practical separates increased in wear between 1947 and 1951, as production of blouses and skirts climbed much more rapidly than manufacture of dresses. Nonetheless the fashion norm of the late 1940s represented a regression from the war years. Higher heels, narrower toes, and more voluminous skirts reduced mobility. The waist-cinching corsets, wired brassieres, and other undergarments necessary to mold the female shape to the New Look diminished comfort. The image of woman projected in the dominant fashion mode exaggerated her decorative function as well as her specifically female—and feminine— attributes.[36]

By its very nature, popular culture reflects the public's experiences, attitudes, hopes, and anxieties. Consequently, most of the popular media represented and validated women's novel wartime roles and confirmed their ability to rise to new challenges. At the same time, the public's anxieties about those departures from convention were equally well represented. The glorification of the housewife, the stress on femininity, the emphasis on romantic relationships, the warnings about careerism, all indicated ambivalence about or opposition to changes in women's activities and life-styles. That these themes, along with negative, even hostile imagery, gained in prominence after the war testified to the endurance of older attitudes about what women should be and fears of what they might become.

Models of womanhood were, of course, produced in systems largely controlled by men. Although women, when they did not design them, promulgated clothing styles and produced much of the copy for women's magazines and many of the scripts for soap operas, the motion-picture, advertising, professional-sports, and comic-strip industries were thoroughly male dominated. But masses of women did consume these media. For some women they were likely no more than a form of escape, easily dismissed as lacking relevance to their own lives. Yet, the female imagery in the popular culture surely spoke to women's own ambivalence about their changing situation, an ambivalence produced not just by the novelty of their experiences, but by the failure of social and economic institutions to change in ways that would ease women's accommodation to different roles. While validating women's new activities, the wartime media also fastened those departures to a context of conventional femininity and domesticity. In the postwar period, popular culture reassured those women who resumed their traditional place, while its dominant messages discouraged those with aspirations in conflict with the traditional sex-gender system.

NOTES AND REFERENCES

1. Richard R. Lingeman, *Don't You Know There's a War On? The American Home Front, 1941–1945* (New York: G. P. Putnam's Sons, 1970), pp. 318–19; Russel Nye, *The Unembarrassed Muse: The Popular Arts in America* (New York: Dial Press, 1970), p. 239; Milton Caniff, "The Comics," in Jack Goodman, ed., *While You Were Gone: A Report on Wartime Life in the United States* (New York: Simon and Schuster, 1946), p. 504.

2. Maurice Horn, *Women in the Comics* (New York: Chelsea House Publishers, 1977), pp. 89-91, 104.

3. Ibid., pp. 126-27, 130–31; *Wonder Woman*, with an Introduction by Gloria Steinem (New York: Holt, Rinehart and Winston, 1972), unpaginated.

4. Robert Sklar, *Movie-Made America: How the Movies Changed American Life* (New York: Random House, 1975), p. 250.

5. Marjorie Rosen, *Popcorn Venus: Women, Movies and the American Dream* (New York: Avon Books, 1974), pp. 201–207; Frank Manchel, *Women on the Hollywood Screen* (New York: Franklin Watts, 1977), p. 164.

6. Rosen, *Popcorn Venus*, pp. 201–205, 276; Manchel, *Women on the Hollywood Screen*, pp. 64–67; Melva Joyce Baker, "Images of Women: The War Years, 1941–1945. A Study of the Public Perceptions of Women's Roles as Revealed in Top-Grossing War Films," Ph.D. dissertation, University of California, Santa Barbara, 1978, pp. 81–105, 214–44, 251–73.

7. Ibid., pp. 218–33; Donald Bogle, *Brown Sugar: Eighty Years of America's Black Female Superstars* (New York: Harmony Books, 1980), pp. 73–90.

8. Ibid., pp. 91–106; Horne is quoted in Jeanne Noble, *Beautiful, Also, Are the Souls of My Black Sisters: A History of the Black Woman in America* (Englewood Cliffs, N.J.: Prentice-Hall, 1978), p. 252.

9. Bogle, *Brown Sugar*, pp. 97–106.

10. John A. Lucas and Ronald A. Smith, *Saga of American Sport* (Philadelphia: Lea and Febiger, 1978), pp. 342–63; M. Gladys Scott, "Competition for Women in American Colleges and Universities," *Re-*

search Quarterly 16 (March 1945):56–71; Nancy Norton, "Mildred (Babe) Didrikson Zaharias," in Barbara Sicherman and Carol Hurd Green, eds., *Notable American Women: The Modern Period* (Cambridge, Mass.: Harvard University Press, 1980), pp. 756–57.

11. Ellen W. Gerber, Jan Felshin, Pearl Berlin, and Waneen Wyrick, *The American Woman in Sport* (Reading, Mass.: Addison-Wesley, 1974), pp. 40–41, 64–66.

12. Dan Parker, "The World of Sports," in Goodman, ed., *While You Were Gone*, pp. 291–94; Lucas and Smith, *Saga of American Sport*, pp. 364–66. The most complete history of the league is Merrie A. Fidler, "The Development and Decline of the All-American Girls Baseball League, 1943–1954," M.S. thesis, University of Massachusetts, 1976.

13. Ibid., pp. 53–54, 84–87, 245, 253–54, 262–66, 286, 357–61.

14. Kathryn Weibel, *Mirror, Mirror: Images of Women Reflected in Popular Culture* (New York: Anchor Books, 1977), pp. 205–209; Sally Kirkland, "Claire McCardell," in Sicherman and Green, eds., *Notable American Women*, pp. 437–39.

15. Michael and Ariane Batterberry, *Mirror Mirror: A Social History of Fashion* (New York: Holt, Rinehart and Winston, 1977), pp. 330, 347; Annalee Gold, *Seventy-Five Years of Fashion* (New York: Fairchild Publications, 1975), pp. 69, 75.

16. Lingeman, *Don't You Know There's a War On?*, pp. 123–26; Prudence Glynn, *In Fashion: Dress in the Twentieth Century* (New York: Oxford University Press, 1978), p. 57; Weibel, *Mirror, Mirror*, pp. 208–209; Marilyn J. Horn, *The Second Skin: An Interdisciplinary Study of Clothing* (Boston: Houghton Mifflin, 1968), p. 183; Mimi Blaker, "Fashions in 1943," *Journal of Home Economics* 35 (February 1943):73–76.

17. Ibid.; William Giddon, "Footwear in 1944," ibid. 36 (March 1944): 129–31.

18. George A. Wiley, "The Soap Operas and the War," *Journal of Broadcasting* 7 (Fall 1963):339; Madeline Edmondson and David Rounds, *From Mary Noble to Mary Hartman: The Complete Soap Opera Book* (New York: Stein and Day, 1976), pp. 34, 56–57; Raymond William Steadman, *The Serials: Suspense and Drama by Installment* (Norman: University of Oklahoma Press, 1971), pp. 320–21.

19. Wiley, "The Soap Operas and the War," pp. 343–44; Steadman, *The Serials*, pp. 333, 338; Edmondson and Rounds, *From Mary Noble to Mary Hartman*, pp. 55, 84–85.

20. Ibid., pp. 56, 80–82; Wiley, "The Soap Operas and the War," pp. 343, 345–46.

21. Steadman, *The Serials*, pp. 275–77, 281, 313, 320–21; Edmondson and Rounds, *From Mary Noble to Mary Hartman*, p. 249; Mary Jane Higby, *Tune In Tomorrow* (New York: Cowles, 1968), p. 136; L. Lloyd Warner and William F. Henry, "The Radio Day Time Serial: A Symbolic Analysis," *Genetic Psychology Monographs* 37 (February 1948):3–71.

22. Gold, *Seventy-Five Years of Fashion*, p. 69; Lingeman, *Don't You Know There's a War On?*, p. 126; Batterberry, *Mirror Mirror*, p. 347; E. J.

Dingwall, *The American Woman* (New York: Rinehart and Co., 1957), pp. 179–80.

23. Caniff, "The Comics," pp. 508–10; Horn, *Women in the Comics*, p. 128.

24. Rosen, *Popcorn Venus*, pp. 221–29, 284–90; Robert Sklar, "Marilyn Monroe," in Sicherman and Hurd, eds., *Notable American Women*, pp. 487–89.

25. Hildegarde Fillmore, "Little Girl on a Big Plane," *McCall's* 70 (April 1943):104; ibid. (August 1943):62, 87; ibid. (March 1943):31.

26. "A McCall's Survey," ibid. (November 1943):14–15, 30; Stuart Raleigh, as told to Toni Taylor, "I'm Proud of My Wife," ibid. (September 1943):41, 84; ibid. 71 (July 1944):31; ibid. 70 (June 1943):67.

27. Donald Robin Makosky, "The Portrayal of Women in Wide-Circulation Magazine Short Stories, 1905–1955," Ph.D. dissertation, University of Pennsylvania, 1966, pp. 27–29, 49–70, 87–88, 97–99, 290, 22. Makosky's study is based on 1,115 stories which appeared in each decade's mid-year in *Woman's Home Companion*, *Cosmopolitan* (not then a woman's magazine), *Saturday Evening Post*, *Harper's*, *Smart Set* (1905–1915), and the *New Yorker* (1925–1955).

28. Baker, "Images of Women," pp. 243–44, 251–73.

29. Rosen, *Popcorn Venus*, pp. 207–11; Molly Haskell, *From Reverence to Rape: The Treatment of Women in the Movies* (New York: Holt, Rinehart and Winston, 1974), pp. 129, 144, 179–80.

30. Ibid., pp. 189–204; Rosen, *Popcorn Venus*, pp. 238–42.

31. Ibid., pp. 233–38; Haskell, *From Reverence to Rape*, pp. 195–96.

32. Horn, *Women in the Comics*, pp. 128–29, 154–56, 165–69; Gloria Steinem, "Wonder Woman: An Introduction," in *Wonder Woman*.

33. Christian Dior, *Christian Dior and I* (New York: E. P. Dutton, 1957), pp. 40–41; Kurt Lang and Gladys Lang, "Fashion: Identification and Differentiation in the Mass Society," in Mary Ellen Roach and Joane Bubolz Eicher, eds., *Dress, Adornment and the Social Order* (New York: John Wiley and Sons, 1965), pp. 324–29.

34. Letter to the editor, *Seventeen* 6 (November 1947):4; Lang and Lang, "Fashion," pp. 325, 329; Dior, *Christian Dior and I*, p. 71.

35. "Smoother Shoulders; Longer, Fuller Skirts . . . ," *Seventeen* 6 (August 1947):124–25; Wilhela Cushman, "Outline of Fashion . . . 1947," *Ladies Home Journal* 64 (September 1947):59–61; Nora O'Leary, "Your Favorite Clothes Go to New Lengths," ibid. (October 1947):72–73; "Christian Dior: Bright Meteor of Paris Fashion," ibid. (November 1947):53.

36. Fessenden S. Blanchard, "Revolution in Clothes," *Harper's Magazine* 206 (March 1953):60.

Chapter Eleven

War, Economic Growth, and Social Change

The degree to which World War II improved women's status and reshaped sex roles in the United States is a question which has claimed increasing attention since 1972, when William Chafe published his groundbreaking study of American women in the twentieth century. While Chafe recognized the strength of ideological and institutional constraints on women's activity and opportunities, he was much more impressed with the war-impelled changes in women's behavior. In Chafe's view the war represented a watershed, by promoting new patterns of female behavior which eventually altered attitudes about what women could and should do. Succeeding historians, investigating in greater detail more discrete aspects of women's wartime experience have taken issue with Chafe's conclusions. Reversing his emphasis, they argued that continuity rather than change is the key to understanding sex roles in the 1940s.[1]

The complex nature of female roles and the variety of war-related factors which affected them preclude sweeping generalizations about war and social change. World War II brought with it scarcities of domestic goods, the absence of men, technological innovation, a greater emphasis on egalitarian ideals, and a comprehensive set of benefits for those who fought the war. But these developments had no uniform effect on women. Some of them were beneficial, some made women's lives more difficult, and the impact of others was mixed. In addition, a woman's race, age, economic class, and educational and marital status determined how she would experience the force of war on domestic America. While many of the changes generated by war were reversed after victory, others, particularly the economic boom stimulated by the war, continued to reshape the lives of women. Indeed, that economic regeneration effected a more profound and lasting change than any wrought by war alone.

The most dramatic impact of war was its withdrawal of men from their customary positions, its extraordinary demands on the productive system, and the consequent need for women to undertake novel activities. This imperative produced an atmosphere for women workers which was unprecedented. Along with plentiful job opportunities, women experienced higher wages; a lessening of discrimination, especially that based on marital status, age, and race; greater attention from labor unions; public recognition of their value as workers; and a measure of concern for their dual responsibilities as wives and workers.

While women's employment underwent the largest and most visible change during the war, the absence of men also expanded women's involvement in a variety of educational, civic, cultural, and recreational activities. Educational opportunities widened as colleges sought to compensate for declining male enrollments, and the national emphasis on science and technology encouraged more women to prepare for traditionally male fields. Some institutions admitted women for the first time, and others relaxed quotas which had restricted women's admissions. The shortage of men also increased women's participation in civil and political affairs. Several states admitted women to jury service for the first time. Women replaced men as political party workers and leaders at the local level, and they enjoyed their greatest gains as state office-holders since the 1920s.

Accompanying the actual opportunities for women created by the war was a climate of opinion more cognizant of women's worth and capabilities and more sensitive to the injustices they experienced. In their efforts to maximize women's contributions to the war effort, public officials, employers, and media writers emphasized female competence and women's vital part in achieving victory. Public rhetoric which cast the war as a struggle for freedom and democracy, moreover, highlighted the disparity between American ideals and practice. While civil-rights groups more readily capitalized upon wartime necessities and ideals, women's organizations were also energized by an atmosphere more hospitable to their feminist goals. They drew attention to sexual inequities and achieved modest victories for women in the areas of equal pay, military service, citizenship rights, and married women's autonomy. Even the progress made by proponents of the equal rights amendment, while underscoring divisions among collective womanhood, also invigorated women's organizations on both sides and did not foreclose cooperation on other goals of mutual interest. Although issues of women's status never moved from the periphery of the national agenda, the new vitality given to such concerns during the war years kept the issues visible and sustained a small body of feminists into the 1950s and beyond.

Along with its potential for refashioning sex roles, World War II also contained powerful forces which put checks upon women's aspirations and options. Most of the initiatives for women were based on a temporary wartime need: those powers which tolerated, even urged, women to step outside their customary sphere couched that invitation in terms which fortified traditional convictions about sex roles. Mothers were warned about the dire effects their employment might have on their children. Propaganda appealed to women's patriotism; such a focus emphasized women's obligation to their country rather than the personal satisfaction of employment and signified the temporary nature of that duty. Military as well as civilian propanganda highlighted women's femininity and posed their wartime contributions in terms of their relationships to men. As Leila Rupp has demonstrated, the appeals to women "allowed the public to accept the participation of women in unusual jobs without challenging basic beliefs about women's roles."[2] Playing upon these deeply entrenched social values was for propaganda-makers the most expedient means to meeting recruitment goals.

Other wartime priorities also thwarted the potential for change. As industrial and agricultural production was diverted to meet military needs and scarcities occurred in food, clothing, household goods, and appliances, women's domestic tasks, which had always set limits on their public pursuits, became more burdensome. In the face of huge military expenditures, legislators were reluctant to appropriate adequate funds for child care or other services necessary to reduce the conflict between women's private duties and employment outside the home. Rapid production of war materials took precedence over effective enforcement of the executive order prohibiting discrimination against racial minorities and consequently limited the economic advance of black women. And mobilization propaganda as well as the attractions of jobs induced young women to give priority to immediate employment over further education, which might have increased their future options. Despite the greater educational opportunities created by the absence of men, women's college enrollments actually declined during the war.

Because men bore the most dangerous and direct burdens, the war also placed a premium on men's lives, cast them in heroic roles, and increased the disparity between the sexes in important respects. Women's military service represented one of the greatest assaults on traditional practice and values, but relatively few women enlisted, and consequently their experience had little effect on women's status in general. In contrast, the 16 million servicemen enjoyed the products of a nation's gratitude on a number of levels. Civilians, and especially female relatives of veterans, were exhorted to assist soldiers' social reintegration by adapting their own behavior to the veterans' needs. Ex-servicemen benefited from informal employment preference as well as from laws which secured their right to former jobs and gave them precedence over civilians in competing for government work. Veterans also took advantage of the GI Bill's educational benefits, and by 1950 men had increased their share of college degrees to 75 percent of the total.

The fear that women's wartime experiences threatened the traditional sex-gender system was evident in the media, where a variety of authorities sought to restrict women's public activities. What Leila Rupp has termed "the antifeminist backlash" began even before the war ended and constituted a major effort of social control. Businessmen, labor leaders, and government officials told women to relinquish their jobs. Returning veterans compared American women unfavorably to those "womanly" ones they had met abroad. Social welfare and child-care experts called upon women to pay more attention to their maternal duties. Psychologists and psychiatrists emphasized women's biological destiny and diagnosed feminists as neurotic or worse. And, in articles, stories, and advertising, women's magazines glorified the housewife and mother.[3]

Such writings also indicated a growing emphasis on family life related, in part, to the destabilizing effects of war. The social dislocation of the war years directed public concern to rising incidences of juvenile delinquency, divorce, and illegitimacy. Social scientists and popular commentators often made women scapegoats for these problems, but even the more sophisticated analyses stressed the centrality of family life in preserving social order and assigned women the crucial role in family stability. This emphasis on women's private roles meshed with the writings of psychologists and educators during and after the war who rooted women's destiny in marriage and motherhood and sought to adjust women's socialization and education to prepare them more adequately for these roles. But the war not only underscored women's familial roles in prescriptive literature; it also increased the appeal of domestic life. Economic recovery made marriage and childbearing possible for larger numbers of Americans, and the risks and uncertainties faced by men of draft age lent a particular urgency to family formation.

The successful conversion of the economy to peacetime production and the various benefits extended to veterans sustained high marriage and birth rates into the 1950s. One-third of the nation remained near the poverty level, but in contrast to the Depression years unemployment was relatively low and most women were materially better off than ever before. Large numbers of women enjoyed more comfortable homes and a variety of household appliances and products which eased the physical demands of domestic work. Although it became more difficult to obtain therapeutic abortions, women had greater control over reproduction through the increasing availability and popular acceptance of contraception, and they gave birth under conditions which reduced the risks both to them and to their infants. Experts and advertisers set ever higher standards of housekeeping and childrearing, thereby increasing the psychological strains of wifehood and maternity, but in physical and material respects women's domestic roles became easier.

Economic recovery also produced jobs for most women who needed or wanted them. These were not the higher-paying positions which they had claimed during the war, for the prewar sexual division of labor renewed itself. Most of the lasting changes in women's economic behavior during the 1940s represented the continuation of long-range trends and depended upon the growing demand for labor in clerical, service, and some professional sectors of the economy. The war did encourage greater labor-force participation by married and older women and promoted increasing employer acceptance of these workers. But the new monopoly of the female labor force by married and older women also depended upon other circumstances. As Valerie Oppenheimer has shown, the decreasing pool of young, single women combined with the increasing demand for workers in traditionally female fields forced employers to alter their hiring practices.[4] Moreover, women workers had incentives beyond any personal satisfactions that might derive from their employment. The inability of the economy to provide jobs at adequate wages for all men continued to push married women into the labor market. Postwar inflation, social pressures to consume, and the desire to purchase homes, education, and a variety of goods which had lain beyond their reach during the Depression and war led additional millions of women into paid employment.

World War II did promote momentous changes in the lives of individual women. Historians who emphasize continuity should not ignore what it meant for a married woman to learn welding and earn unprecedented wages; for a black woman to exchange domestic service or field work for a factory job; for younger women to nurse soldiers under enemy fire or to train combat pilots; for a musician to have a chance at playing with a major symphony. That most of these experiences were ephemeral and failed to add up to profound changes in women's status demonstrates the tenacity of male power and sex-role socialization, the conservative forces of war itself, and the ability of a nation to use its citizens—women and men—while containing expectations that it was unwilling to fulfill.

While recognizing the overall continuities in women's lives between 1940 and 1950, it is also possible to identify in that decade seeds of change which worked a deeper transformation in women's consciousness, aspirations, and opportunities a generation or so later. Rupp has pointed to the survival of feminist ideology and feminist group culture in the National Woman's party and to its links with the women's movement of the 1960s. In the 1950s a few other groups continued to agitate for an equal rights amendment, federal equal pay legislation, and other proposals which had gained saliency during the war years. The proposal for a national Commission on the Status of Women which grew out of the progress made by the equal rights amendment failed to win approval, but the idea was kept alive. When President John F. Kennedy appointed such a body in 1961, in part to diffuse pressure from amendment advocates, the commission contributed to the development of the women's movement by legitimizing issues of sexual inequity, by gathering women to discuss these issues and by raising expectations for institutional change. While these developments helped to inspire the reform wing of the women's movement, women's experiences in the civil-rights movement, whose roots lay in the war years, brought forth a radical critique of the sex-gender system.[5]

Broader and deeper changes in the social fabric prepared a considerable number of women to be responsive to the ideas of the new movement. William Chafe has linked the growing incidence of paid employment among married women to more gradually changing attitudes. The critical importance of women workers both to the functioning of the economy and to the material security of their families belied the cultural imagery of women as dependent, domestic beings. Women were more ready to recognize the inferior conditions of their employment and to question a system which continued to assign them responsibility for the home regardless of their public roles. Moreover, although the postwar expansion of higher education increased the gap between men and women, it also produced larger numbers of college-educated women. The sharp disparity between horizon-expanding education and the isolation of domesticity or the routine of work below their capabilities also helped to open women's minds to a political analysis of their discontent. Finally, the suburban dream made possible by the economic revival of the 1940s turned out to be not so fulfilling after all. Women whose total devotion to home and family life failed to measure up to their interests or abilities provided a receptive audience for Betty Friedan, who in 1963 defined women's domestic isolation, boredom, and frustration as a collective issue.[6]

The conservative forces of war, the antifeminist backlash, and a general desire for the "normalcy" denied by depression and war undermined the war's potential for challenging sex-role behavior and attitudes. Nonetheless, other developments of the 1940s—the growing importance of women's work outside the home, the expansion of higher education, the sustenance of a small body of feminists, the rise of the civil-rights movement, and the growth of suburbia—laid the preconditions for an awakened womanhood in the 1960s.

NOTES AND REFERENCES

1. The interpretations of Chafe and others are discussed in the Essay on Sources.

2. Leila J. Rupp, *Mobilizing Women for War: German and American Propaganda, 1939–1945* (Princeton: Princeton University Press, 1978), p. 177.

3. Leila J. Rupp, "American Feminism in the Postwar Period," in Gary Reichard and Robert Bremner, eds., *Reshaping America: Society and Institutions, 1945–1960* (Columbus: Ohio State University Press, forthcoming).

4. Valerie Kincaid Oppenheimer, *The Female Labor Force in the United States* (Westport, Conn.: Greenwood Press, 1976), pp. 141–89.

5. Rupp, "American Feminism in the Postwar Period;" Cynthia E. Harrison, "A 'New Frontier' for Women: The Public Policy of the Kennedy Administration," *Journal of American History* 67 (December 1980):630–46. The civil-rights movement during the war is discussed by Richard M. Dalfiume in "The 'Forgotten Years' of the Negro Revolution," ibid. 55 (June 1968):90–106, and by Harvard Sitkoff, "Racial Militancy and Interracial Violence in the Second World War," ibid. 58 (December 1971):661–81. Sara Evans, *Personal Politics: The Roots of Women's Liberation in the Civil Rights Movements and the New Left* (New York: Random House, 1979): describes the rise of radical feminism.

6. William H. Chafe, *The American Woman: Her Changing Social, Economic and Political Roles, 1920–1970* (New York: Oxford University Press, 1972), pp. 234–37; Betty Friedan, *The Feminine Mystique* (New York: Dell Publishing Co., 1963).

Essay on Sources

The manuscript sources used in this study consist primarily of government records, papers of individual women, and papers of organizations which devoted considerable attention to women's affairs. Among the most important government records are the following: Women's Bureau; Children's Bureau; War Manpower Commission; War Production Board; Office of War Information; Office of Community War Services; Office of Price Administration; General Records of the Department of the Navy; Bureau of Naval Personnel; Bureau of Aeronautics; Operational Archives, Naval History Division; War Department General and Special Staffs, especially the WAC Historical File.

Abundant information is contained in the papers of individuals whose careers embraced a major concern for women's interests. The largest number of these collections are in the Schlesinger Library, Radcliffe College, and include the papers of Mary Anderson; Clara M. Beyer; Elinore M. Herrick; Lucy Somerville Howorth; Florence Kitchelt; Alma Lutz; Emma Guffey Miller; Frieda Miller; Elizabeth Reynard; Edith Nourse Rogers; and Jane Norman Smith. Manuscripts in the Sophia Smith Collection, Smith College, include the papers of Dorothy Kenyon; Mary van Kleeck; Emma F. Ward; and Ruth F. Woodsmall. Other useful collections were the papers of Mary T. Norton, Rutgers University; Margaret Hickey, University of Missouri–St. Louis; Agnes Meyer, Mary Church Terrell, and Anna Kelton Wiley, Library of Congress; and Westray Battle Boyce Long, Truman Library, Independence, Missouri.

Major collections of organizational records include the papers of the National Consumers League, the National League of Women Voters, the National Women's Trade Union League, and the Women's Joint Congressional Committee, all in the Library of Congress; the American Association of University Women Archives, Washington, D.C.; the National Council of Negro Women, in the National Archives for Black Women's History, Washington, D.C.; the American Federation of Labor, State Historical Society of Wisconsin, Madison; and the United Automobile Workers, Labor History Archives, Wayne State University, Detroit. Smaller collections of the American Association of University Women and the National League of Women Voters papers are in the Schlesinger Library.

Among the most important contemporary print materials are the Bulletins of the Women's Bureau, and business and employer publications at the Baker Library, Harvard University. Major periodicals include the *Journal of the American Association of University Women*; *Journal of the National Association of Deans of Women*; *Women Lawyer's Journal*; *Independent Woman*, published by the National Federation of Business and Professional Women's Clubs; *Equal Rights*, published by the National Woman's party; *Aframerican Woman's Journal*, published by the National Council of Negro Women; *Journal of Home Economics*; *Monthly Labor Review*; *American Federationist*; and *CIO News*. *Annals of the American Academy of Political and Social Science* devoted the September 1943 issue to the family, and the May 1947 issue to the status of women.

Historical studies of women have begun to appear only very recently, but a considerable measure of attention has been devoted to World War II. William Chafe's *The American Woman: Her Changing Social, Economic, and Political Roles, 1920–1970* (New York: Oxford University Press, 1972) was the first scholarly study of women's roles after 1920. The war years formed the centerpiece of his book, and in this section he concentrated primarily upon women's economic behavior. See also Chafe's *Women and Equality: Changing Patterns in American Culture* (New York: Oxford University Press, 1977) for a comparative approach to the war and issues of race and sex. In another fine comparative study, *Mobilizing Women for War: German and American Propaganda, 1939–1945* (Princeton: Princeton University Press, 1978), Leila Rupp demonstrated how images of womanhood were manipulated to encourage women's paid employment while simultaneously upholding traditional definitions of sex roles. Eleanor Straub emphasized the haphazardness and inadequacies of government policies, noting the exclusion of women from policymaking and the absence of a unified women's movement which might have made government more responsive to women's interests. See Straub's "United States Government Policy toward Civilian Women during World War II," *Prologue* 5 (Winter 1973):240–54; and her unpublished dissertation, "Government Policy toward Civilian Women during World War II," Emory University, 1973. Karen Anderson in *Wartime Women: Sex Roles, Family Relations, and the Status of Women During World War II* (Westport, Conn.: Greenwood Press, 1981), discusses women's family roles as well as their labor-force participation. Her monograph concentrates on the defense production communities of Baltimore, Detroit, and Seattle and includes the fullest discussion thus far of the experiences of black women. In her unpublished dissertation, "Wives, Workers, and Womanhood: America During World War II," University of North Carolina, 1979, D'Ann Campbell provides important demographic information and analysis of popular attitudes regarding gender roles, along with discussions of housewives, female workers, and labor unions. While Campbell joins Rupp, Straub, and Anderson in stressing continuity, she roots that continuity in women's satisfaction with the status quo, while Rupp and Anderson emphasize the power of social controls.

Several scholars have provided background for the 1940s by examining aspects of women's experience in the preceding decade: Lois Scharf, *To Work and To Wed: Female Employment, Feminism, and the Great Depression* (Westport, Conn.: Greenwood Press, 1980); Winifred D. Wandersee, *Women's Work and Family Values, 1920–1940* (Cambridge, Mass.: Harvard University Press, 1981); and Susan Ware, *Beyond Suffrage: Women in the New Deal* (Cambridge, Mass.: Harvard University Press, 1981). Ruth Milkman has published two valuable articles: "Women's Work and the Economic Crisis: Some Lessons from the Great Depression," *Review of Radical Economics* 8 (Spring 1976):73–97; and "Organizing the

Sexual Division of Labor: Historical Perspectives on 'Women's Work' and the American Labor Movement," *Socialist Review* 49 (January—February 1980):95—150.

Women's military experience has received little historical analysis. Mattie E. Treadwell has written the official history of the Women's Army Corps, in which she makes some comparisons with the other women's services: *The United States Army in World War II, Vol. VIII, The Women's Army Corps* (Washington, D.C.: Department of the Army, 1954). Sally Van Wagenen Keil's *Those Wonderful Women in Their Flying Machines: The Unknown Heroines of World War II* (New York: Rawson, Wade, 1979) is a highly readable account, much of which is based on oral histories of former Wasps.

Women's employment has received the most extensive historical treatment, although most of the work does not go beyond the war years. Two useful early studies are Constance McLaughlin Green, *The Role of Women as Production Workers in War Plants in the Connecticut Valley* (Northampton, Mass.: Smith College Studies in History, 1948), and International Labour Office, *The War and Women's Employment: The Experience of the United Kingdom and the United States* (Montreal: ILO, 1946). Recent articles on particular aspects of women's employment reinforce Rupp's and Anderson's emphasis on the limits of change. The best of these are Alan Clive, "Women Workers in World War II: Michigan as a Test Case," *Labor History* 20 (Winter 1979):44—72; Nancy Gabin, "Women Workers and the UAW in the Post—World War II Period: 1945—1954," *Labor History* 21 (Winter 1979—80):5—30; Marc Miller, "Working Women and World War II," *New England Quarterly* 53 (March 1980): 52—61; and Karen Beck Skold, "The Job He Left Behind: American Women in the Shipyards during World War II," in Carol R. Berkin and Clara M. Lovett, eds., *Women, War and Revolution* (New York: Holmes and Meier, 1980). Frank Stricker's "Cookbooks and Law Books: the Hidden History of Career Women in Twentieth Century America," *Journal of Social History* 10 (Fall 1976):1—19, presents a valuable overview of professional and career women.

The most important longitudinal study of women's employment is Valerie Oppenheimer, *The Female Labor Force in the United States* (Westport, Conn.: Greenwood Press, 1976). See also Glen

Cain, *Married Women in the Labor Force: An Economic Analysis* (Chicago: University of Chicago Press, 1966), and Clarence D. Long, *The Labor Force under Changing Income and Employment* (Princeton: Princeton University Press, 1958).

Two excellent studies of wartime child-care programs are Karen Anderson's chapter in *Wartime Women*, and Howard Dratch, "The Politics of Child Care in the 1940's," *Science and Society* 38 (Summer 1974):175–77. For an overview, see Margaret O'Brien Steinfels, *Who's Minding the Children? The History and Politics of Day Care in America* (New York: Simon and Schuster, 1973).

The best sources on women's education are Mabel Newcomer, *A Century of Higher Education for Women* (New York: Harper and Brothers, 1959); Jessie Bernard, *Academic Women* (University Park: Pennsylvania State University Press, 1964); Jeanne L. Noble, *The Negro Woman's College Education* (New York: Columbia University Press, 1956); and Marian Elizabeth Strobel, "Ideology and Women's Higher Education, 1945–1960," Ph.D. dissertation, Duke University, 1975, which is based on case studies of four institutions.

Although there exists no systematic treatment of women's legal status, important information is conveyed in "Sex Discrimination and the Constitution," *Stanford Law Review* 2 (July 1950):691–730; Barbara Allen Babcock et al., *Sex Discrimination and the Law: Causes and Remedies* (Boston: Little, Brown, 1975); and Judith A. Baer, *The Chains of Protection: The Judicial Response to Women's Labor Legislation* (Westport, Conn.: Greenwood Press, 1978). Leo Kanowitz, *Women and the Law: An Unfinished Revolution* (Albuquerque: University of New Mexico Press, 1969), provides a useful overvi w. Good introductions to the particular oppressions of black women and Japanese-American women are Gunnar Myrdal, *An American Dilemma: The Negro Problem and Modern Democracy* (New York: Harper and Brothers, 1944), and Roger Daniels, *Concentration Camps, U.S.A.: Japanese Americans and World War II* (New York: Holt, Rinehart and Winston, 1972).

Information on women and politics during the 1940s is scattered throughout broader studies written by political scientists. The most important of these are Sandra Baxter and Marjorie Lansing, *Women and Politics: The Invisible Majority* (Ann Arbor: University of Michigan Press, 1980); Emmy F. Werner, "Women in the State

Legislatures," *Western Political Quarterly* 21 (March 1968):40−50; Emmy F. Werner, "Women in Congress: 1917−1964," *Western Political Quarterly* 19 (March 1966):16−30. Hope Chamberlin, *A Minority of Members: Women in the U.S. Congress* (New York: New American Library, 1974), contains lively biographical sketches; while Eleanor Roosevelt and Lorena A. Hickok, *Ladies of Courage* (New York: G. P. Putnam's Sons, 1954) and India Edwards, *Pulling No Punches: Memoirs of a Woman in Politics* (New York: G. P. Putnam's Sons, 1977) offer the best accounts by activists.

The private side of women's lives has received scarce attention from historians. Most of the literature on marriage, sexuality, and reproduction is in the form of statistical analyses by social scientists. The most helpful studies include Paul C. Glick, *American Families* (New York: John Wiley and Sons, 1957); Richard A. Easterlin, *Population, Labor Force, and Long Swings in Economic Growth: The American Experience* (New York: National Bureau of Economic Research, 1968); Ronald Freedman, Pascal K. Whelpton, and Arthur A. Campbell, *Family Planning, Sterility and Population Growth* (New York: McGraw-Hill, 1959); Paul H. Gebhard, Wardell B. Pomeroy, Clyde E. Martin, and Cornelia V. Christenson, *Pregnancy, Birth and Abortion* (New York: Harper and Brothers, 1958); Sam Shapiro, Edward R. Schlesinger, and Robert E. L. Nesbitt, Jr., *Infant, Perinatal, Maternal and Childhood Mortality in the United States* (Cambridge, Mass.: Harvard University Press, 1968); Wilson H. Grabill, Clyde V. Kiser, and Pascal K. Whelpton, *The Fertility of American Women* (New York: John Wiley and Sons, 1958); and Alfred C. Kinsey, Wardell B. Pomeroy, Clyde E. Martin, and Paul H. Gebhard, *Sexual Behavior in the Human Female* (Philadelphia: W. B. Saunders, 1953).

Linda Gordon, *Woman's Body, Woman's Right: A Social History of Birth Control in America* (New York: Grossman Publishers, 1976), discusses the birth-control movement in the 1940s and contains a section on female sexuality and sex counseling. Richard C. Wertz and Dorothy C. Wertz, *Lying-In: A History of Childbirth in America* (New York: Free Press, 1977), provides an overview of childbearing. Two good surveys of women's domestic work in the twentieth century are JoAnn Vanek, "Time Spent in Housework," *Scientific American* (November 1974):116−21; and Ruth Schwartz Cowan, "The 'Industrial Revolution' in the Home: Household Technology and Social Change in the 20th Century," *Technology and Culture* 17 (January 1976):1—23. Childrearing literature is analyzed insightfully by Nancy Pottishman Weiss, "Mother, the Invention of Necessity: Dr. Benjamin Spock's *Baby and Child Care*," *American Quarterly* 29 (Winter 1977):519—46; and Martha Wolfenstein, "Fun Morality: An Analysis of Recent American Child-Training Literature," *Journal of Social Issues* 7 (1951):15—25. Carl N. Degler's *At Odds: Women and the Family in America from the Revolution to the Present* (New York: Oxford University Press, 1980) provides a good survey of the tension between women's family ties and their public activities.

Little scholarly work has been done on women and popular culture. A notable exception is Melva Joyce Baker, "Images of Women: The War Years, 1941—45. A Study of the Public Perceptions of Women's Roles as Revealed in Top-Grossing War Films," Ph.D. dissertation, University of California, Santa Barbara, 1978. A number of general studies contain some information on the 1940s. For movies, see Marjorie Rosen, *Popcorn Venus: Women, Movies and the American Dream* (New York: Avon Books, 1974), and Molly Haskell, *From Reverence to Rape: The Treatment of Women in the Movies* (New York: Holt, Rinehart and Winston, 1974). The best survey of women's athletics is Ellen W. Gerber, Jan Felshin, Pearl Berlin, and Waneen Wyrick, *The American Woman in Sport* (Reading, Mass.: Addison-Wesley, 1974). Raymond William Steadman pays considerable attention to soap operas in *The Serials: Suspense and Drama by Installment* (Norman: University of Oklahoma Press, 1971). Although often superficial, a historical overview of various forms of popular culture is provided in Kathryn Weibel, *Mirror, Mirror: Images of Women Reflected in Popular Culture* (New York: Anchor Books, 1977).

Two historical discussions of male sex roles include interesting sections on the 1940s: Peter Gabriel Filene, *Him/Her Self: Sex Roles in Modern America* (New York: New American Library, 1976), and Joe L. Dubbert, *A Man's Place: Masculinity in Transition* (Englewood Cliffs, N.J.: Prentice-Hall, 1979).

Index